Caught Between Borders

The Norwegian Refugee Council (NRC) is a voluntary organisation. For more than 50 years the organisation has worked to provide humanitarian assistance to people fleeing from their homes and to defend their fundamental human rights. It is currently active in projects to assist both refugees and internally displaced in Africa, Europe, Latin American and Asia. The Norwegian Refugee Council has no political or religious affiliation.

For more information please contact:
Norwegian Refugee Council
Grensen 17, P.O. Box 6758 St. Olavs Plass
0130 Oslo, Norway

Phone: (47) 23 10 98 00
Fax: (47) 23 10 98 01
E-mail: nrc-no@online.no
website: www.nrc.no

Caught Between Borders

Response Strategies
of the Internally Displaced

Edited by

Marc Vincent and Birgitte Refslund Sorensen

Pluto Press

LONDON • STERLING, VIRGINIA

in association with

NORWEGIAN REFUGEE COUNCIL
CONSEIL NORVEGIEN POUR LES REFUGIES

First published 2001 by Pluto Press
345 Archway Road, London N6 5AA
and 22883 Quicksilver Drive,
Sterling, VA 20166–2012, USA

www.plutobooks.com

British Library Cataloguing in Publication Data
A catalogue record for this book is available from
the British Library

ISBN 0 7453 1819 3 hardback
ISBN 0 7453 1818 5 paperback

Library of Congress Cataloging in Publication Data
Caught between borders : response strategies of the internally displaced
/ edited by Marc Vincent and Birgitte Refslund Sorensen.
    p. cm.
Includes bibliographical references and index.
    ISBN 0–7453–1819–3 — ISBN 0–7453–1818–5
  1. Refugees. 2. Migration, Internal. 3. Global IDP Survey. I.
Vincent, Marc. II. Sorensen, Birgitte Refslund.
    HV640 .C38 2001
    325—dc21
                                                              2001003500

10   09   08   07   06   05   04   03   02   01
10   9   8   7   6   5   4   3   2   1

Maps by András Bereznay <http://www.historyonmaps.com/>
Designed and produced for Pluto Press by
Chase Publishing Services, Fortescue, Sidmouth, EX10 9QG
Typeset from disk by Stanford DTP Services, Towcester
Printed in the European Union by TJ International, Padstow, England

Contents

Latin America

Europe

Lists of Tables, Maps and Photos

List of Abbreviations

ADRA	Acção para Desenvolvimento Rural e Ambiental
AFP	Agence France-Presse
AHRC	Asian Human Rights Commission
ANC	African National Congress
AR	Autonomous Republic (of Abkhazia)
ACCU	Peasant Farmers Self-Defence Group of Córdoba and Urabá
BERG	Burma Ethnic Research Group
CAD	Corpo de Apoio ao Deslocado
CHA	Consortium of Humanitarian Agencies
CIA	Central Intelligence Agency
CIDKP	Committee for Internally Displaced Karen People
CIS	Commonwealth of Independent States
CODHES	Consultoría para los Derechos Humanos y el Desplazamiento
DKBA	Democratic Karen Buddhist Army
DKBO	Democratic Karen Buddhist Organisation
DRC	Danish Refugee Council
DRC	Democratic Republic of the Congo
FARC	Revolutionary Armed Forces of Colombia
Fbu	Burundian Franc
FGM	female genital mutilation
FNLA	Frente Nacional de Libertação de Angola (National Liberation Front of Angola)
FRODEBU	Front Démocratique du Burundi
GDP	Gross Domestic Product
GEL	Georgia Lara
GURN	Government of Unity and Reconciliation
IASC	Inter-Agency Standing Committee
ICRC	International Committee of the Red Cross
IDEE	Institute of Democracy in Eastern Europe
IDP	internally displaced persons
IFRC	International Federation of the Red Cross
INCORA	Colombian Institute for Agrarian Reform
IRC	International Rescue Committee

IRIN	Integrated Regional Information Networks
KHRG	Karen Human Rights Group
KIC	Karen Information Centre
KLA	Kosovo Liberation Army
KNLA	Karen National Liberation Army
KNU	Karen National Union
KORD	Karen Organisation for Relief and Development
Ls	Sudanese Dinar
LTTE	Liberation Tigers of Tamil Eelam
MINARS	Ministry of Social Affairs
MPLA	Movimento Popular de Libertação de Angola (People's Movement for the Liberation of Angola)
MRRDR	Ministère en Charge de la Réinsertion et de la Réintégration des Déplacés et des Réfugiés
MSF	Medécins sans Frontières
MTB	Mosque Trustee Board
NGO	non-governmental organisation
NIF	National Islamic Front
NRA/M	National Resistance Army/Movement
NRC	Norwegian Refugee Council
NUPI	Norwegian Institute of International Affairs
OAU	Organization of African Unity
OFP	Popular Women's Organisation of Barrancabermeja
OSCE	Organisation for Security and Cooperation in Europe
PCS	Project Counselling Service
PRA	Participatory Rural Appraisal
RDF	Rural Development Foundation
RRA	Rapid Rural Appraisal
Rs	Sri Lankan Rupees
SPLA	Sudanese People's Liberation Army
UN	United Nations
UNCHR	United Nations Commission on Human Rights
UNDP	United Nations Development Programme
UNGA	United Nations General Assembly
UNHCR	United Nations High Commissioner for Refugees
UNICEF	United Nations Childrens Fund
UNITA	União Nacional para Independência Total de Angola (National Union for Total Independence of Angola)
UNMIK	UN Mission in Kosovo
UNOCHA	UN Office for the Coordination of Humanitarian Affairs

UNOMIG	UN Observer Mission
UNRCO	United Nations Resident Coordinator Office
UPDF	Uganda Peoples Defence Forces
UPRONA	Party of Unity and National Progress
USAID	United States Agency for International Development
USCR	United States Committee for Refugees
WFP	World Food Programme

Acknowledgements

We would like to thank the many people who played a part in producing this book.

Special mention goes to Marilyn Achiron who helped edit the country chapters. She managed her task with style and professionalism and accepted our innumerable added requests and changes without complaint.

We would like to thank the staff of the Global IDP Project and the Norwegian Refugee Council for their generous support to the project, and we are grateful to those who offered comments, advice or assistance along the way, including Brita Sydhoff, Tone Faret, Bjorn Pettersson and Simone Cosma.

We would also like to thank András Bereznay <http://www. historyonmaps.com> for preparing the maps.

Lastly, we would like to thank the following donors of the Global IDP Project who have supported all the activities of the project, including this publication.

Department for International Development (DFID-UK)
Department of Foreign Affairs and International Trade, Canada
European Community Humanitarian Office
Ministry of Foreign Affairs, Denmark
Ministry of Foreign Affairs, Norway
Ministry of Foreign Affairs, Switzerland
Swedish International Development Agency
International Development and Research Centre, Canada
Norwegian Church Aid
World Vision International
Save the Children UK

It should be noted that the views expressed in this book are those of the authors alone and do not necessarily represent the views of the Norwegian Refugee Council or any of the donors of the project.

Foreword

Internal displacement has emerged in recent years as one of the most pressing humanitarian, human rights and political issues facing the international community. Globally, there are an estimated 20 to 25 million persons who are forcibly displaced within the borders of their own countries by conflict and human rights violations, often in acute need of protection and assistance. Millions more are internally displaced as a result of natural disasters and other causes.

Responding to increasing concern at their numbers and their need for assistance and protection, the international community has sought, with varying levels of success, to facilitate a more timely, predictable and effective response to the challenges facing the internally displaced. However, to be truly effective in addressing the crisis at the field level, the international response must acknowledge, take account of, and supplement the efforts of local and national authorities. Although national authorities have the primary responsibility for addressing the needs of their displaced citizens, they often lack the capacity and sometimes the will to provide them with protection and assistance. The international community is therefore called upon not only to supplement the efforts of local and national authorities, but also to pay due regard to the efforts of the displaced themselves to cope with, and respond to, their situation.

This book, edited by Marc Vincent and Birgitte Refslund Sorensen, constitutes a timely and most welcome initiative in this direction. Bringing together case studies from countries in all regions of the world, it provides an important insight into the diverse strategies employed by internally displaced persons in responding to the formidable challenges that confronts people who are forcibly displaced from their homes and communities. Using the *Guiding Principles on Internal Displacement* as its methodological framework, the book focuses on strategies through which the displaced seek protection and strive to meet their basic subsistence needs. As such, it constitutes a valuable contribution to our understanding of the dynamics of displacement and underlines the importance of approaching a given displacement crisis from the perspective of assisting the displaced populations to help themselves. Moreover, it is a book which bears witness to the courage and ingenuity of people who have lost almost everything except the will to live and ensure the survival of their families. I hope and trust that this book will receive the attention it deserves and help provide constructive guidance for international cooperation on behalf of the internally displaced populations around the world.

Dr Francis M. Deng
Representative of the UN Secretary-General
on Internally Displaced Persons

Introduction and Background

Marc Vincent

The global crisis of internally displaced persons (IDP) appears finally to have caught the attention of the international diplomatic and humanitarian community. Yet amid all the discussions on the legal, political and institutional dimensions of the crisis, something is missing: the roles and responses of the internally displaced themselves. With all the attention focused on issues of state sovereignty versus state responsibility, institutional mandates within the United Nations (UN), and humanitarian concerns regarding security and access, the one aspect of the problem that has been too frequently overlooked is the ability of internally displaced people to adapt to the experience of displacement. This oversight robs the displaced of their voice and belittles the substantial contributions they make in shaping their own lives. It also reinforces the incorrect perception that the international stage is the only venue for action.

A GROWING TREND

The number of internally displaced persons has grown alarmingly over the last decade. By conservative estimates, there are between 20 and 25 million persons worldwide who are internally displaced because of conflict – almost twice the number of refugees.[1] In a study commissioned by the Norwegian Refugee Council (NRC) for the 1998 Global IDP Survey, Susanne Schmeidl noted that in 1970 there were 5 million IDPs from five countries; by the end of the 1980s, there were 7 million in 10 countries (Schmeidl 1998).

Between 1980 and 1990, the numbers both of internally displaced persons and refugees nearly tripled, to 22 million from 23 countries and about 17 million from 50 countries, respectively. From 1990, significant demographic changes took place in the two groups. While the estimated number of refugees declined from 1990 onwards, internal displacement increased sharply, peaking at 27 million in 32 countries in 1994 (Hampton 1998:27).

Statistics are necessary to appreciate the size of the problem; but they are, at best, estimates and, at worst, misleading. Disagreements over definitions and the lack of institutional resources mean that internally displaced persons are rarely counted. Even if those receiving some form of international or national assistance are counted, those who never receive such assistance and who are far from the cameras and notebooks of the international media may never be counted, as this book illustrates.

It is difficult to give a full analysis of the factors contributing to the apparent increase in internal displacement within the space of this introduction, but two principal reasons emerge. First is the changing nature of conflict and the rise in communal violence since the end of the Cold War (Stremlau 1998). Increasingly, civilian displacement has become a military or political objective of communal violence. The International Committee of the Red Cross (ICRC), which normally follows a discrete path in advocacy, has for several years publicly deplored the use of civilians as intentional targets (ICRC 1999).

Another reason for the increase in internal displacement is the declining willingness, on the part of some states, to accept large refugee inflows. That attitude effectively denies the right to asylum and limits the ability of internally displaced persons to escape national boundaries (UNHCR 1997). European governments are frequently singled out for their restrictive policies towards asylum-seekers; but those kinds of policies are now cropping up all over the world. The inhospitable climate towards refugees among countries neighbouring Afghanistan, for example, has had a demonstrable impact on internal displacement in Afghanistan, as this book shows.

UN efforts to improve capacity and response to internal displacement really started in 1992 when, at the request of the Commission on Human Rights, the then UN secretary-general, Boutros Boutros-Gali, appointed a representative, Francis Deng, to raise awareness of the problem and to investigate ways to improve protection and response. In his first comprehensive study, presented to the Commission on Human Rights in 1993, Dr Deng observed that, unlike the case of refugees, there was 'no single organisation' within the UN system responsible for protecting and assisting the internally displaced. He suggested that one of his objectives would be to study the available options and recommend action (E/CN.4/1993/35). Three years later, in 1996, he concluded:

Because there is no one organisation, or collection of organisations, mandated to take responsibility for the internally displaced, there are institutional gaps in the international system. At the same time, there is no political will to create a new organisation mandated to protect and assist these persons. Nor is it likely that an existing institution will be mandated to assume full responsibility for the internally displaced. The residual option is that of a collaborative arrangement among a wide variety of bodies and organisations whose mandates and activities are relevant to the problems of internal displacement. (E/CN.4/1996/52, 1996, paragraph 16)

The collaborative arrangement is centred on the UN Inter-Agency Standing Committee (IASC), created in 1991. The IASC is chaired by the Emergency Relief Coordinator and is composed of the heads of major humanitarian and development organisations, including UN agencies, the Red Cross Movement, The World Bank and the International Organisation for Migration, plus three non-governmental organisation (NGO) umbrella groups. It was intended to strengthen coordination in emergency situations. The so-called 'collaborative approach', as defined by IASC policy, is a management model for assistance and protection in situations of internal displacement that involves the government and local authorities, UN agencies, international organisations, and international and local NGOs working together.

Not everyone had faith in the collaborative approach, however. In 2000, US Ambassador to the UN, Richard Holbrooke, lamented 'the inadequate and uneven protection afforded to internally displaced persons'. He demanded a reassessment of the institutional structures to deal with the problems of internal displacement:

It's unacceptable that legalistic distinctions prevent people from receiving the same assistance simply because they're classified as something called IDPs instead of refugees. ... I do not personally believe that shifting responsibility of different agencies to head the operation in different areas will work. I believe that 'co-heads' means no heads and I'm glad that we have an opportunity to keep attention on this enormous issue that affects tens of millions of people.[2]

The chapter on international response has yet to be closed, but it continues to be dominated by the collaborative approach. Still, humanitarian actors are beginning to pay more attention to response mechanisms and local capacity. This change in attitude and emphasis has come about for several reasons. The humanitarian community has made significant strides in analysing both the negative and positive effects of assistance. Studies on how assistance contributes to conflict have forced humanitarians to reconsider their self-image as benefactors. Instead, they are making greater efforts to understand the dynamics of assistance during conflict and their potential role in upsetting the delicate balance of interests and group dynamics that may inadvertently contribute to the conflict or even create new problems.

Furthermore, the recent emphasis on capacity building has forced humanitarian agencies and the development community to look more closely at local capacity to find complementarity (Lautze and Hammock 1996). Although capacity building, as a term, has become a catch-all phrase, as an activity, if properly managed and implemented, it requires an in-depth understanding of what communities are already doing, as well as an understanding of cultural norms and locally defined aspirations. For capacity building to be successful, it must be based on an analysis of who the local communities are, their internal social structures and the different vulnerability patterns within them.

Even as civilian populations have been increasingly targeted and turned into displaced populations, no institutional framework has been developed to guarantee assistance and protection in this precarious situation. In many cases, the government involved, which is legally charged to protect and assist its citizens, including those who are displaced, has been either a direct instigator of displacement or a collaborator. This meant that internally displaced persons often had to rely on their own support mechanisms and resources.

RESPONSE STRATEGIES: THE BACKGROUND TO THIS STUDY

The genesis of this project on response mechanisms was the observation that while the vulnerability of internally displaced people was generally recognised, little attention was being paid to how they perceived and responded to displacement. Nor was there much understanding about the longer-term social consequences of their various response strategies. By studying internally displaced persons in different countries, different settings and different phases of displacement, we hoped to contribute to a greater understanding of response mechanisms during displacement. The goal was to be able to answer such questions as:

- What do internally displaced persons do for themselves and among themselves to survive or cope with the ordeal?

- How do they address the material and protection needs of the community or individual?
- What are their resources and goals?
- And what are the constraints they face in different phases of the process?

Finally, the study aimed to shed light on the question of universality or particularity in responses. To what extent do similarities or common patterns emerge in different geographic and cultural contexts? To what extent are the strategies dependent on culture, geography or lifestyle prior to displacement?

We wanted to examine the response mechanisms of those internally displaced people who struggle in isolated and inaccessible areas far from the consciousness of the international community. For obvious logistical and security reasons, the international community has, until now, been more familiar with the visible and accessible internally displaced. There is little or no information on the many internally displaced persons who never make it to camps and who struggle through a cycle of displacement far from humanitarian aid organisations. This is the case with some of the displaced in Burma, for example, or the so-called dispersed in Burundi and Colombia, many of whom survive in the jungles alone, relying exclusively on their own wits and resources. This category of the 'unseen' displaced would also include the internally displaced who do make it to cities and larger population centres but who become lost among the urban poor or prefer to remain anonymous.

We also wanted to study the known and lesser-known response mechanisms of the visibly displaced. In Angola and the Sudan, response mechanisms are more obvious and can be seen in displaced persons' participation in the informal economy or in the establishment of camp bars and restaurants. Indeed, even in cases when the internally displaced choose to reside with friends and family in the city, it is often not difficult to identify them in local markets as they sell handicrafts or farm produce so they can buy needed utensils. While these kinds of economic response mechanisms are obvious, they require further analysis. Plus, there are many strategies of which an observer may be completely unaware. These include informal information networks that warn the displaced of impending danger or inform them of events occurring in their home villages during their absence.

Finally, we also wanted to address the lack of appreciation, among many development and humanitarian actors, of the sheer complexity of building or rebuilding a community when the displaced finally return to their home villages or resettle elsewhere. Unrealistic assumptions about the time it takes to develop sustainable livelihoods and social identities often betray this lack of understanding.

The findings of the study provide a convincing argument against the tendency, especially within the humanitarian community, to view the internally displaced as mere victims. By doing so, humanitarians blind themselves to the resourcefulness of the communities and individuals. As argued by Birgitte Refslund Sorensen in a conference in Oslo in 1997, acknowledging the effectiveness of coping strategies provides us with a 'counter-discourse' to the traditional hegemonic humanitarian labels of 'vulnerable groups', 'beneficiaries and recipients' (Sorensen 1998). The displaced have personal and social histories, they constitute heterogeneous groups with competing interests, and they act with different goals and ambitions in mind. Generally speaking, the universal categories of humanitarian assistance ignore these distinctions and, because of that, displaced communities are treated as relatively homogeneous groups, solely or mainly defined by their experience of war and displacement. In addition, a more actor-oriented perspective would allow response strategies and reconstruction activities to be seen as not simply reproducing pre-conflict societal patterns, but also as contributing to the emergence of a new post-conflict society.

Overall, our objectives were to promote greater awareness and understanding of individual-, family- and community-level response strategies. We also hoped to use the increased understanding to guide international organisations in designing policies and in developing relief plans and programming in internal displacement crises so that they recognise and support, rather than inadvertently damage or destroy, existing mechanisms.

DEFINITION OF INTERNAL DISPLACEMENT

The definition of internal displacement used in this study is based on the working description of the UN *Guiding Principles on Internal Displacement*:

> ... persons or groups of persons who have been forced or obliged to flee or to leave their homes or places of habitual residence, in

particular as a result of or in order to avoid the effects of armed conflict, situations of generalised violence, violations of human rights or natural or human-made disasters, and who have not crossed an internationally recognised State border. (UNOCHA 1999)

Given the broad scope of the description, the research project chose to focus only on those internally displaced who have been forced to flee from 'armed conflict, situations of generalised violence, violations of human rights ...' Those who have been internally displaced as a result of natural or human-made disasters or who are economic migrants were not included in the study.

During temporary settlement and the return/reintegration phase, internally displaced persons often mix with the local population. In some cases, response mechanisms may be very similar to or the same as the local community's response to armed conflict, human rights abuses or even poverty. The researchers were asked to pay attention to the similarities and differences among displaced and host populations, and not automatically assume that the two groups have the same options and respond in similar ways. Rather, researchers were asked to look at the particular ways in which the response strategies of the internally displaced were received by, and related to the position and strategies of, the local host population, and what kind of relationships developed between the two groups.

DEFINITION OF RESPONSE STRATEGIES

The definition used in this study was based on Sorensen's definition of self-help strategies:

A self-help activity is any voluntary action undertaken by an individual or a group of persons, which aims at the satisfaction of individual or collective needs or aspirations. The main contribution to that activity must stem from the individual's or group's own resources. (Sorensen 1998)

In this study, we have used the term 'response strategies' rather than 'self-help strategies' or the more common 'survival and coping strategies'. The latter term was rejected because of its limited view of who internally displaced people are and what they do. As many of the case studies show, the activities of most internally displaced persons reach far beyond merely securing physical survival, even when that is critical. Internally displaced persons, and others living under dire circumstances, are also social and cultural beings, and issues of identity, dignity and social standing remain important to them and are incorporated in their strategies. Contrary to the common assumption about refugees and internally displaced persons, they are not all poor, resourceless people who think only of surviving their present, difficult circumstances. Some of them have many skills and plan and work for a better future.

The term 'self-help strategies' was initially introduced in the common research framework, highlighting actions that are instigated from within the community rather than from an outside source. The term also stipulated that the resources for the activity or mechanism had to come from within the community or from members of the community. As will be apparent, it was not easy to maintain a strict delineation between community-based activities and outside resources. In many cases, response mechanisms were woven into the broader context of the state and international assistance and were difficult to separate. In fact, gaining access to such external resources was a major strategy for many.

The decision to work with the term 'response strategies' reflects these considerations. The term is meant to stress the *motivation* of internally displaced persons, the *creativity and comprehensiveness* of their strategies and actions, and their *reflectivity* regarding their situation, position and options.

As victims of displacement, internally displaced persons may rely on friends and family for food and shelter. They may set up communication networks to transmit and receive information. Sometimes they may even set up their own court system to deal with transgressions of cultural norms or laws. Some response mechanisms are a direct result of being displaced; others may have been undertaken by the community both before and during displacement and therefore are not directly linked to displacement but reflect the wider behavioural patterns of the community. To identify those mechanisms that were a direct response to *displacement*, the authors were requested to distinguish between those response mechanisms that were initiated as a result of displacement and those that were self-help strategies rooted in cultural tradition. In reality, of course, the two are often intertwined.

Furthermore, researchers were asked to be aware that not all response strategies have a universal positive impact; some may have a detrimental effect on, for example, some members of the community or the environment. Prostitution, child soldiers and mob justice may all be considered response mechanisms that have a negative impact on the community and communal values. Researchers were asked to pay attention to all response mechanisms, whether positive or negative and, when possible, to obtain the displaced person's own assessment of past strategies.

Finally, the researchers were encouraged to include various members of a group in their study to reflect any differences in response that may be based on gender, age, social position, past occupation, ethnicity or religion.

THE RESEARCH FRAMEWORK: APPLYING THE GUIDING PRINCIPLES ON INTERNAL DISPLACEMENT

One of the more significant achievements in the last ten years of the UN response to internal displacement has been the development of the *Guiding Principles*. In addition to examining the UN's institutional response to internal displacement, Deng studied the degree to which the internally displaced were protected under existing international human rights and humanitarian law. In 1996, Deng presented the Compilation and Analysis of Legal Norms in which he concluded that international law provided substantial protection to internally displaced persons. However, there were areas where the law failed to provide an adequate basis for their protection and assistance. To follow up on the assessment, the Commission on Human Rights requested that Deng prepare a normative framework, and this later became the *Guiding Principles*.

The *Guiding Principles* were drafted by a team of lawyers and international legal experts. The *Principles* are not binding in law but reflect and are consistent with international human rights law, humanitarian law and refugee law. While there is hope that the principles will eventually attain the status of customary law, they now guide states, non-state actors and international organisations in their policy-making and programming to meet the needs of the internally displaced.

When the *Guiding Principles* were first presented to the Commission on Human Rights in 1998, they were received primarily as a legal framework, and much attention was given to their legal status. Three years on, there is a tendency among international legal experts not to see beyond the legal dimensions of the *Principles*. For NGOs, however, the value of the *Principles* as an advocacy tool was immediately recognised.[3] The Norwegian Refugee Council, for example, developed country profiles contained in the Global IDP Database based on themes drawn from the Principles. This book, and the research project on which it is based, took the profiles created by the Global IDP Project one step further by developing a research framework based on themes inspired by the *Principles*.

There were two reasons for choosing the *Guiding Principles* as the methodological framework of this study. First, and primarily, the *Guiding Principles*, although a legal framework, are based on a *needs approach* and therefore provide an excellent structure for categorising potential response mechanisms. Those who drafted the *Principles* identified the immediate and long-term needs of the internally displaced in a variety of sectors, such as protection, subsistence needs and education, and then correlated the needs to the appropriate rights within the human rights, humanitarian and refugee legal regimes. The process generated an extensive and comprehensive list of needs. Since it follows that internally displaced persons would seek to meet those needs whenever possible, the *Guiding Principles* can therefore be 'turned upside down' to act as a categorisation of possible responses.

The choice of the research framework was also influenced by the fact that there appeared to be no other appropriate structures. Some are similar but not suitable, such as Michael Cernea's Risks and Reconstruction Model (Cernea 1997). Cernea claims the model, which identifies impoverishment risks for resettlement, can, with 'appropriate adjustments', be useful in analysing the resettlement of victims of forced displacement, such as internally displaced persons and refugees. While the model does provide useful diagnostic and predictive elements, it diverged from our needs in two areas. First, its focus is principally on resettlement and so its use to assess the 'flight phase' of displacement was untested. Second, as other observers have noted (Muggah 2000), its ability to test 'protection responses', or physical security, is not as detailed.

Another similar, but unsuitable, form of classification of responses could have been the more traditional humanitarian/refugee needs assessment. Since the project hoped to measure the capacities and responses of the internally displaced, the applied framework was considered more appropriate because the risks facing internally displaced persons are often different from those facing refugees. Refugees, by definition, have crossed an international border and are therefore entitled to international protection. Internally displaced persons have not left their country and are thus much more likely to be in closer proximity to the conflict and elements that caused their displacement. Also, while the two groups face the same or similar risks at the point of displacement and during return, their experiences during the temporary settlement stage can be markedly different.

STRATEGY CATEGORIES: THE FRAMEWORK OF THE STUDY

To facilitate cross-cultural comparison, all the case studies were based on a common system of categorisation and divided into the following groups.

Protection strategies:

- *Strategies that protect the right to life and personal security.* Defined as activities that attempt to shield the individual or group from acts of violence, terrorism, or physical threats. Acts of violence were considered to include armed attacks, killings, enforced disappearances, ill treatment and torture.
- *Strategies that protect the right to personal liberty.* Defined as strategies that attempt to shield victims from arbitrary detention, or strategies that attempt to mitigate the problems associated with detention for members of the group or relatives of members of the group. Mechanisms may include networks and methods for locating, identifying and assisting members of the group held in detention.[4]
- *Strategies that protect movement-related needs.* Actions/strategies that promote freedom of movement, including the right to seek safety in another part of the country and the right to leave, or return to, the country, and methods of leaving or circulating freely within enclosed areas, such as supposed IDP camps.

Subsistence strategies:

- *Strategies that improve access to basic goods and services or materially improve conditions of displacement.* Activities include methods or mechanisms that improve or provide the delivery of health care, such as care to vulnerable individuals or elderly members of the community, and can also include activities that improve sanitary conditions and access to food and water or that address shelter needs.

- *Strategies that offer or increase the opportunities for employment and other economic activity.* These include activities such as cultivating land, keeping crops and livestock, or finding employment.

Access to education:

- *Strategies that provide access to education.* These strategies include activities either within camps or host communities that allow for adult training or apprenticeship. Particular attention was paid to efforts made to ensure equal access to the education system for women and girls.

Civic strategies:

- *Strategies that improve access to or public participation in community, governmental and public affairs.* Activities that protect the right to associate freely and participate equally, and the right to vote.
- *Strategies that provide access to documentation.* Mechanisms to gain access to passports, personal identification documents, birth certificates, marriage certificates, and death certificates.
- *Strategies that protect or maintain family unity, social identity and culture.* Family reunification programmes, efforts to maintain unity of the village and/or community; also, mechanisms for maintaining or protecting indigenous language, culture, identity or religion.

Property issues:

- *Strategies that protect property.* These include strategies that protect property in areas of original residence as well as mechanisms that provide for the restitution of property or the compensation for the loss of property.

Researchers were not expected to look for specific examples from all categories but, rather, were asked to choose the categories or responses that best reflected the specific cases and that would be most illustrative or interesting. While researchers were asked to be aware of different phases of displacement (a flight situation, temporary settlement or return/resettlement), it was recognised that displacement situations are rarely linear and certainly not homogeneous. In many displacement situations, all phases are occurring simultaneously: some people are fleeing while others are returning. Moreover, since many internally displaced persons are displaced more than once, the opportunity to learn about their own reflections on the different phases, as well as on changes in their responses to displacement over time, was welcome.

Wherever possible, local researchers were chosen or teamed up with international experts. We believed that local authors would be in a better position to recognise and understand culturally based strategies and provide appropriate analysis. Also, we believed that local authors would be able to do their research less obtrusively.

CASE STUDIES

The book begins in Africa, home to at least half of the world's displaced persons. We start in Angola, where Nina M. Birkeland and Alberta Uimbo Gomes look at the response of the displaced to one of the continent's longest wars. Despite a large international presence in Luanda, the constant insecurity, a weak state and a destroyed economy means many displaced are left to cope on their own. The chapter focuses on the recent wave of *deslocados* to Huambo province and pays particular attention to economic survival.

Following Angola, we look at Burundi, where Geneviève Boutin and Salvatore Nkurunziza examine several different displaced populations. Despite the pervasive insecurity, Boutin and Nkurunziza were able to talk to both Tutsi and Hutu displaced groups and include some analysis on regroupment sites, where the government forced the rural population into camps, ostensibly for security reasons.

The next chapter looks at the Sudan, which hosts the world's largest internally displaced population. Karen Jacobsen, Sue Lautze and Abdal Monim Kheider Osman look at the response mechanisms of the displaced in Khartoum. Displaced from areas in the southern and western regions of the Sudan, those in Khartoum face a continual struggle against the government's land policies.

The last African country examined is Uganda, where Ambrose Olaa examines the importance of cultural traditions and family among the displaced Acholi people in Kitgum District.

After Africa we turn our attention to South Asia. First we look at Afghanistan, where Grant Farr examines how, in the most desperate of situations, coping strategies rarely help. Farr is able to look, albeit from a distance, at some of the response mechanisms of Afghan women.

On the other side of the South Asian region, Chris Cusano studies displaced Karen in Burma. The Karen, like other ethnic groups on the Thai–Burma border, have been left to struggle against displacement in almost total isolation. Although a trickle of assistance gets through, they have basically been forgotten by the international community and have developed such strategies as cultivating rice and pre-positioning food while on the run from military forces.

The opacity of the situation in Burma is contrasted by the transparency of the conflict in Sri Lanka. Birgitte Refslund Sorensen investigates the responses of the minority Muslim community who were forcibly displaced more than ten years ago.

In Latin America, Esperanza Hernandez Delgado and Turid Laegreid examine the situation in Colombia, where generalised socio-political violence is inextricably linked with displacement.

The last two studies look at displacement in Europe. In Georgia, Julia Kharashvili looks at the response mechanisms of ethnic Georgians displaced from Abkhazia and the remarkable infrastructure they brought with them. The last chapter, by Vladimir Ilic, looks at another lesser-known case of displacement: that of Serbs displaced from Kosovo during and immediately after the NATO bombing campaign.

NOTES

1. There were an estimated 11.6 million refugees worldwide at the end of 1999 (UNHCR 2000).
2. Statement by Ambassador Richard C. Holbrooke, US Permanent Representative to the United Nations (UN), 'Maintaining Peace and Security: Humanitarian Aspects of Issues before the Security Council', UN Security Council, 9 March 2000.
3. See *Report of the International Colloquy on the Guiding Principles on Internal Displacement*, Vienna, 21–23 September 2000, Brookings Project on Internal Displacement.
4. Detention in this sense is not referring to IDP camps, but to official, unofficial or even illegal detention centres, including jails, prisons, etc. in which people are being held for committing, or because they are accused of committing a crime.

Africa

1
Angola: *Deslocados* in the Province of Huambo

Nina M. Birkeland and Alberta Uimbo Gomes

Angola has the fastest growing economy in Africa, but is ranked as number 160, out of 174 nations, on the United Nations Human Development Index 2000. Angola produces 800,000 barrels of oil every day, yet public hospitals do not have enough diesel fuel for their generators. Of Angola's population of 12 million, 3.8 million are internally displaced. This is one of the highest populations of internally displaced persons in the world, both in sheer number and in percentage of the population. In addition, several hundred thousand persons have fled to neighbouring countries and live as refugees, primarily in Zambia.

Forced migration is nothing new to Angolans. During the colonial era, which began as early as 1576 in some parts of the country, forced relocation and displacement were common. But since the end of Angola's 14-year war for independence from Portugal in 1975, larger and larger segments of the population have been forcibly displaced from their homes and homelands. Indeed, it is fair to say that the majority of the population is or has been displaced since Angola became an independent country. During 2000 alone, at least 457,000 persons were displaced for the first time (IRIN 2001). Displacement in Angola is both a history of war and devastation and a tale of advanced survival strategies among the displaced.

BACKGROUND

Angola is located in south-west Africa and shares borders with Namibia to the south and Zambia and the Democratic Republic of the Congo (DRC) to the east and north. The enclave Cabinda, which is situated on the north shore of the Congo River, also belongs to Angola. Congo-Brazzaville abuts Cabinda to the north and east, and the DRC to the south and east. The Atlantic Ocean lies to the immediate west of Angola. The country is the second largest in Africa (DRC is the largest) with an area of 1,246,700 square kilometres. Most of the country is highlands or plateau with an

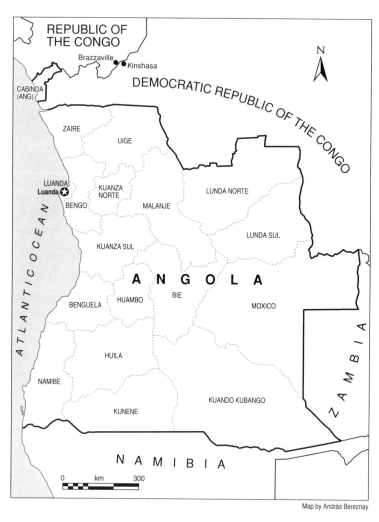

Map 1   Angola

elevation between 1,000 and 1,800 metres above sea level. Angola is divided into 18 provinces. The province of Huambo, the site of this chapter's case study, is one of the smallest in the area, but has the densest population.

Most Angolans survive on subsistence agriculture. In 1999, oil production accounted for 45 per cent of the country's Gross Domestic Product (GDP) and 90 per cent of its exports. Industry, services and agriculture, in decreasing order of percentage, accounted for the remaining 55 per cent of GDP (CIA 2001).

Large-scale displacement has resulted in rapid urbanisation throughout the country, estimated at 50 per cent (UNDP 1999:47). Cities and towns may be safer than rural areas, but livelihoods are harder to come by in urban zones. The massive migration into urban areas has not been followed by the necessary investments in infrastructure to provide basic sanitation, water, health care and schools.

Of the nine ethnic groups living in Angola, the Ovimbundu (37 per cent of the total population), Mbundu (25 per cent) and Bakongo (15 per cent) are the largest. Although the ethnic groups, which also include the Tschokwe, Ganguela, Nhaneca-Humbe, Ambo, Herero, and Xindonga, are spread out over the entire country, there remain core areas for certain groups: the Ovimbundu are concentrated in the Central Highlands, the Mbundu in and around the capital, Luanda, and the Bakongo in the north.

Civil Wars

Civil wars and unrest have tormented the country continuously since independence, except for two periods of relative peace during 1991–92 and 1994–98 (Hodges 2001:7). Throughout the 1970s and 1980s, the war(s) were linked to Cold War geopolitics and to the apartheid regime in South Africa, whose goal was to weaken the Angolan government's support for the African National Congress (ANC). Since 1992, external actors, interests and ideology have played less a role in the civil war than personal ambition to control the country's wealth of natural resources, especially oil and diamonds.

The Warring Parties: The MPLA, UNITA and the FNLA

The three nationalist movements began their fight against the Portuguese colonial regime in the early 1960s.

The MPLA (Movimento Popular de Libertação de Angola [People's Movement for the Liberation of Angola]) was founded in Luanda in

1956 and drew its constituency from the Mbundu population and the *mestiço* (mixed population). The MPLA was a Marxist organisation, but has evolved into a 'social-democratic party' in the hands of President José Eduardo dos Santos. Through the late 1950s and early 1960s, the MPLA received assistance and support from the Soviet Union. In the race for Luanda in 1975, and until the late 1980s, Soviet military assistance and Cuban troops played a key role in the MPLA's victory and, later, its control over the country. Since the elections in 1992, the MPLA has held the majority of seats in parliament and ministerial posts in the government.

UNITA (União Nacional para Independência Total de Angola [National Union for Total Independence of Angola]) was founded in 1966 by Jonas Savimbi, who remains the leader of the military faction of UNITA. In the 1960s, UNITA enjoyed little external support; but later, UNITA received assistance from South Africa and the United States. Much of UNITA's funding comes though its control over large parts of the diamond-mining areas in the northeast of the country. Although Savimbi built his movement among the Ovimbundu population, UNITA is an not an ethnic Ovimbundu organisation, nor do the majority of Ovimbundu support UNITA. UNITA has traditionally been based in rural areas and in the Central Highlands and southern parts of the country. In 1998, frustration within UNITA over Savimbi's war strategy and refusal to assume his position in the Government of Unity and Reconciliation (GURN) prompted one group to split from Savimbi and proclaim UNITA Renovada as the 'real' UNITA. Not all members of UNITA's parliamentary bench supported this initiative; they, in turn, formed a third group. Today, many members of UNITA call for peace negotiations and an end to the war.

The FNLA (Frente Nacional de Libertação de Angola [National Liberation Front of Angola]) was founded in 1962 in Kinshasa, then Congo, and is rooted in the Bakongo population from northern Angola. The FNLA received support from, among others, the late Congo President, Mobuto Sese Seko. After its failed race for Luanda, the FNLA more or less disappeared from the political scene, but returned as a political party in the 1992 elections.

The Post-Independence War (1974–91)

The first independent Angolan government was formed from a coalition of the three liberation movements, the FNLA, UNITA and the MPLA. The 'post-independence war' began when the three inde-

Photo 1   Displaced persons in Angola (UNHCR, C. Sattlberger 1944)

pendence movements fought each other for control of the capital, and thus political supremacy, when the Portuguese left. The MPLA, bolstered by Cuban troops, won and established a single-party socialist government in November 1975. Since then, Angola has been in a constant state of civil war.

From the mid-1970s, the MPLA government has largely controlled the cities and parts of the countryside in the coastal areas; UNITA has controlled most of the interior and rural areas, particularly those in the central and southern parts of the country. Since war is not waged all the time, in every part of the country, there are great regional variations in how the fighting affects the population. Some areas in the southern provinces and along the coast have been almost untouched by war; while the interior provinces of, for example, Bié, Malanje and Huambo have witnessed fierce fighting.

In 1991, UNITA and the MPLA signed a cease-fire agreement known as the Bicesse Accord. The parties agreed to hold multi-party elections for parliament and president in September 1992 and to unify their armed forces. They also agreed that the government should establish its authority over former UNITA territory, and that the UN should oversee the implementation of the peace accord and the elections.

The Post-Multi-Party-Elections War (October 1992–November 1994)

The first free multi-party elections were held in September 1992. When UNITA unexpectedly lost to the MPLA, the two movements returned to full-scale war, which lasted until 1994. Because the government demobilised many troops in 1991 as part of the peace accord, UNITA forces were able to occupy and hold five of the 18 provincial capital cities: Uíge, Huambo, Caxito, M'banza Kongo and Ndalatando. In Huambo, UNITA established an alternative government. On 20 November 1994, the Lusaka Cease-Fire Protocol was signed by the Angolan government, headed by the MPLA, and UNITA. As part of the Protocol, the GURN was established in April 1997. Under the Protocol, UNITA troops were to be integrated into the government army or demobilised. However, UNITA used the demobilisation camps as feeding and resting areas for their soldiers until a new war began in 1998.

The Latest War (December 1998–   )

The country was plunged back into full-scale civil war in the beginning of December 1998, after a year of infrequent attacks and confrontations between government troops and the opposition's guerrillas. UNITA used the time after the Lusaka Protocol to shield itself from further territorial losses and to rebuild its military. It refused to hand over territory to the government (Vines, 1999:4). The government attacked UNITA headquarters in Bailundo and Andulo as part of its political campaign during the fourth MPLA party congress in December 1998. What was expected to be a short period of fighting has lasted for more than two years.

This war is described by some as more devastating for the population and the infrastructure than the previous wars (MSF 2000). Villages have been attacked, houses and food stocks have been burned, domestic animals have been stolen, men and women have been raped and molested, cities have been shelled, convoys carrying food and medicine to besieged populations have been attacked and robbed. Reports estimate that 2.6 million people have been newly displaced since 1998, tens of thousands have been killed and hundreds of thousands have died indirectly from the effects of the war (see UNOCHA 2000b:10).

During 1999, rising oil prices and UN sanctions against UNITA bolstered the FAA, and in October 1999 they took back important UNITA strongholds and headquarters. UNITA returned to guerrilla-style warfare.

Despite peace and reconciliation initiatives launched by the UN and the civil society, particularly the churches, there are few signs of a political resolution to the conflict. The Angolan government has recognised and accepted UNITA Renovada, while Savimbi's UNITA is considered a terrorist organisation. In December 2000, the government gave amnesty to all UNITA soldiers. It urged all UNITA troops still in the bush to surrender to government authorities and participate in the reconstruction and development of the country.

THE TERM 'INTERNALLY DISPLACED PERSON' IN AN ANGOLAN CONTEXT

In Angola, displaced persons label themselves as *deslocado* (singular). Directly translated into English, *deslocado* means 'dislocated' or 'out of place'. However, such a pure linguistic translation of the term does not necessarily capture the implicit understanding of forced relocation as is implicit in the Angolan context. In a society where movement and relocation of villages, tribes, families and individuals are normal, the term *deslocado* is used to describe an abnormal situation: a relocation that is forced, not voluntary or part of normal practice. It is therefore necessary to highlight the element of force that is implied in the term.

The *deslocado* identity is a social identity. Those whom we label *deslocados* or displaced in this chapter have multiple facets of identity, such as 'woman', 'old', 'Ovimbundu' (ethic group), 'Sambo' (tribe), 'peasant', 'head of family', 'Catholic', 'MPLA supporter', etc. These facets assume different levels of importance at different times (Bordo 1990:136–45). *Deslocado* is only one facet of the identity of the people we interviewed.

In Angola, the displaced population is often divided into two categories: 'new' and 'old' *deslocados*. This is a classification that is commonly used by the displaced themselves, by NGOs and by government representatives. New *deslocados* are all those who have been displaced after July/August 1998, regardless of the cause of their displacement, although the war is the predominant cause. Among the new *deslocados*, some have fled from government-controlled areas, others from UNITA-controlled areas.

This division between new and old *deslocados* can be related to Susan Bordo's multiple 'axes' of identity, whereby the various axes are given varying degrees of importance by the *deslocados*, the established population, and others (1990:139). Based upon the information culled from our interviews, the *deslocado* axis is more important to the new *deslocados* than to the old. This is not to suggest, however, that the old *deslocados* have stopped using that word to describe themselves. Rather, other identifying axes are more important in their daily lives.

Sorensen argues that for rural populations identity is embedded in their land and their agricultural practices (1998:82–3). Even though the displaced in Huambo province have not fled far from their homes, they often find it impossible to cultivate the land where they settle after flight. Displaced persons have described a loss of cultural identity after they leave their home villages. Our interpretation is that, with the loss of their land and normal life, an important facet of their identity is lost too.

STORIES FROM SELF-SETTLED NEW *DESLOCADOS*

Vinte-e-Sete is a village located 14 kilometres east of Huambo City. It is a settlement that was established to provide housing for agricultural workers at the Chianga Research Institute. Today, only a handful of those who live there permanently have a job at Chianga. In March 1999, some 400 families lived there.[1] More than half were displaced and the majority of them were new *deslocados*. The *soba* (traditional leader) described a situation in which everyone, established groups and the displaced 'lack everything ... we have a lot of suffering, no food, no clothes, no health clinic, no school ...' The village received the first displaced persons in 1975; since then, there have been regular influxes. Many of the displaced have returned to their homes, in areas around Sambo, Bailundo and Kilengue, at various times.

The *soba* explained that the *deslocados* came to Vinte-e-Sete because 'they do not want to live in the city [Huambo]. Some had tried that first but did not manage.' There were some empty houses to accommodate the displaced when they arrived '... since many had fled from here to relatives in [the cities of] Huambo and Benguela when the "trouble" began [November/December 1998]'. The Angolan NGO, Corpo de Apoio ao Deslocado (CAD), ran a food-for-work project in cooperation with the local authorities and the World Food Programme (WFP). The beneficiaries were the most vulnerable *deslocados* in Vinte-e-Sete. One hundred households had been chosen to participate.

In all locations around Huambo that had welcomed displaced persons, both established groups and new *deslocados* struggled to survive. However, where the established groups had housing and land they could tend, the new *deslocados* often did not have access to fields. If they did, it was land that was far away and of low fertility. The new *deslocados* pointed out that even if they could rent land from someone, they lacked other essentials, such as seeds, fertilisers and tools. Elderly *deslocados* and female-headed households had great difficulty in constructing houses or repairing abandoned houses for shelter against rain and cold nights.

Fourteen *deslocado* families fled from Sachitemo (27 kilometres south-east of Vinte-e-Sete) during late October and November 1998. They left Sachitemo during the nights, alone or in small groups of five to ten persons. They only walked on roads in secure places, such as near Missão do Cuando; otherwise, they travelled through the bush. They had fled their village, without knowing where they were headed, because of the killings and robberies taking place around them. 'UNITA kills with machetes, whereas the government troops use weapons', one of them told us. There were very few adult men among the families; only two elderly men. The women said that they did not know where their husbands were. Most had probably been forcibly recruited. In addition, there were few women between the ages of 18 and 40. Many of them had also probably been captured by UNITA to be used as labourers.

These *deslocados* did not want go to a displaced camp, because 'there, we will have to cooperate with the government', one said. It was only by coincidence that they came to Vinte-e-Sete. They were warmly received there and so decided to stay. Others from their village went to the city of Huambo or to the Co-Alfa camp on the outskirts of Huambo.

This was the second time these people were displaced; the first time, they fled to Missão do Cuando. 'This time life is much more difficult than the other time we were *deslocados* [during 1993–94]. We do not have access to *naka* (low-lying, fertile soil)', one of them said. They said they wanted to return home as soon as it was safe there.

Nearly all the new *deslocados* interviewed wanted to return home as soon as possible, citing bad living conditions and no opportunity to acquire their own land as displaced persons. It was only among those few who were displaced for the first time that there was some reluctance to return. Perhaps that is because those who have had previous experience with displacement believe it is a better survival strategy to re-establish their livelihoods at home, despite the destruction and losses they have suffered there. Quite a few of the *deslocados* pointed out that they will be dependent on government assistance, such as seeds for maize, since everything at home has been stolen or destroyed.

OLD *DESLOCADOS*

Most of the old *deslocados*, while identifying themselves as *deslocado*, also regard themselves as part of the established groups where they are settled. The old *deslocados* seem to have evolved from a state of survival to a state of fight for livelihood. There were three main causes of displacement of the old *deslocados:* during the colonial era, the authorities gave settlers permission to displace the local populations from land they wanted for themselves; degradation of agricultural land to the point that peasants cannot sustain themselves from what they are able to produce; and earlier phases of the civil war.

A PROFILE OF ANGOLA'S DISPLACED

The number of internally displaced persons in Angola varies from month to month and year to year. As some displaced return home, new people become displaced. As a result, there is continual disagreement between the Angolan government, particularly the Ministry of Social Affairs (MINARS), and many international NGOs and agencies, such as the International Committee of the Red Cross (ICRC) and the United Nations High Commissioner for Refugees (UNHCR), even over estimates of the number of displaced persons in the country. The estimates for April 2000 ranged between that of the UN Office for the Coordination of Humanitarian Affairs (UNOCHA), 2.3 million, and MINARS's 3.7 million (NRC 2000a:26). The discrepancy in figures is partly due to insufficient information, but also to basic differences of opinion in what constitutes forced migration. In addition, many displaced individuals do not register themselves as such since they are self-settled and do not receive any assistance from the government or from NGOs. Many displaced persons are afraid to present themselves to the local authorities as displaced, since they fear that the authorities may then consider them to be 'infiltrators' from UNITA (UNDP 1999:87).

During the past two decades, more than 25 per cent of Angola's population has been displaced (UNOCHA 2000b:10). Humanitarian agencies estimate that 1 million people were still displaced in 1997 as a result of the 1992–94 war. Since 1998, another 2.6 million persons have become displaced. Of these, just over 1 million have been registered by various NGOs and humanitarian agencies. Some 393,000 live in IDP camps and transit centres and another 187,000 are temporarily resettled (UNOCHA 2000b:10). Both groups receive some form of assistance, but self-help activities are essential to their survival. The remaining 520,000 of the NGO-registered displaced persons are integrated into urban and semi-urban societies and, to a large extent, survive on their own or with assistance from host populations.

The majority of the displaced population, perhaps as much as 75 per cent, are women and children. Many men are soldiers, or have been killed in the wars; often men flee to others areas, such as forest or unpopulated places, to hide from the armies of both sides. Female-headed households tend to go to camps or other places that do some kind of registration more often than male-headed households. Inevitably, the distorted social structure of the displaced population plays a decisive role in how the population copes with displacement.

Displaced persons generally move either from rural and remote areas to more urban and central places in the provinces (such as the coastal towns of Luanda, Lobito and Benguela and the interior cities of Malanje, Luena, Menongue and Huambo), or from the interior to the coastal areas. Some estimate that 80 per cent of Angola's displaced population fled to the coastal areas and larger cities (NRC 2000b:2). Although some researchers have said that most displaced persons do not return to their place of origin (Vines 1998:93), the displaced who remained behind in Huambo province said that many of their number had been displaced several times, and thus must have gone back to their places of origin more than once (Birkeland 2000:112).

Table 1.1   Displaced persons by province, at 30 September 2000

Province	Reported number of IDPs since January 1998	Confirmed number of IDPs since January 1998
Bengo	46,106	25,827
Benguela	142,636	73,425
Bié	352,900	123,041
Cunene	62,137	7,051
Huambo	331,401	126,566
Huíla	178,503	125,309
Kuando Kubango	90,971	51,606
Kuanza Norte	180,115	46,651
Kuanza Sul	127,781	89,752
Luanda	495,130	11,104
Lunda Norte	31,798	13,047
Lunda Sul	68,970	61,970
Malanje	252,003	131,931
Moxico	138,859	83,179
Namibe	14,121	14,121
Uíge	155,280	97,486
Zaire	14,869	3,877
Total number	2,683,580	1,085,943

Source: UNOCHA (2000b:13).

While people seem to be continually on the move, the Angolan government has, in cooperation with UNOCHA, organised return and resettlement schemes for some of the displaced persons staying in camps and transit centres in the same provinces as their home villages. By the end of December 2000, 288,000 displaced persons had been temporarily resettled, but large-scale return was limited because of persistent insecurity in many areas (IRIN 2001). MINARS has decided not to return displaced persons to their villages unless the 'Minimum Standards for Return and Resettlement' are fulfilled. Central to these standards are voluntariness, security and the participation of the displaced themselves. As discussed in the section on protection strategies below, some observers say these standards are not always met when the displaced are asked to leave camps and transit centres.

CASE STUDY: THE DISPLACED IN HUAMBO PROVINCE

Before the last war started in 1998, there were between one and 1.5 million inhabitants in Huambo province. With the outbreak of war, many residents fled to other provinces, but at least 350,000 displaced persons remain in government-controlled areas. The number of displaced persons and the conditions in which they live in UNITA territory are unknown; but the number of people in those areas is likely to be only a fraction of the number of persons in government-controlled zones. A large percentage of the displaced population originate from Huambo and other parts of the Central Highlands.

Huambo province is a place of great real and symbolic importance for both the government and UNITA. It was here that UNITA declared independence on 11 November 1975, after the group had lost its struggle with the MPLA for control of Luanda. Later, Huambo City was retaken by the MPLA; but the countryside remained, for the most part, under UNITA control.

In 1992, when UNITA rejected the election results and resumed the war, the rebels set up their own national government in Huambo. When UNITA was forced out of Huambo in late 1994, their headquarters was moved to Jamba in the province of Cuando Cubango. After the signing of the Lusaka Protocol in 1994, UNITA moved its headquarters to Bailundo, again in Huambo province. In October 1999, the government forced UNITA out of Bailundo. Throughout the past decade, the province's population has been stuck in the middle of this military and political see-saw.

Huambo province has been called Angola's 'Garden of Eden' (Bender 1978; Russo 1993) because of its favourable climate and the belief, not borne out by reality, that the land is fertile. After 25 years of civil war and, prior to that, 35 years of intense exploitation by the Portuguese, the area has seen the greatest drop in standard of living, including in social and cultural life, of all Angola's provinces.

The Ovimbundu are the predominant ethnic group in Huambo province, as in the rest of the Central Highlands. The Central Highlands and the Ovimbundu are often presented as the core of UNITA's and Savimbi's supporters. However, large segments of the population liken the difference between the government and UNITA as one between plague and cholera. The MPLA are seen as thieves and UNITA as assassins (Munslow 1999:551–2). Although some observers characterise the war as an ethnic conflict, Ovimbundu men make up the majority of both the government's and UNITA's armies.

Most of the displaced population that remains in Huambo – originating from both government- and UNITA-controlled areas – fled to and within the government-controlled areas – along the Benguela Railway (CFB) corridor and concentrated in the municipalities of Caála and Huambo. The CFB corridor includes urban areas and the surrounding agricultural zones, but UNITA has held the most productive agricultural land in the south and north of the CFB corridor.

It is only the most affluent of the displaced, those with economic resources or good contacts in the government or army, who have been able to leave the region entirely.[2] Since the resumption of war in December 1998, UNITA's strategy seems to have been to force the whole rural population into government-controlled areas. The rationale behind this is two-fold: to strain the government's resources and capabilities with large influxes of displaced persons and, since UNITA drove the peasants off their land shortly after the 1998–99 planting season, to secure access to food for UNITA troops the following year.

Providing assistance and protection to *deslocados* in the province is difficult given the limited human and economic resources available and since many areas are inaccessible because of the security risk and lack of good infrastructure. While there are a substantial number of displaced persons in Huambo who have developed a dependency on external aid, most of the displaced know they cannot 'trust' external actors to provide sufficient food, shelter and education. Indeed, they would be extremely vulnerable if they had to depend solely on fluctuating levels of international aid and the presence of international NGOs in the region. Therefore, many displaced persons have developed strategies to survive independently.

METHODOLOGY

The data used in this study were collected during field work in the region from February to May 1999 and in September and October

2000. The interviews were both semi-structured and open. Among those interviewed were also representatives from host populations, NGOs and the government. Most of the interviews were conducted in Umbundu, the local language, and were simultaneously translated into Portuguese. Interviews were held in various locations in the municipalities of Huambo, Caála, Ekunha and Longonjo among self-settled displaced, those living in camps and transit centres, resettlement camps, and displaced persons who were in the process of returning to their villages after one to two years of displacement.

RESETTLEMENT IN HUAMBO

On 5 August 2000, the provincial government in Huambo began a resettlement programme to move thousands of displaced persons from the 'inadequate' transit centres in the town of Caála to locations closer to their home villages. The authorities had identified two sites, Cantão Pahula and Kassoko, for the resettlement camps. This resettlement operation was the focus of heated debate among various international and national humanitarian agencies. The ICRC, for example, did not regard these locations as safe enough for resettlement. Agency representatives also expressed their fears that the resettled population would be used as an 'early warning system' by the government. However, the Angolan NGO Acção para Desen-volvimento Rural e Ambiental (ADRA) argued that people should be assisted when they wanted to move away from the deplorable conditions in the transit centres.

The centres were often set up amid the ruins of factories or storage buildings where there was only limited access to water and firewood. Latrines were dug in the courtyards and back gardens. Either plastic sheeting was used for roofing or families sheltered in tents. There was usually only limited or, more often, no access to cultivable land. The displaced described the conditions in these centres as unfit for their animals.

UNOCHA and international NGOs were uncomfortable about moving thousands of displaced persons to new locations before access to water and sanitation facilities had been established. Never-theless, the local governor pushed the resettlement scheme through. Zoraida Mesa, the UN Humanitarian Coordinator in Angola, said at the time: 'It is certainly good news that these transit centres will no longer be used to accommodate displaced persons. However, the UN would like to … emphasise that resettlement of IDPs in Angola should take place in the context of the government's minimum operational standards. Security is a prime condition, as are acceptable living conditions and the means for self-reliance through the provision of arable land and seeds and tools' (IRIN 2000a).

UNOCHA had already raised concern over the forced resettlement of displaced persons in its Rapid Assessment report of April 2000 (UNOCHA 2000a). Local authorities, represented by MINARS, stressed that no involuntary resettlement has taken place; but many of the displaced said they had never been consulted before being resettled.

Teresa is a 25-year-old peasant who lives with her husband and their two children in Caála. She spoke with us in September 2000 in 'Centro de Reassentamento do Kassoko', a resettlement camp in Caála municipality:

We had to flee from our village because of attacks in May 1999. We fled at night from our village, first to Lupili, and later continued to Caála. We arrived in Caála without anything. We left almost everything in our village. The little we brought with us was stolen by UNITA during the flight. I, for example, brought with me 10 kilogrammes of maize and 5 kilogrammes of beans. They took everything from me. I asked to keep something for the baby I carried at my breast, but they did not accept that. Then we arrived in Caála and struggled badly to survive. Many people starved, became sick and some died. Even today I have 'pains in my breast' [am very sad] when I think of that situation.

When we arrived in Caála, we went to the Salsicharia [a transit centre]. We rather wanted to stay in the *bairros* [quarters] than in a transit centre, but there we would have to rent a room or house, and we did not have any money to pay rent.

The stay in Salsicharia was very difficult because we could hardly do anything. We had to collect firewood in the woods of Kassoko and sell it in Caála to get money to buy food. Those who had cards from ICRC received food, but we did not receive anything from them since we arrived at Salsicharia after the ICRC registration.

In some ways, it was not difficult to adapt to life in the IDP camp because I already had some experience in small-scale trading. In Salsicharia, the children could study because we had a brother named Artur who gave classes to the children; but the youth and the adults did not study. When we became sick, we went to the hospital in Caála for consultations and they gave us remedies.

In Salsicharia, we did not have access to land to cultivate or employment. In the displaced peoples' camp, although we lived in a very difficult situation, we had to respect the others since we all lived in more or less the same place. At night, it was very difficult because we all had to sleep together in the same room. We did not know whether it was a man or a woman lying next to us or who it was ... Children and adults also had to sleep in the same space.

At the moment, I do not have an identity card because my old one was destroyed when my house in our village was burned down during the attack, but I am thinking of getting a new one now.

We stayed in the Salsicharia camp one year and eleven months. Three months ago, we moved from Salsicharia to here at Kassoko. When the government asked us to move here, we came to a place that was not a good place, but it is closer to our fields and village. Therefore, we can cultivate our own land now.

We were very happy to be able to make that decision of moving, because at Salsicharia we had to live very crammed; so we did not have problems in moving here to Kassoko. Here, we move around freely without any problems. For example, our fields in our village are located far away, but we do not go there every day. Here in Kassoko we have problems with water and food, but we do not have health problems. We are still staying together, the whole family. Also, I am active in all the activities that the administration gives us.

PROTECTION STRATEGIES

Lack of security is a major concern for the displaced population in Huambo province, even after flight. Although most of the population now lives in areas controlled by the government, people are not necessarily protected against violence and attacks. Displaced persons living in various locations, such as Caála, Ekunha, Lepi and Huambo, all report incidents of robbery and attack by soldiers from both sides of the conflict. Indeed, the warring parties assume that the local population sympathises with whichever party controls their area at any given time.

UNITA carry out guerrilla-style attacks on villages and towns and also attack transport vehicles. Displaced persons reported that when

UNITA seizes a village, the soldiers do not waste bullets to murder villagers, but use machetes, instead.

But it is not only UNITA soldiers who harass civilians. Government soldiers, too, steal from, and sometimes rape, the population they are sent to protect. When soldiers do not receive their salaries, which, because of mismanagement and corruption, occurs more often than not, pillage and robbery become a strategy for their own survival. The soldiers tend to behave better when they are located closer to administrative centres, therefore many displaced persons prefer to stay in those areas.

Given this insecurity, both displaced persons and the local population carry guns when they go into the fields. It is startling to note that the farther from the towns one goes, the more weapons one sees among the civilians. Civil defence groups, composed of both men and women, have been organised both by the local population and the authorities. Men carry the weapons, women patrol the paths and roads. Some members of the civil defence teams carry light weapons to protect settlements and markets. On the roads into towns, members of the civil defence regularly check that people are not carrying weapons and bombs hidden in their bags and baskets. Sometimes, a small civil defence group is left to protect houses and crops in villages from which most of the population has already fled.

Flight

Since the people in Huambo province lived through many years of forced displacement, they have developed good instincts about when they should flee. The displaced who had settled in Vinte-e-Sete and in Caála reported how people from the same village or area chose to flee at different times within a three- to four-month period. One man recounted how he and his family left their village in May 1998, three months before most of the village's population fled. He had arrived in Caála before the main influx of displaced persons in late 1998–early 1999, and thus had been able to stay with friends of the family instead of going to the IDP camp. He recalled:

> We regarded the situation as unfavourable and left our village in late May with some of our belongings. We even brought 16 cattle with us. These were later stolen here in Caála. For those who remained in the village until August, some are dead now and others went to Salsicharia.

Most villagers fled in small groups, usually at night, and avoided main roads where they could fall victim to robbery and assault. Some displaced women said that their husbands and other men went to UNITA-controlled areas because they were afraid they would be regarded as spies by the FAA if they remained in government-controlled areas while under attack from UNITA forces. Sometimes, representatives of the government or army would come to villages and order the population to leave, saying the area was considered unsafe. Villagers then had only a few hours to gather the goods they wanted to bring with them.

SUBSISTENCE STRATEGIES

Through their multiple displacements, the people of Huambo province have gained a great deal of experience in how to survive forced migration, including how to obtain assistance from international NGOs and other humanitarian organisations. Over the years, increasing numbers of agencies have opened offices in Huambo. Indeed, Huambo City is second only to Luanda in the number of humanitarian agencies located there. Most agencies are based, and conduct nearly all of their projects, in or close to Huambo City. As a result, the displaced who want access to the agencies' assistance and protection generally flee to those areas.

While international humanitarian agencies cannot operate in many areas because of the security risk, national NGOs can and do. In those locations, mission stations, such as Missão do Cuando, often provide food and medical assistance to the displaced. In addition, many displaced persons have developed valuable skills in how to survive in locations where humanitarian agencies do not operate. One such location is the resettlement camp Caliamama, which was established by local authorities in the southern part of Ekunha municipality, about 18 kilometres north of Caála town. Some 5,086 displaced families were living there in the beginning of October 2000. They had fled from the northern parts of Ekunha municipality in January and February 2000. Some had fled because of attacks by UNITA; others, because they were told by police and government forces to leave for security reasons.

The families first went to the new IDP camp, Kasseque III, in Huambo, but the municipal administration soon asked them to move on to Caála. Because of the abysmal living conditions in the transit centres there, the local authorities sent the displaced back to Ekunha, just on the other side of the Caála municipal border. The local administration told the families to build grass huts in an area next to Calia Mblingo village, which was identified as the site for the new resettlement camp.

Since Caliamama resettlement camp has received only minimal and sporadic assistance from external actors, and there is no agricultural land available nearby, malnutrition is a constant threat. The families subsist by collecting firewood and providing labour for others. Women explained how they are paid for their labour in sweet potatoes: 0.5 to 1 kilogramme for one day's work. In the camp, the women dry the sweet potatoes to make flour from which they then make their traditional, usually maize-based, porridge, *funge*. Those who cannot obtain sweet potatoes dry bananas to make flour. Others return home at night, a distance of approximately 40 kilometres, to collect food from their fields there. The journey is not only long, it is extremely dangerous: the area is littered with landmines. According to the *soba* (traditional leader), 17 people in that camp were killed or wounded by mines in the month of September 2000 on their trips back to their home areas to collect food or firewood. People living in the camp said that despite their considerable efforts to meet their basic needs, 'We live like animals here.' But to remain in UNITA-controlled areas was not an option: 'People who stay behind on the UNITA side are used as slaves', they said.

In general, people forced to flee go to areas that are secure but still far enough from cities and towns to offer access to fields and firewood. Because of the almost complete collapse of the economy, urban areas do not provide many options for subsistence other than agriculture; but after years of intensive use, the soil there is exhausted. Although agricultural land is relatively plentiful in the province, fertile land, that is, land that can be successfully cultivated without the use of fertilisers, is scarce. For the newly displaced, it is almost impossible to get access to fertile land near urban centres since it is already used by the established population. Even with access to land, a family can barely manage to cultivate one or two hectares if hand-hoes are all they have with which to tend their plots.

Carrying the Tools to Survive

The displaced have also learned, through experience, what is essential to bring with them. Food for their time on road and at the new location, and goods that can be sold for cash are most important. Having agricultural tools and the special tools used by carpenters and bricklayers makes it easier to build a livelihood in a

Table 1.2   Summary of the main income-generating activities in the informal sector for the displaced and host populations in the city of Huambo in September 2000 (US dollar = 13.5 kwanza, September 2000)

Main income-generating activity	Income in cash/goods	Participation by IDPs
Firewood	5–7 kwanza/day	Very common
Charcoal burning	5–10 kwanza/day	Common
Biscatos = working for others. Working the land of others, small businesses, washing clothes, collecting and carrying water and other household chores	4–10 kwanza/day or the equivalent to 1.5–2 canecas of *fuba* (maize flour)	Very common
Manufacture of natural-fibre mats	30–35 kwanza/week	Rare
Trading in fruits and vegetables	Depending on the season; during dry season: 7–15 kwanza/day	Common
Trading staple foods	7–30 kwanza/day	Rare
Farming own land	15–30 kwanza/day (depending on the amount of land and the crops produced)	Rare (due to lack of land for IDPs close to camps and resettlement camps)
Boleias (porter services)	Depending on the demand, weights and distance. 10–30 kwanza/day. On occasion, no income from this work. Therefore, it is likely that they engage in parallel trading activity.	Rare
Trading in luxury items	10–200 kwanza/day	Insignificant (due to large up-front capital requirements and lack of safe storage facilities).

Sources: Ana Gerlin, ICRC nutritionist, and authors' observations and interviews.

new location. A tailor who fled from Sambo and lives in Kasseque III IDP camp brought his sewing machine with him when he fled. He has taken it along with him to every place he has stayed before he was moved to the camp. He can now make enough money to live on by offering his services to others in the camp.

Collecting Firewood

Collecting firewood is probably the most common survival strategy used by displaced persons, whether they live in or outside camps. There has been a shortage of energy throughout Huambo province for the past eight years. With infrastructure largely destroyed, very little fossil fuel (gas, diesel and gasoline) reaches the interior, thus prices have skyrocketed.[3] In addition, since the 1992–94 war, deforestation has taken place on a massive scale in the most populated areas, specifically the corridor along the Benguela railway. The deforestation can be partly attributed to the lack of other energy sources, but mostly because firewood collection has been one of the best survival strategies for displaced and other vulnerable populations. Workers charge so little for their labour that even when road transport is functioning, consumers will opt for the cheaper firewood rather than other fuels.

Firewood is collected by all family members in a variety of locations:

- *Remaining trees on the savannah.* Trees have become scarce within secure walking distances from where displaced populations are concentrated. Areas within 30 to 50 kilometres from populated areas are more or less deforested. The host population explained that this change in the landscape has occurred gradually, through the decades, but accelerated after the 1992 war started. Even in areas in which fewer displaced have settled, access to wood requires a 3–8-kilometre trek each way. In these areas, further from the energy markets of the larger cities and towns, the wood is made into charcoal before it is transported.

  Though a sack of charcoal sells for more than firewood, it is not the producers who make the profit. Truckers buy the coal, then resell it at a 300 to 400 per cent mark-up. Some of the displaced who are strong enough will walk to the markets themselves, balancing a sack or two of coal on their heads, just to squeeze out a bit more profit for themselves. Near urban areas, elderly displaced dig for tree roots that may also be used for firewood.

- *Illegal cutting in forest reserves.* The reserves, protected by armed guards, are the only places near populated areas where dense forest can be found. Displaced persons either sneak into the forests to cut trees or pay the guards a small bribe to be let in. The displaced know that this illegal activity leads to deforestation which, in turn, leads to a lack of firewood and to wind erosion. They recall how their home areas used to be full of forests, with plentiful firewood and other natural bounty, such as insects, honey and wild animals. However, neither the displaced population nor the local population has much incentive to use the forest in a sustainable manner, given the level of insecurity in the region.

Petty Trading and Small-Scale Markets

As described in the UNDP's *Human Development Report for Angola* (1999), informal markets are the main survival strategy for displaced persons across the country. From our interviews and observations, however, we found that, for the displaced in Huambo province, firewood collection and *biscatos* (work for others) are more important sources of income.

Petty trading in streets and markets is most common in urban areas, but is occasionally also practiced in rural areas. Among the displaced in Huambo, it is mostly women who use petty trading as a source of income. Women who have access to some cash place themselves on the outskirts of markets or in markets, such as São Pedro, where they buy from local producers. A farmer may not have the experience or skill to sell his produce to consumers, so he may prefer to sell his goods in bulk to these trade women. The women do not make a great profit from their work: they may buy a wheelbarrow-load of cabbage to resell at the market, and make only enough to provide one or two meals for their families. Others sell fruits and vegetables in residential areas, or anything from used clothes and shoes to washing powder.

Informal trading also takes place inside the IDP camps and transit centres. Cigarettes, soap, matches, cooking oil and firewood are sold there in small quantities. Women dominate as sellers of low-priced goods. High-priced merchandise is generally sold by men, but few displaced men have the financial resources to enter that sector of the market.

Biscatos (Work for Others)

A common survival strategy among the newly displaced is to work for the more established population, either other displaced individuals or members of the host population. Some displaced persons may get an agreement to work for a week or longer, but usually work is a day-to-day arrangement. If someone wants to have his/her yard cleaned, he/she will go to a transit centre or to displaced persons living in the neighbourhood and say he/she needs someone to work that day. Payment for biscatos is almost always in kind, usually a can of maize meal (which, in September 2000, cost the equivalent of US$0.15). Given the meagre wages, families divide their labour and time in various income-generating activities to earn enough for food, fuel, soap, medicines, etc. Generally, men will clear new agricultural land and do construction work as their biscatos, while women collect firewood, wash clothes and trade. Children may help in all activities, but collecting firewood and water are typically children's work.

Handicrafts

Poverty among the host population, partly the result of earlier flight, does not leave much of a market for the sale of products made by the displaced. However, a few displaced persons have been able to set up small-scale businesses making and selling mats and clothes. The mats are made of either straw that is collected along the riverbanks or sisal. These mats are used for everything from sleeping mats to walls in huts and latrines.

Craftsmen such as tailors and construction workers sell their services to other displaced individuals as well as to the host population. Many masons and carpenters have been engaged to help reconstruct or build schools and health posts through food-for-work projects.

Many women produce and sell the traditional drink, chissangua, made from roasted maize grains, sugar and water. The drink is sold by the cup as a soft drink to other displaced persons, members of the host population and also to soldiers.

Negative Subsistence Strategies

There have been some instances of stealing among the displaced. In Ekunha, the local population reported an increase in produce stolen from their fields and yards and blamed the thievery on the desperate circumstances of the displaced persons living among them. In general, though, there has been little of this kind of activity, despite the poverty and desperation of the displaced. Displaced persons themselves said that only the most desperate, and those who had no social conscience, stole. They emphasised that these kinds of negative survival strategies were not accepted by the society.

Cheating with food ration cards, however, is not regarded as stealing, and is done more frequently. Families split up and go to different camps/transit centres to register, and thus benefit from multiple sources of food. Sometimes, families will build huts in different locations where NGOs and/or the ICRC provide food rations and then travel back and forth to get double rations. Since food is given out on certain days in each location, it is not difficult to move between the camps at the appropriate times. The government and various NGOs tried to stop this practice by registering all displaced persons by name, but since most displaced persons have no identity cards, the system is often ineffective.

SELF-RELIANCE STRATEGIES

Before the civil wars began, most Angolans lived in rural areas and farmed, mostly subsistence crops, but also cash crops used to buy goods like soap, salt, cloth and medicines. Families in the Central Highlands relied on three sources of income: growing food in their own fields, working as forced labourers for the Portuguese during the colonial era and, after independence, as migrant labourers in the coastal zones, and working for the urban population in the Central Highlands.

The civil wars started a chain of migration of all sectors of society. The work providers in cities and towns fled to Luanda and Benguela, causing upheaval in the secondary and tertiary sectors of the economy in the Central Highlands. People were pushed back to their small plots in the villages for subsistence. These fields were too small to sustain a family, particularly when many families hosted displaced relatives from areas more vulnerable to attacks.

The displaced constantly struggle to feed themselves. In Ekunha, a mother of five told us how she and her children had first fled from a hamlet near Sambo to Huambo City. But she was not able to get access to agricultural land or *biscatos* in Huambo and after two months they fled Ekunha. At that time, Ekunha was considered unsafe because of regular attacks by UNITA rebels. But this woman decided that it was better to have access to fertile agricultural land, even if that meant living with war, than to live without the means to sustain herself and her children.

Even for the established population, food scarcity is a major problem in the Central Highlands. There are simply too many people living in small areas where the land has been degraded and fertilisers are too expensive. In a mid-December 2000 report, WFP noted that the agency had been trying to provide the displaced population with seeds and agricultural tools: '... the resettled IDPs were expected to grow their own food and become self-sufficient within at least two harvest cycles. But a lack of safe, arable land, seeds and tools had slowed down this process ... people are likely to end up eating the seeds they're supposed to plant if they have no other source of food' (IRIN 2000c:1).

In some of the villages in which the displaced are resettling, the returning population and NGOs working in agricultural extension, such as ADRA-Angolana, OIKOS (Cooperacao e Desenvolvimento) and Development Workshop, organise agricultural campaigns to repair and build irrigation systems, propagate seeds, and introduce and promote greater varieties of produce. The latter is founded on a concern for food security and future access to cash income. With a greater variety of crops, the resettled population will be less vulnerable to changes in rainfall patterns and thievery.

ADRA-Angolana, which runs an agricultural programme for persons returning to their villages in the 'Quilometre Vinte-e-Cinco' area south of Caála, found that the local church has great influence in whether a village embraces agricultural change or not. Protestant villages seem to be more open to change and innovation, such as introducing new vegetables for sale and personal consumption, while the more traditional Catholic villages want to keep to maize and sweet potatoes as their main crops.

ACCESS TO EDUCATION

Three decades of civil war have devastated the educational system in Angola. Two out of three children will never reach the fifth grade. In 1995, 44 per cent of the male population and 74 per cent of the female population were illiterate, with much higher illiteracy rates in rural areas than in urban areas (NRC 2000a:67). There are more schools and teachers in urban areas, since that is where both the government and NGOs invest in infrastructure for education and since many teachers fled from rural municipalities to seek safety in more central areas. Schools in these areas are overcrowded, since many displaced children also attend these schools. When their home areas are safe, some displaced families who have settled in urban areas send their men and male adolescents back to their villages while the mother or an older sister remains in town so the younger children can continue going to school.

Although there is great awareness of the importance of education among the displaced, there is a long way to go before most displaced children receive even a basic education. Displaced parents often cannot pay the 'extra fees', or bribes, which the teachers and administrative staff at the schools demand to provide certificates of matriculation. (The request for 'extra fees' is not surprising: teachers' salaries average about US$20 per month, and payment is often two to six months late.) Interestingly, this seems to be less of a problem in Huambo than in, for example, Luanda. A significant number of parents who were displaced from Huambo province to Luanda (that is, some of those families who fled in December 1998) sent their children to schools in Huambo, when the city became safe again, because they didn't have to pay as many bribes and the quality of the education was better than in Luanda.

Education provided by external actors, such as the United Nations Children's Fund (UNICEF), is concentrated in the IDP camps and urban areas. One displaced woman described how her children only got access to education when they moved to Kasseque III camp. They had first fled from Sambo to Missão do Cuando and later Escóla 113 (both of which were large IDP settlements, accommodating several thousand persons, that received minimal assistance from agencies). They arrived at Kasseque III one and a half years after they first took flight. Even though Kasseque III is regarded as one of the best IDP camps and transit centres in Angola, most of the children living there do not get past the first year of school. Parents cannot afford to keep their children in school when they need their labour; and hunger and illness among the pupils and a lack of qualified teachers keeps children away. Because most children have either not finished their schooling or have never attended school before, the ages of those in the first grade can range from six to 14 years.

Some displaced persons we spoke with told how they had organised education for their children in transit centres by asking the teachers among them to teach their children in return for a small amount of food or cash. Later, some of these schemes were supported by outside agencies, such as UNICEF. In villages where the displaced have resettled and others are returning home, several schools and health centres are being built as part of food-for-work projects. ADRA-Angolana, together with the government and WFP, provide food for the workers and some construction material for school buildings. The agencies only become involved when the projects are initiated by the villagers.

PUBLIC PARTICIPATION

After the MPLA came to power, party committees were set up in every village. But villages are generally led by a *soba*, who is elected by the population and can be replaced if the population grow dissatisfied with his performance. Each village also has one or more *seculo*, or deputy *soba*, and a council of elders that is responsible for the daily administration of the villages. When an entire community flees, this structure of government is kept intact. When only part of the community flees together or reunites after flight, the *soba* will remain leader as long as he stays with a group from the village. In the IDP camps near Huambo City in early 1999, a typical village group consisted of women, children and either the male *soba* or administrator; the men had either been recruited by UNITA or government forces or refused to come to an area where they knew they were likely to be recruited.

For displaced communities that settle among the host population, the *soba*'s authority is greatly diminished, since the displaced then fall under the leadership of the host population's own *soba*. MINARS emphasises that no resettlement takes place without prior consultations with and approval from the displaced populations' *sobas*. Yet one may wonder how open these meetings are to objections from the *sobas*.

Public participation for most displaced persons, as for most of the rest of the population, is limited to participating in discussions held in the *jango*, or communal hut. These consultations usually revolve around community developments, such as the construction of schools and health posts, organising civil defence or setting up lending facilities for members of the community who need money for investments. The *jango*, which is also the site of traditional dances and story-telling, is so important in village life that it is often the first structure to be erected in resettlement camps.

For those displaced persons who live on their own, public participation may be more difficult since they are newcomers in a neighbourhood or village. But before settling in a new place, displaced individuals contact the local *soba* and ask for permission to stay. Normally, they will then be given the right to use a piece of land and told where they may build a hut. In urban areas, where acquiring new housing is a matter of finances, displaced persons rarely integrate fully into the social and political life of the host community.

DOCUMENTATION AND CITIZENSHIP

When displaced persons arrive at a checkpoint or at their destinations they are supposed to present themselves to the local authorities as displaced and show their identity (ID) cards or passports. Many Angolans, however, have neither. Among the 43 households we interviewed in Caála municipality, none had passports and only a quarter had ID cards. Some explained that they used to have ID cards, but they either didn't have time to find the cards before they fled or the cards were lost during flight.

In Angola, a person has to register with the local authorities if he/she travels to a different province, despite the 'free circulation' policy adopted in 1997. People without ID cards cannot flee far without being stopped at a checkpoint. Many displaced persons described how they fled through the *mata* (savannah) both to avoid regular attacks by troops and to avoid ID controls along the roads. If a person cannot provide a valid ID card, he/she has to bribe the police or government representative or risk a jail term.

If displaced persons have access to the offices that issue ID cards, they may be able to buy a card without the necessary documentation if they can pay enough. Those who have some form of employment, usually in urban areas, are more likely to have ID cards than peasants. A woman who lives in an IDP camp outside Lepí explained that she wanted to flee to Benguela, but could not do so since she did not have an ID card. As long as she fled within the municipality, the people at the control posts knew her and she did not have any problems. To get an ID card, she would have had to produce a birth certificate, travel about 30 kilometres to Caála, where the nearest government office that issues ID cards is located, pay for photos to be taken, and pay, again, to obtain a card. For her, the task was too daunting and too expensive and so she decided to remain in a place that was relatively safer than her village, but that was not where she had wanted to resettle.

Among those displaced persons we interviewed who originated from areas that were usually controlled by UNITA, no one had an ID card. This is not surprising, since many regard the national ID card, issued by the government, as a 'pro-government' card. In addition, many in UNITA-controlled areas do not want to use the ID cards they have because they fear that authorities would consider them as 'infiltrators' (UNDP 1999:87). However, when a person does not have an ID card, the police and other authorities are likely to believe that the person is a UNITA supporter. As one local administrator said: 'Those who do not have an ID card are not Angolans.'

PROPERTY ISSUES

The Land Act, which regulates the use of arable land, was approved in 1992 but it has not been widely applied in the province of Huambo, except in 1997, when local authorities allocated about 59,000 hectares to 785 farmers (UNDP 1999:57). Not surprisingly, a few commercial farmers won control over most of the land. According to the UNDP (1999), out of 41,457 hectares allocated in three municipalities, eleven farmers now own 46 per cent of the arable land. Those who were awarded the large concessions were usually political or military leaders. The government gave an old *fazenda* (commercial farm) to an NGO, despite the fact that the land supported the crops of several hundred families who were then forced to leave in favour of the NGO's tree-planting project.

Traditionally, land is controlled by the communities and the *sobas* divide the land among the population. Displaced persons we interviewed who were still living in exile, and some who had just repatriated to their areas of origin, said that no one is allowed to claim another family's land, even in their absence, because of the belief that they may someday return. Only family members are allowed to use the abandoned land. Those who return, however, can ask if they may use a field that is, at the moment, untended. Ultimately, the *soba* has the right to re-allocate land if he wants to.

There are few conflicting claims for land among the subsistence peasants who return to their original areas. But that is likely to change when large landowners return to what they believe is still their land. During the decades of war, very few of these landholders remained in the Central Highlands. During this time, much of their land was appropriated by the local communities and given to displaced persons. At present, there are no mechanisms in place to prevent or solve these prospective conflicts.

CONCLUSION

Forced displacement and the complex humanitarian emergency in the Central Highland region have become 'normal' life for the population. Yet in spite of their adaptation to this 'normalcy', both the host populations and the displaced long for a future of peace, with no need for displacement. For the displaced, collective and individual knowledge and the capability of surviving during, and of re-building their lives after, displacement are valuable assets, especially since host authorities are usually weak and the NGO presence is inconstant.

Since many of the displaced cannot rely on the government or on outside agencies to provide assistance, they devise low-cost self-help activities that can be taken with them if they have to move again. The survival of these displaced populations is, to a large extent, dependent upon their own resilience, tenacity and considerable efforts. The host authorities and humanitarian agencies could do more to support the displaced through focused activities and projects, even during times of conflict.

ACKNOWLEDGEMENTS

The fieldwork for this chapter was made possible with a research grant from the NRC, Programme on Forced Migration, Resource Conflicts and Development.

André Kapingãla Imbo Ndjamba, Pedro Changolo Manuel Chipindo, Chikemba Claudeth, Sandra Mussungo, Isabel Graça Macedo Aurélio, Belamino Jelembi, Inocêncio Katiavala and Cidália Gomes provided research assistance.

The authors would also like to thank Carlos Figueiredo, Director, DW Huambo, Fernando Arroya, field advisor, UNOCHA Huambo, António Víctor Nobrega, coordinator, ADRA-A Caála, Bjørg Leite, Norwegian Ambassador to Angola and all the interviewees who gave their time.

NOTES

1. The family unit generally consists of three to seven members.
2. The FAA, for example, provides *deslocados* with transport out of the area in military planes – for a high fee.
3. One litre of diesel cost two to three US dollars in Huambo in September 2000; 1 litre cost US$0.1 in Luanda during the same period.

2
Burundi: Developing Strategies for Self-Reliance. A Study of Displacement in Four Provinces

Geneviève Boutin and Salvatore Nkurunziza

Since the 1993 assassination of its first elected President, Melchior Ndadaye, Burundi has been racked by political and social upheavals. Between bouts of violence perpetrated by the army and armed rebels and targeted mainly at civilians, instability, economic decline and human suffering continue unabated. The current crisis is only the most recent in a long history of violent conflict in the country. Since Burundi became independent in 1962, there have been recurrent outbreaks of political violence caused by tension between the Tutsi minority and Hutu majority, the most significant of them occurring in 1965, 1972, 1988 and now, since 1993.

Large numbers of people were forced to leave their homes as a result of past fighting, notably in 1972, when over 300,000 people fled to Tanzania. Most of them have not returned. Since the army and armed rebel movements continue to target civilian populations, displacement continues to be a primary consequence, and characteristic, of the conflict that has raged since 1993. Patterns of displacement in Burundi are complex. Some internally displaced persons find refuge in camps, others hide in forests and swamps, and large numbers of people flee to neighbouring Tanzania. Some people have had to flee their homes more than once, only to have to rebuild their lives from scratch each time.

An estimated 630,000 people, or more than 10 per cent of Burundi's total population, are believed to be displaced inside Burundi (MRRDR 2000). As Francis Deng, Representative of the UN Secretary-General on Internally Displaced Persons, reported in 1994: 'Displacement has become a way of life for many of the people of Burundi.' Since his report, the situation for most of them has only worsened.

This study focuses on internally displaced persons who have been displaced during the latest crisis – since 1993 – and exclusively on

Map 2   Burundi

those persons who have been forced to flee from armed conflict, situations of generalised violence, or violations of human rights. Interviews and participatory research exercises were conducted among displaced persons and/or former displaced persons in four of Burundi's 17 provinces. The provinces chosen are among those most affected by the conflict. The aim of the study was to learn from the displaced individuals about how they cope at both the individual and community levels prior to, during, and after forced displacement.

Findings from the province of Bujumbura Rurale, where displacement during 1999–2000 was the result of a deliberate policy of forced relocation carried out by Burundian authorities, will be discussed separately. This is because forced relocation, also called regroupment, puts targeted individuals and communities into circumstances where it is particularly difficult for them to sustain themselves and their families. Forcibly relocated populations benefit from little or no access to social services or basic hygiene and sanitation. They are often forbidden to cultivate their land and are forced to leave in haste, often abandoning their belongings to do so. As a result, they have few means at their disposal to cope with their circumstances, and are often more dependent on external assistance than are other displaced persons. Given that it implies violations of human rights and international conventions, and has serious consequences for food security, forced relocation presents a special challenge to the international community.

In general, we have found that individuals devise numerous strategies to cope with the causes and circumstances of internal displacement. These are not self-help strategies in the strictest terms, where people act on their own determination and without any form of external assistance. Given that Burundi was already one of the poorest countries in the world prior to the latest crisis, and that there are few resources available to peasants in Burundi (little or no savings, little education, almost no access to information), it is clear that most individuals would not survive internal displacement without at least minimal assistance. What we found, however, was that once given limited assistance in the form of protection, shelter and food, people developed a large array of coping strategies. It is thus critical to understand the response mechanisms of communities and individuals so that any assistance provided to them can be targeted effectively and can reinforce, rather than discourage or counteract, the initiatives developed by the internally displaced.

BACKGROUND

Geography and Population

Burundi is a small, landlocked country in east Africa that covers less than 28,000 square kilometres. It is bordered by Tanzania to the east and south, Rwanda to the north, and the Democratic Republic of the Congo (DRC) to the west. Like neighbouring Rwanda, Burundi has one of the highest population densities in the world. With a total population of about 6.2 million,[1] Burundi has an estimated population density of about 222.8 inhabitants per square kilometre.

Burundi has a complex and multilayered administrative structure. The country is divided into 17 administrative provinces.[2] Each province, in turn, is divided into communes, then into zones, *secteurs* (sectors), *collines* (hills), and *sous-collines* (sub-hills). Each of these units has a chief, who is responsible for various duties. Most inhabitants tend to identify themselves with the *colline* from which they originate. There is no tradition of centralised human settlement in Burundi. Instead, populations have always lived scattered across the *collines*, in isolated houses surrounded by the family land and banana plantation. However, as a result of internal displacement and subsequent resettlement programmes, some displaced camps are being transformed into semi-permanent or permanent villages.[3] There is no telling how this important change in the social landscape will affect political and economic interactions in Burundi over the long term.

More than 90 per cent of the population live by subsistence farming. For these people, displacement means more than being forced to live far away from their cultivated plots; it can mean starvation, since they generally have few sources of cash income and very little savings and/or other resources.

The population of Burundi is generally believed to be 80 to 85 per cent Hutu, 15 to 20 per cent Tutsi and approximately one per cent Twa.[4] However, these numbers are not based on recent statistical data. In fact, none of the successive governments of Burundi since independence has conducted an ethnic census. The percentages, based on data gathered under Belgian colonial rule, do not necessarily reflect ethnicity as perceived by Burundians, themselves, because of the methodology used by the Belgians. When they conducted the census in 1934, Belgian administrators arbitrarily classified anyone owning more than ten cows as a Tutsi (USCR 1998). Since independence, Tutsis have held most political offices and have dominated the military and the judiciary. Most Hutus are cultivators; the Twas, a marginalised ethnic group, live off small crafts and subsistence agriculture.

While the existence of real differences among the three main ethnic groups is debatable (see below), to many Burundians, repeated incidents of ethnic violence have reinforced the notion that ethnicity is a divisive issue. This, in turn, feeds the violence between ethnic groups. This standard view of Burundian society as divided into three ethnic groups ignores a web of complex regional, sub-ethnic, caste and patrimonial categories (see Lemarchand and Martin 1974) that have a profound impact on Burundi's political, economic and social systems.

History

There are two dominant historical narratives about Burundi, each with its own distinct interpretation of the background to the ethnic clashes and the present crisis in the country.

It is widely agreed that, unlike most countries in Africa, Burundi was not a pure invention of European colonialism (USCR 1998). It had been a kingdom for centuries prior to the arrival of the Europeans, with its king (the *Mwami*) the leader of all Burundis who spoke one language, Kirundi, and shared a common culture. Conquered by Germany in 1899, Burundi became a Belgian mandated territory after the First World War. As such, it was administered jointly with neighbouring Rwanda as Rwanda-Urundi.

Some Burundians argue that tensions between the Hutus and Tutsis in Burundi existed before colonisation. According to this version of history, the inhabitants of Burundi arrived in three waves. The Twas were the original inhabitants of the country. Later, the Hutus, of Bantu origin, migrated to the Great Lakes region from Central Africa. The Tutsi pastoralists, originally from north-eastern African, according to this theory, arrived last. Although they were not always in violent conflict with each other, this history argues that the pastoral Tutsis slowly gained control over the Hutu farmers and the Hutus have been dominated by Tutsis since. This view is widely held among Hutu leaders in Burundi and those in exile (Malkki 1995).

The second historical narrative is mostly told in government circles and has become, since 1989, the official version of Burundi's history (see Government of Burundi 1989). According to this version, the conflict among the inhabitants of Burundi is the direct result of Belgium's colonial policy, which favoured the Tutsis as allies in ruling the colony. The 'hamitic' myth, according to which Tutsis arrived from the north after the Hutus, is said to have been created in colonial writings on Burundi. There is no historical or linguistic evidence for this claim, argues the current Burundian President, Pierre Buyoya (Buyoya 1998:53).

When the people of Burundi were finally allowed to vote in 1956, they did not mobilise along ethnic lines. Prince Rwagasore created the Party of Unity and National Progress (UPRONA), whose main platform was to reject ethnic divisions and strive for national unity.

In 1962, the same year Burundi gained independence, a bloody rebellion took place in Rwanda. Hutu politicians overthrew the minority Tutsis. This event had a lasting impact on the political consciousness of the Tutsi elite in Burundi, who feared that the same fate awaited them. Indeed, Prince Rwagasore was assassinated in October 1963, and from then on, the dominant party, UPRONA, was divided along ethnic lines. Between 1963 and 1972, Burundi was transformed from a constitutional monarchy into a one-party presidential system. After the country's first episodes of ethnic violence and political chaos erupted during 1965 and 1966, the nation's politics increasingly crystallised along ethnic lines.

In 1972, a Hutu rebellion, followed by violent repression by the Tutsi-dominated army, led to an unprecedented wave of violence. An estimated 80,000 to 100,000 people died during the violence (Lemarchand and Martin 1974:29–30). About 3.5 per cent of the population was physically eliminated – either killed or exiled – in the space of a few weeks. Some analysts have called this event a 'selective genocide' because, they argue, the ruling political elite planned the elimination of all Hutu political and economic leaders and intellectuals (Lemarchand 1998:6). This is a sensitive issue, and political leaders in Burundi still argue over whether the Hutus were victims of genocide in 1972.

Following these events, the government, under the leadership of President Bagaza, ignored the question of ethnicity. It was literally forbidden to discuss the issue. At the same time, a newly adopted constitution declared that UPRONA was to be the sole political in Burundi; all others were outlawed. Power was consolidated in the hands of the Tutsis (Kay 1987:7–8). President Bagaza was deposed in 1987 and, in a bloodless palace revolt, was replaced by the current President, Major Pierre Buyoya.

Socio-Economic Conditions

To understand the responses to displacement during the 1993–2000 crisis, it is important to recognise that at the beginning of 1990s, Burundi was already one of the poorest countries in the world. Its high population density, lack of natural resources, and ineffective social policies left the majority of Burundians in a state of poverty. In 1990, the UNDP Human Development Index, a measure that aggregates per capita GDP, literacy rates and life expectancy, gave Burundi one of the lowest ratings in the world (UNDP 2000). That index has continuously decreased since 1993. In 1998, Burundi's index was lower than the average for Sub-Saharan Africa, and Burundi was ranked 170 out of a total of 174 countries surveyed (UNDP 2000). The rate of illiteracy has increased from 48 per cent in 1992 (*L'État du Monde 1995*) to 64 per cent in 1995 (*L'État du Monde 1999*). Since 1992, per capital GDP has decreased in absolute terms while prices have increased. Life expectancy has also dropped since the 1970s. Less than 35 per cent of Burundians will now live past the age of 60 (UNDP 2000).

THE PRESENT CONFLICT AND PATTERNS OF DISPLACEMENT

In 1988, President Buyoya launched a 'unity' process. A national commission, charged with studying the topic of national unity, made a number of recommendations. This, however, only increased the population's awareness of ethnic divisions. A unity government was formed, with an equal representation of Hutus and Tutsis at the ministerial level, but this democratisation of public institutions did not apply to the army or the judiciary.

Burundi's first elections in three decades took place in 1993, with the Front Democratique du Burundi (FRODEBU), overwhelmingly Hutu, winning 71 per cent of the vote in the legislative elections. In June of that year, the FRODEBU candidate, Melchior Ndadaye, won nearly 65 per cent of the popular vote to become the first elected – and first Hutu – president of Burundi.

Four months later, Melchior Ndadaye was killed in an unsuccessful coup attempt. The assassination was followed by spontaneous Hutu uprisings and mass killings of Tutsis by civilians. The Tutsis fled their *collines* and found refuge in camps near urban centres, where they were protected by the army. Following the violence, the army launched a wave of repressive assaults that left many Hutus dead. Hutu peasants could not count on the protection of the army or the police; in fact, in most cases, they were fleeing in fear of the army. They sought safety either in the forests or in remote areas populated almost exclusively by Hutus. In addition, large numbers of Hutu peasants fled to Tanzania, swelling the camps of Burundian refugees along the border. From the camps in Tanzania, armed rebel groups, supported by many of the Hutu families hiding in forests in Burundi, organised counterattacks on army positions. The striking difference in patterns of displacement between Tutsis and Hutus had significant impact on their respective coping strategies.

After three years of political and social chaos, during which more than 800,000 people were displaced, a coup on 26 July 1996 returned President Buyoya to power. His government implemented a policy of forced regroupment. Tutsi populations gathered around army positions while Hutus were forced to move to regroupment camps. Most of these regroupment camps were closed in 1997 in response to considerable international pressure. The deterioration of the country's social and economic conditions resulting from the political crisis was only exacerbated by the economic sanctions imposed on Burundi by the Organization of African Unity (OAU).

In 1997, the two main political parties reached an internal power-sharing agreement, and peace talks began in Arusha, Tanzania, in 1998. Initially under the leadership of Tanzanian President Julius Nyerere, the talks involved a number of political parties, but not the armed factions that were at war with the government. Attacks continued all over the country, especially in the southern provinces, even as the peace talks went on. In August 1999, the government resumed its policy of forced regroupment, this time in the province surrounding the capital city, Bujumbura Rurale.

On 12 October 1999, two UN officials were killed when unidentified armed men attacked their convoy in the province of Rutana. Most UN operations in the country were then suspended. After the death of Julius Nyerere the same month, Nelson Mandela became the mediator at the Burundi peace talks. Under his guidance, an agreement among 19 parties, including the government, was finally reached and signed in the autumn of 2000. On 29 September 2000, the UN Security Council issued a statement welcoming the signing of the Arusha peace plan and calling for an end to hostilities in Burundi. The Security Council demanded that all attacks on civilians end and advocated the gradual resumption of external assistance to Burundi. However, the agreement did not include a cease-fire and has not yet been ratified by the three major armed movements. Attacks around

Bujumbura, and in the eastern provinces such as Ruyigi and Rutana, have recurred frequently since. As a result, people continue to be displaced – some for the second time in less than a decade.

As of June 2000, more than 670,000 Burundians were considered to be 'affected by displacement', meaning they were refugees outside of Burundi or displaced internally, living in some 320 sites scattered around the country. (This figure does not include the 300,000 Burundians who have been living as refugees in Tanzania since 1972). The affected population therefore represents about 10 per cent of the total population (NRC 2000). The ministry in charge of displaced persons and refugees, MRRDR, counted 630,000 individuals living in 218 sites in mid-2000. The living conditions in displacement camps are harsh. The UNOCHA estimates that 91 per cent of camps do not have access to potable water (UNOCHA 1999:3).

FORCED REGROUPMENT: A DISTINCT FORM OF DISPLACEMENT

Forced relocation was implemented on a large scale by Burundian authorities during 1996–97 and again during 1999–2000. The policy, known as regroupment, is defined as, 'the forced movement of entire communities, usually by a government, to permanent or semi-permanent sites often directly under the control of military units' (Bennett 2000:1).

In 1996, the army forced large numbers of people into regroupment camps in the provinces of Muramvya, Kayanza, and Karuzi. Authorities claimed that the goal of the policy was to protect the populations from rebel attacks. However, rebel groups and Hutu political leaders argued that the government was forcing people, mainly Hutu peasants, into regroupment camps to make it impossible for them to assist the rebellion. Conditions in these camps were appalling.

The Humanitarian Law Consultancy, an organisation based in The Hague, conducted an inquiry into the legality of Burundi's regroupment policy. It found that, despite the fact that humanitarian law is ambiguous on the issue, 'it can be demonstrated that the regroupment policy of Burundi is not consistent with international humanitarian law'. Two principal reasons were cited: first, the policy is carried out in such a way that acceptable levels of hygiene, health, shelter and nutrition cannot be ensured in the camps. This, in itself, is a violation of the Geneva Conventions. Second, 'serious doubts can be raised about the purportedly humanitarian nature of the camps, since they are, at least in part, established for strategic reasons. Burundian military personnel, sometimes without wearing a uniform, are present in the camps, thus inviting attacks' (Humanitarian Law Consultancy 1997:36).

The government's regroupment policy posed a great challenge to the UN system and all humanitarian actors in Burundi. In 1997, the *Griffith Memorandum* outlined the UN's official policy on the issue. Regroupment was understood to be a military strategy used by the government to bring peace to the country. The *Memorandum* also judged that the policy rendered regrouped populations dependent on relief, and had a negative impact on agricultural production, since people were regrouped far from their lands. Therefore, the *Memorandum* concluded, UN agencies should not support any involuntary regroupment, defined as 'cases when populations in areas subject to systematic destabilisation by rebel activities are required to leave their homes and relocate to camps guarded by armed forces'. In concrete terms, this meant that whenever the UN judged that forced regroupment had occurred, only short-term assistance would be provided. Food rations would not exceed a week's worth and no permanent access to water would be set up, to discourage the permanent settlement of populations. Faced with this UN position and considerable international pressure, the government abandoned its regroupment policy in 1997 and all regroupment camps were dismantled.

But the war dragged on and rebel attacks moved closer to the city during the second half of 1999. Beginning in September that year, the government forced some 300,000 civilians to move into about 50 new camps in the province of Bujumbura Rurale, which surrounds the capital city (NRC 2000). Most of these camps reportedly had no access to water or sanitation, and most inhabitants suffered from hunger and disease. Francis Deng visited a camp of some 40,000 residents at Kabezi and said: 'Just the sheer concentration of so many people, the needs they have ... It is not sustainable' (Kriner 2000:1).

UN agencies and foreign governments condemned the policy, and the peace negotiator, Nelson Mandela, likened the regroupment camps to concentration camps and called for their immediate closure. The guidelines for humanitarian assistance to regrouped populations remained the same as in 1997. Only life-sustaining assistance was to be provided, and displaced persons would receive help in accessing local services and basic education for their children. But the UN stated that 'no assistance should be provided to the creation of permanent structures in the site, or administration of the sites' (UNOCHA 2000:6).

While most of the camps were dismantled by July 2000, many former residents still lived in limbo between the camps and their homes. In fact, the government's announcement that it was considering turning some of these camps into permanent villages raised doubts about the sincerity of its intention to let people go home.

Nevertheless, our research team visited Bujumbura Rurale in September 2000 and found some of the camps still inhabited. For security reasons, it was not possible to conduct lengthy Participatory Rural Appraisal (PRA) exercises, but we discussed response strategies with groups of IDP representatives. Regrouped populations tend to be suspicious of external visitors; as a result, our findings from the regroupment camps are more cursory than the information we were able to gather elsewhere. However, the few discussions we were able to have in the camps demonstrated clearly that, as a distinct type of internal displacement, forced regroupment has serious implications for individuals' and communities' ways of coping with forced displacement.

METHODOLOGY OF THE STUDY AND CHOICE OF PROVINCES

This survey of community and individual response strategies during internal displacement is based on a participatory rural study conducted in four of Burundi's 17 provinces: Ruyigi, Gitega, Rutana and Bujumbura Rurale. PRA is an intensive, iterative process during which small, multidisciplinary research teams use a variety of tools to elicit local knowledge and then combine those findings with 'scientific' methods of analysis and enquiry, such as sampling and comparative analysis. PRA and Rapid Rural Appraisal (RRA) were developed in the 1970s to learn about rural populations from the populations themselves. For this reason, we believe that this methodology was particularly well suited to our research.

The research conducted in the province of Ruyigi is the most extensive and so constitutes the core of this study. Whereas most of those who were displaced in Ruyigi have now left the camps, the province was one of the hardest hit during the 1993–94 conflict. Other provinces were specifically chosen to complement the findings from Ruyigi. For example, the policy of forced regroupment was never implemented in the province of Ruyigi, but it has been a central aspect of internal displacement in Bujumbura Rurale and, to a lesser extent, in Rutana. Reintegration strategies among displaced persons also differ from province to province. In Ruyigi, for example, all displaced persons are encouraged to return to the land they occupied before the crisis, while in Gitega, a number of IDP camps are being transformed into permanent villages. The provinces located in the south-west of the country, namely Makamba and Bururi, were most affected during the later phase of the crisis, from 1996 to 1999. They remain unstable and were not visited because of security concerns.

In Ruyigi, a team of six researchers visited three different sites. The first day was devoted to meeting with local officials and representatives of the displaced populations. During the second day, exercises including social mapping and resource mapping were conducted. On day three, the team discussed the results with participants and addressed possible solutions to some of the problems the populations had identified. Researchers noted that participants expected to receive assistance for participating in the study. Researchers also found that it was difficult for the participants to discuss sensitive issues, such as their experience of displacement. In other provinces, semi-structured interviews were conducted with representatives of the displaced populations.

Ruyigi

In October 1993, more than 10,000 people, mostly Tutsis, arrived at the provincial capital from the hills. During the months that followed, many Hutus fled towards the Mosso region, which is almost entirely Hutu and was thus considered safe, where they lived 'dispersed', often for more than a year. However, most displaced persons in Ruyigi were able to return to their homes between 1995 and 1997. Research was conducted in three different zones: Rugongo in Butaganzwa commune; Rusengo in Ruyigi commune; and Butezi in Butezi commune. Many of the inhabitants of Rugongo were killed at the onset of the crisis, during 1993–94. Most of those who were displaced from that zone returned to their homes in 1996; 50 persons still live in a camp. In Rusengo, more than 10,000 persons were displaced during 1993–94. All of them have since returned to the land they occupied before the crisis. Butezi was the scene of a tragedy in 1993 when more than a hundred persons were killed as the communal administrative building in which they had found refuge was set afire. Inhabitants from that zone are severely traumatised; few of them have returned home. In total, 209 persons, either currently or formerly displaced, took part in the research.

Gitega

As of June 2000, there were 21,350 persons living in IDP camps in the province of Gitega. They live in 16 semi-permanent village settlements. Interviews were conducted in one of these sites, named Intankoma. Intankoma is located about 5 kilometres away from the town of Gitega. The total population of Intankoma at the time of the visit was 1,578 persons from 408 families who originally hailed from seven different communes within the province of Gitega. Of these families, 208 are female-headed households, 87 are headed by children and 72 are headed by widowed male (MRRDR 2000). The research team met with a group of 22 representatives of Intankoma's inhabitants.

Rutana

In Rutana, over 5,000 people were still displaced in June 2000. Since there have been recent attacks and roadblocks in Rutana, this number may have increased. The participants in that province are what the government calls 'stabilised displaced', meaning people who do not expect to return to their previous homes. They live in a site at Kangoma, province of Rutana, but are all originally from the commune of Buraza, province of Gitega. Out of the 50 families who live on the site, 36 people participated in the study, including 20 men, ten women, and six young adults.

Bujumbura Rurale

The research team visited two regroupment sites in Bujumbura Rurale: Kivoga, in the commune of Mutimbuzi, which hosts more than 10,000 people; and Mugendo, commune of Mutambu, where over 5,000 people lived at the time of the study. The first site has been in existence since 1996, but became much larger during the autumn of 1999. The second site was established when the authorities launched their forced regroupment policy in Bujumbura Rurale. Semi-structured interviews were conducted with a group of 50 representatives in each camp. For reasons explained earlier, findings from this province will be discussed separately.

COMMUNITY AND INDIVIDUAL RESPONSES TO DISPLACEMENT

Although they may be closely interrelated, individual and community responses and strategies will be discussed in separate categories. Throughout this section, the reader may want to refer to the matrix[5] presented in the Annex 1. This matrix was drawn up during the PRA sessions conducted with participants in Ruyigi. It shows their perceptions of which social grouping is more apt to devise strategies to fend for themselves (in areas such as protection, subsistence, self-reliance, etc.), and which individuals and groups are more vulnerable and dependent on assistance to achieve the same objectives. In many cases, those individuals within families and communities that were more capable developed strategies to assist the most vulnerable. These examples could offer guidance to the international community in how best to support the coping initiatives taken by the displaced populations before, during and after displacement.

PROTECTION STRATEGIES

Protection is a key concern for all Burundians, but especially for displaced persons who live in constant fear of their neighbours, the army and/or the armed rebel groups. Discussions with displaced persons and former displaced persons in Ruyigi, Rutana and Gitega revealed that protection strategies were developed in response to the different phases of the conflict (see Background, above). In provinces that had been relatively untouched by earlier crises, such as Ruyigi, individuals and communities developed strategies and learned how to protect themselves as the crisis evolved. In general, they considered themselves better able to identify threats and to distinguish real threats from rumours, assess the level of risk and share that information among themselves than they had been in 1993. It is useful to describe the protection strategies employed by individuals and communities in the context of three phases.

Phase 1 – Individual Responses: To Each His own

The people met in Ruyigi were mostly Tutsis. When the crisis started in 1993, they were concerned about unusual movements among their Hutu neighbours, who were holding meetings and rallies, and about rumours and threats. Yet they stayed in their homes and, in most cases, did not believe that their lives were in any real danger. More than 70 per cent of participants claimed that at this stage they did not make plans for an escape or devise protection strategies. About 20 per cent of them said that they had discussed, within their households, ways to flee and hide in case of attack. Today, those who have returned to their homes consider that they are much better informed and able to evaluate the risk of an attack and to plan an escape because of their experiences during the previous seven years. In many cases, they now have contingency plans for flight, something that they did not have before 1993.

As the massacres and looting started in 1993, individuals fled in search of refuge, either to administrative centres at the zone or commune levels, or to the provincial capital. Leaving in haste, they often became separated from members of their families: parents left children behind; husbands and wives were separated. In some cases this happened accidentally. However, many in Butezi testified that men often left their wives and children behind, and mothers abandoned their children to save themselves.

In a few instances, people organised themselves into groups to flee. Students from a school in Rusengo fled together to make sure that the boys could protect the girls.

As they fled, most people avoided major roads and rural tracks so they would not be caught. Many hid in the forests during daytime and walked towards safety at night. It took people two weeks, on average, to reach the town of Ruyigi, a distance of between 10 and 25 kilometres from their homes. Under normal circumstances, the journey can be made in one day, on foot.

Marie Bukuru, 42, is a widow and the mother of three children. As of August 2000, she was still living in the IDP camp at Butezi in Ruyigi province. She tells the story of her flight in late October 1993:

I fled immediately after my husband was killed right before my children's eyes, while I was hiding in the banana plantation behind our house. With my three children and the three children of my neighbours (they were with me because I was not sure their parents were still alive), I decided to try to reach Ruyigi. I had to take a long detour and spend one week in the jungle to avoid getting killed. After a week in hiding – without food – we had to come out of the jungle to find some food and join the main road to Ruyigi. We ran into a man, a Hutu, whom I did not know. He asked me where I was going and when I said that I was fleeing the killers, he proposed to hide us in his house. We stayed with him for seven days but eventually left because I did not want to cause our benefactor any trouble. We finally met the *chef de zone* of Rugongo who accompanied us part of the way. In the end we reached a camp near Ruyigi. I thank God for that generous man who protected us and gave us shelter and food even though he was from a different ethnic group than us.

A number of Tutsi parents left their children with Hutu neighbours before they fled. When asked if they trusted that their children would be protected, they explained that they felt this was the only choice and that they should take the risk. They often quoted a Kirundi proverb, *Uwuhana umurozi umubitsa umwana*, which means, 'He who wants to punish an assassin trusts him with his own child.'

In a few exceptional cases, Tutsis were rescued by Hutus (see the testimonies of Marie Bukuru, opposite, and Caritas Harabahiriwe, pp. 69–70). However, while women and children could sometimes count on the protection of Hutu neighbours, others, especially young men, were not so lucky. They would be killed if they were caught before reaching the town centre.

Reports of cases in which members of different ethnic groups assisted each other were more frequent in Ruyigi than elsewhere. That may be due, in part, to the relatively high rate of intermarriage in Ruyigi. In addition, some of the *collines* in Ruyigi boasted a good balance between the number of Hutu and Tutsi families. In those circumstances, people tend to perceive the risk to their communities as 'external' to the *colline* and would cooperate in defending themselves against this external threat. This was not the case in most other provinces.

Phase 2 – Spontaneous Sites

Refuge meant very different things to Tutsis and Hutus. Displaced Tutsis found refuge in town centres, close to army posts where they felt they would be protected. They spontaneously organised themselves around the existing infrastructures and moved into public buildings, such as churches, schools and administrative offices. Generally, they claimed, the camps were organised quickly. The displaced population chose site leaders, often the chiefs of their *colline* or zone of origin. They also ensured that the most vulnerable members of their community – elders, handicapped persons, the wounded and sick, women and children – had shelter. Men had the responsibility of protecting the site. Adult men and young men took turns doing night patrol.

Hutus, who were targeted by the army, found refuge as far as possible from military bases and town centres where they felt their lives would be in danger. They hid in forests, mostly dispersed in small groups, eating roots and sleeping outdoors. They had to move constantly, which made it difficult to develop coping strategies in other areas, such as self-reliance, education and health care.

Phase 3 – Transit Sites

In the province of Ruyigi, more than 90 per cent of the internally displaced population gathered in and around the centre of Ruyigi. Aid agencies reached them quickly and provincial officials devised plans to manage the displaced population, often without consulting the displaced. Transit sites were created to ensure that displaced persons would reside no more than 5 kilometres away from their plot of land. The goal of this policy was to give people the chance to cultivate their plots, and therefore feed their families. During the first week, the military escorted displaced persons to their land. This made the Tutsis feel safer, but provoked panic among those Hutus who had remained on the hills.

Semi-Permanent Sites

Most of those displaced in Ruyigi went back to their homes relatively quickly. But that has not been the case for many other displaced populations. People interviewed in Kangoma, in Rutana province, recalled that after a number of months the military post charged with protecting the camp was withdrawn. During periods of insecurity, adult men and young men took turns making rounds at night, while women slept outside for additional protection. Only young children were allowed to sleep inside. As a result, they said, men and women became weak from lack of rest and so had difficulty tending their plots during the day.

Shelter

Most persons interviewed believe that the question of shelter is closely associated with protection. In general, flight took them either to the forests, where they slept outside, or to abandoned buildings and infrastructure in which they could sleep. But most of those who reached the camps said that they were given insufficient assistance. They didn't receive enough plastic sheeting, they said, to properly protect an entire family. Others in Rutana noted that as parents and children had to share such a small space, the proximity changed their living habits and created tensions within the family. To compensate, many families built mud huts, or built walls with anything they could find, with hay roofs covered with plastic sheeting, so their homes could be larger than the simple tent they could erect with just the sheeting. In contrast, the 'dispersed' populations often spent the nights hiding in the forest and attempted to return to their homes on the hills during the day to rest. The lack of stable shelter and access to services had significant implications for the health of the dispersed.

SUBSISTENCE STRATEGIES

As noted earlier, more than 90 per cent of the population of Burundi have small plots and cultivate their own land. They are self-sufficient, sometimes trading their produce for food items but usually having little, if any, cash income. When a family needs cash for a special occasion, one of the family's goats or chickens is sold. Thus, when flight took them too far away from their land to cultivate it during the day, people had to make profound changes in their subsistence strategies.

Most reported that they fled in haste and took no food with them. Of those who were able to return in the following days, many found that their livestock had been stolen and their houses burnt or looted. During flight, many people ate roots and plants in the forest. If they had to walk and hide for more than a week, most were near starvation when they reached the camps.

Mamérita Bakundukize, 42, is married and has six children. She talks about the different phases of her exodus:

In October 1993, I fled towards Tanzania with my husband and children. We had never been to Tanzania and did not really know which way to go, so we just followed other Hutus who were going in the same direction. We were not attacked while we walked. But we were so tired and hungry that we walked very slowly and it took us two weeks to reach Tanzania. We were warned that we should hide from the police when we arrived, because it was known that the police beat people and took all their belongings.

We spent one month living with a Tanzanian family. While we worked hard on their land, they barely gave us any food. Children could only eat once every second day. After one of our children died, I told my husband that we should leave the family and go with others from Burundi who lived in a refugee camp at Nya-mutenederi. The situation there was not much better, and our children got sick. Three more of our children died while we were in the camp. I told my husband that we should go back home. We had come here seeking refuge from death but we were still dying. We walked back to our home *colline* in Bunodera. Initially we lived in a camp among our former Tutsi neighbours. Now we have returned to our home to start over.

During the first few days of flight, people gathered in groups of ten or 20 families. They pooled their meagre resources and organised 'collective cooking'. The food they prepared would be given, in order of priority, to children, pregnant women or breastfeeding mothers, and the elderly. Establishing groups like this also created a mechanism to provide for orphaned or unaccompanied children. Young men were responsible for finding food and other goods. Often they went into the *collines* to loot abandoned houses and steal cattle.

Most families in flight were far from health centres and had no access to sanitation or clean water. In addition, many health centres had been destroyed and looted. Before humanitarian assistance reached them, communities often used traditional medicine to cure minor diseases and heal wounds. Some displaced persons in Rugongo also said that they resorted to prayer and spiritual chant to heal the wounded.

Those interviewed noted that there was a considerable change in their eating habits during this period. Children ate two meals a day, but adults were only able to eat only one meal a day. During the first weeks after they left their homes they ate mostly manioc. When they started receiving assistance, their eating habits were again disrupted as they were given corn and other food items they were not used to eating and did not know how to cook. Dispersed families who did not seek shelter in camps tried to get to their fields or were obliged to eat the roots and herbs found in the forests where they hid. As a result, there were extremely high levels of malnutrition among these populations.

SELF-RELIANCE STRATEGIES

Those displaced persons who are lucky enough to reach existing camps or be otherwise assisted by the international community start receiving food very rapidly. Yet, they continue to struggle to maintain some kind of livelihood and to ensure access to basic services, either to compensate for shortages in assistance, to complement the food aid they receive, or to sustain themselves and their families when the flow of aid is cut off. Therefore, even when they receive assistance, internally displaced persons develop strategies to achieve a minimal level of self-reliance. A number of people pointed out that self-reliance is closely linked to dignity, that being dependent on assistance and unable to provide for their families contributed to a loss of status and self-confidence for many of them, especially the men, who are traditionally responsible for providing for their family.

Cultivating the Family Plot

Whenever possible, displaced persons walk to their plots every day to grow enough food to feed their families. Relatively speaking, this is easier for dispersed populations as they usually hide in areas closer to the family land while the camps are further away. However, in both cases, movement is often restricted by the authorities and/or the prevailing insecurity. Often, after walking long distances to reach their plots, the displaced are too exhausted to work. Many complained they were not able to maintain their plots because they were too far away. Neighbours or people passing by would often steal the fruits of their labour in their absence.

Mr Kabura, 49, is married and the father of three children. He is originally from the Kangozi *colline*, commune of Buraza, province of Gitega. As of September 2000, he was still residing in an IDP camp at Kangoma in Rutana province. He tells the story of his flight, in mid-1994, and life in the camp:

> I used to live peacefully on the Kangozi *colline* with my wife and children. I worked my own land and produced enough to feed myself and my family and cover all our needs. When the crisis started, I was forced to flee with all of my family. We first went to the main town of the Ngoma zone, and later to the Kangoma zone. As we fled, we witnessed the murders of family members and close friends by people enraged with ethnic hatred. When we arrived to the Kangoma zone, we received assistance in the form of food, clothes, cooking instruments and agricultural tools. Our main problem was to find shelter. When the assistance stopped, I received help from family members who live in Kangoma zone. I also managed to earn an income by selling my labour. Today, I still live in the camp and find odd jobs to support my family. I am not planning to go back home, at least not as long as those who stayed behind harbour bad intentions towards us.

Agricultural Labour

Those who are physically able, especially men and boys, try to get jobs working other peoples' land. Sometimes they are paid in cash, but most often they receive food. Generally, they are paid less than the going rates because the employers know they are desperate and would take the job for any salary. They earn Fbu150–200 (Burundian Francs) per day when they use the owner's tools, and Fbu300–400 if they bring their own. This, however, tends to reinforce the vulnerability of internally displaced persons because they are tending someone else's land instead of their own. It becomes a vicious circle that traps them in dependence.

Paid Employment

Young men and women are often sent by their parents to find paid employment in the city. Usually, they end up with domestic work or, for the men, jobs as guards. They earn Fbu2,000–3,000 per month, which they usually send back to their families. The disadvantages of this strategy, interviewees recognise, are that children often have to leave school to go to the city, and they generally do not return to their *colline*. More important, they often become part of delinquent circles. Hutu boys are often recruited by armed militias operating in and around cities, while Tutsi boys often join the army.

The Burundian Franc (Fbu)

In September 2000, the official exchange rate for the Burundian Franc was Fbu750 for US$1.

A few examples can give a sense of the cost of living:

- Fbu200 can buy 1 kilo of beans during harvest time (January and July) and 0.5 kilos during the rest of the year.
- A shovel costs Fbu6,000.
- Sending a child to school costs Fbu1,000 for school fees; Fbu5,000 per year for books and pencils; and Fbu4,500 for a uniform.

Prostitution

Some respondents acknowledged that young women and widows turned to prostitution to make a living. Sometimes, sexual services were not sold explicitly but were exchanged for food or protection. This explains why, on the matrix, young women were classified as being relatively more self-reliant than other groups. However, these practices have adverse effects on health, as they spread sexually transmitted diseases including HIV/AIDS; and many young women become single mothers, which tends to make them more vulnerable than other displaced persons.

Small Businesses

Families who can count on an outside source of income or savings, such as having a child who works in the city, often set up small businesses and shops. Most frequently, they establish *kiosques* where they sell a few products, such as salt, oil and cigarettes. Some of them eke out a profit, even though the market is small. One of the negative consequences of this activity, participants noted, is that it changes people's working habits and makes it more difficult for those families to return home and tend their plots again once the crisis is over.

Many displaced families sell goods received as part of humanitarian assistance to soldiers and local government officials. They do this because they need the cash, but also because the aid they receive is not always appropriate (such as when they were given corn, though they did not know how to cook or eat it).

In addition, some individuals were able to start viable businesses, such as *kiosques*, handicrafts, and petty commerce, through the income-generation activities promoted by NGOs.

Caritas Harabahiriwe, 46, is a widow and the mother of six children. Her husband and three of her children were killed in October 1993. Originally from the Nyakibingo *colline*, commune of Gitega in Gitega province, as of September 2000 she was still residing in an IDP camp at Intankoma. She recalls her flight and the living conditions in the camp:

> I fled the house after my husband was killed. At first, I spent one night hiding in the banana trees close to our house. While I was there, I saw my Hutu neighbours stealing our belongings and our cattle, and then burning our house. When night came, I found refuge in the house of a friend, a Hutu. Not all Hutus are bad: while some were involved in destruction and massacres, others protected us and kept us in hiding. My children and I stayed with this friend for three weeks, but there came a point where my presence put him and his family's life in danger.
>
> At that point, I decided to move into this camp. There were so many of us, and the shelters were too small. We often had to sleep outside, and when it rained, we did not sleep at all. I received assistance [from humanitarian organisations], but what they gave me was not enough. Therefore, I have had to search for other sources of income. In the beginning, I did odd jobs and sold some

of the goods we received [from humanitarian organisations]. I sold the cotton oil and used the income to buy food that my children like, such as manioc flour. It is very monotonous to eat the same thing every day, but when they gave us something else [corn grains], we were not able to cook it properly because we did not have enough wood and our children could not eat it.

When I got a small house in the camp I used the Fbu700 I earned [selling my labour] to start a small business. I sold avocados. However, I found that I did not sell the avocados fast enough and I lost a lot of money. Now I am once again selling my labour. I wish that I could be assisted in starting an income-generating activity so that I could be more autonomous.

Two of my children are now going to school. I was lucky because the boy scouts provided them with uniforms and books for school, otherwise I would not have been able to send them.

ACCESS TO EDUCATION

Everyone interviewed considered the lack of access to education to be one of the most crucial problems facing internally displaced persons. Young girls are particularly vulnerable because parents, when they have to choose, tend to send the boys to school first. Young girls are asked to find jobs and provide for the family while boys may be encouraged to go to school. Very few orphans have the means to attend school.

It is not only distance that keeps Burundi's internally displaced children from school. Much of the country's social infrastructure, particularly schools, were destroyed and looted during the crisis. There is also a shortage of teachers, as many were killed or are living in exile. If there is a school near where the displaced families are living, it tends to serve as housing for displaced populations, rather than as a school. In addition, even though the government subsidises schooling for IDP children, parents still have to buy books and pencils, and very few of them can afford to do so. Finally, from 1994 to 1997, fear kept many children away from schools. Parents would not allow their children to attend school if the teacher was from a different ethnic group. Some NGOs introduced peace education and reconciliation programmes; and one international organisation created 'mobile' schools that provided access to education to some IDP children who would otherwise have had none.

STRATEGIES FOR PUBLIC PARTICIPATION

On many occasions during the discussions, participants said they felt they are not sufficiently involved in decisions that concern them. In particular, they feel they should help decide what assistance they should receive, and when, and should help identify the most vulnerable groups among them. They feel they have been more involved in decisions made by humanitarian agencies and the government since 1995, but wish they had been consulted from the early phases of the crisis.

DOCUMENTATION NEEDS AND CITIZENSHIP

All social categories of displaced persons face difficulties in obtaining necessary official documents. In most cases, people lost these documents during flight or left them behind; many official papers were destroyed when peoples' houses were burned down. Burundi's National Identity Card (CNI) must be shown when requesting all other documents, such as proof of training, medical insurance cards, diplomas and other attestations. To obtain this card, people must return to their communes of origin, making it more difficult to obtain the CNI when the displaced are living in a different commune. It is difficult to travel back to get this card because individuals are asked to show the card at every checkpoint: they cannot travel without it. Displaced persons also noted they have no way of getting the required identity pictures taken. Participants said, however, that when one reaches the communal administration and is able to present a photograph, it is fairly easy to obtain the CNI.

ISSUES OF FAMILY UNITY, IDENTITY AND CULTURE

When asked about these topics, participants insisted that dignity and pride were inseparable from issues of family unity, culture and identity.

In many cases, families were separated during flight. It took up to two weeks for all surviving family members to find each other. Usually, inhabitants of the same *colline* tended to flee in the same direction, making reunions more possible. When camps became better organised and the displaced were asked to register, each person declared the names of lost family members and the organisation in charge of the camp helped to trace them.

Separation occurred far more frequently, and with more complications, among ethnically mixed couples. A husband and wife from different ethnic groups would flee separately, as would their children. Because sites for the displaced were relatively mono-ethnic, it sometimes took a long time before they were reunited. In many cases, the separation became semi-permanent.

The respondents described instances when parents brought their own children to an orphanage, claiming that the children's parents were dead. By doing so, they thought their children would be safer.

Participants noted that during displacement and while living in camps, those people considered more vulnerable than others, such as widows and orphans, were well respected and given assistance by the community. However, upon return, communities no longer felt responsible for them when they were back on their land.

Adélaïde Mpfayokurera, 35, is married and has five children. She is originally from the Kangozi colline, Buraza commune, province of Gitega. As of September 2000, she was still living in an IDP camp at Kangoma in Rutana province. She talks about her life since she fled her home in mid-1994:

> Before the crisis, I lived comfortably in Kangozi with my family. When the crisis started, our Hutu neighbours were threatening us and we were aware that they were planning to kill us. We fled towards Ngoma. In the beginning, we received assistance from the communal administration. As the aid gradually came to an end, we started to sell our labour.
>
> The other displaced persons who live here with me are not ready to go back, because those who live in the hills do not trust us. We have attempted to go to cultivate our land, but then we were unable to harvest. The problem is not that we've lost our property; it is that we do not have safe access to our land.

The kinds of assistance they receive in the camps, and the way in which assistance is distributed, undermine dignity, participants argued. For example, a man who used to be able to feed his family and now must stand in line in front of the entire community, only to receive small quantities of food, feels humiliated. His wife and children then regard him differently, which leads to tensions in the family. In this context, young adults, both men and women, tend to detach themselves from their parents much earlier than they would have done in normal circumstances.

Parents who cannot provide for their children feel that they cannot play their parental role properly. This is especially true when camps are located close to major cities or when the camps are essentially transformed into semi-permanent villages. Parents feel incapable of exerting parental authority and transmitting family values to their children. Proximity to towns and villages means that there are more opportunities for delinquency and prostitution; yet when parents try to stop their children from engaging in such activities, they are often ignored. Young adults have less respect for their parents' authority, since they are no longer living under their father's roof, but in a house provided by the government.

However, some important traditions are preserved in the camps, such as teaching the family's history to children in the evenings, or cooking inside the home and eating meals as a family. But many people who were interviewed were concerned that they were not able to conduct proper grieving and funeral ceremonies while they were in the camp. Some fear that the spirits of dead relatives will haunt them because they have not observed the tradition.

In general, life in the IDP camps seems to accentuate the physical and psychological traumas associated with forced displacement. Many of those interviewed felt that their family lives and traditions had changed forever, yet a number of them were still not ready to go home because they did not feel secure.

PROPERTY ISSUES

Most respondents assumed that their property continues to be recognised as theirs even while they are living in camps. When they return, communities designate committees to be in charge of settling property disputes and ensuring that goods stolen during the crisis are returned to the rightful owner. Access is the central problem, they claim, not property.

INDIVIDUAL AND COMMUNITY RESPONSES TO FORCED RELOCATION

As discussed in an earlier section of this chapter, forced relocation, also called 'regroupment', is a very distinct form of forced displacement. Our research team visited two regroupment camps in Bujumbura Rurale and had discussions with groups of representatives in both. The prevailing insecurity did not allow the team to conduct lengthy PRA exercises, therefore the findings from Bujumbura Rurale are not as detailed as the findings gathered in other sites. Yet, they reveal a number of coping strategies specific to populations that have been forcibly relocated.

Living Conditions among 'Regrouped' Populations in Bujumbura Rurale Province

Bujumbura Rurale is a mountainous province, and most of the regroupment sites were established on mountain summits, exposed to wind, heavy rains and hot sun. The mud huts built by residents cannot withstand either the sun or the rain, and very few are equipped with latrines. The sites are located far from potable water sources and social infrastructure. For all the reasons outlined earlier, plus the additional problem of logistics, delivery of humanitarian assistance is irregular and insufficient. In most cases, family-owned plots are far away and people are not allowed to travel freely, which makes it difficult, if not impossible, to provide food for their families. Access to health care and education is limited, at best.

Subsistence is a crucial concern among these displaced persons. Because most were forced to leave in haste, they took few reserves with them. Only those people who are allowed to go to their fields can return with manioc, bananas and other fruits and vegetables to feed their families. Because they are only allowed to leave the camps for a few hours, families generally divide responsibility for the daily tasks. Women try to reach the family plot and cultivate, children search for water and wood, and men go to the capital city to find paid employment. In addition to providing for their own families, children are often forced to fetch water and wood for the military.

In regroupment camps, young men are usually forced to accompany the military to patrol their *collines* and guard the camps at night. When attacks occur, they are often the first victims.

Traditions and customs are rarely observed in the regroupment camps, and the displaced persons we met feel that their dignity and pride have been seriously undermined by this experience. They said that sexual commerce is rampant, as are delinquency and theft. Some parents even encourage their own children to prostitute themselves to get cash.

Nevertheless, the research team was surprised to see that small shops, restaurants and markets have been established in the camps, an indication that the forcibly regrouped have, to a certain extent, adapted to their situation. The team also noted that the regrouped populations kept themselves well informed of the political and military situation in Burundi. They listened to the radio and got news from people travelling back and forth to the city. In general, those people we interviewed stated that they hoped the sites would be closed, that the peace plan and a cease-fire would be implemented, and that they would be allowed to resume a normal life.

CONCLUSIONS

The matrix (see Annex 1, p. 301) provides an interesting overview of how participants in the study perceive their own capacities to cope with the loss and trauma associated with forced displacement. It also outlines participants' perceptions of the relative vulnerability of different social groups.

As stated in Background, above, most persons who have been affected by forced internal displacement in Burundi are subsistence farmers. Although they were certainly among the poorest in the world and had little access to social services before the crisis, in most cases, they were able to provide for their families' basic needs, such as food and shelter.

Because it throws a precariously balanced situation into flux, displacement often means disorientation and confusion at first. Those Burundians who became displaced in 1993 fled in haste. Families were separated, belongings were left behind and looted. One of the interesting, and sad, findings of this study is the existence of a learning curve concerning displacement. In subsequent phases of the crisis, people considered themselves more capable of identifying risks, distinguishing reliable information from rumours, and planning ahead.

At first glance, it may appear that we identified few strategies for self-reliance in the strict sense of the term. Indeed, it is true that reaching safety and a place where external assistance is available is the foremost coping strategy for most displaced persons. In a conflict in which civilians have been targets of both warring parties, it is not surprising that they are dependent on assistance to a certain extent. Yet, during flight and especially once settled in the camps, they developed a number of strategies to fill the gaps in assistance. They sold their labour, opened small shops, organised themselves into small groups to share limited resources, and tended their land whenever possible.

There are, of course, negative consequences to some of the strategies adopted. For example, while young women do better than other social categories in self-reliance and subsistence, they score low on identity, family and culture, which the respondents associated with dignity and pride. Young women's reliance on providing sexual services to obtain cash or goods led not only to the spread of sexually transmitted diseases and HIV/AIDS, but also to a significant loss of respect from others in the community.

According to the matrix, young men do better than other categories when it comes to protection, probably because they are responsible for guarding the camps and making rounds at night. Yet these tasks put their lives at risk; and the long-term impact of such serious responsibilities may be dreadful.

Public participation appears to be relatively unaffected by displacement, and adult men are more involved than other categories. Yet, when confronted with other findings, such as the declared loss of status and respect for men who cannot feed their own families, one must wonder whether social interactions really remain unchanged.

Participants felt that all social categories are relatively helpless when it comes to obtaining official documentation. Yet their needs are simple: they need the services of a photographer and access to administrative offices. This is an area in which external assistance could, fairly easily and at low cost, provide significant help.

We would argue that the fact that the people we spoke with did not demand help related to education, public participation and official documentation reveals that they are more concerned about what they consider to be more immediate issues: protecting their families against perceived enemies and providing enough food to survive. The other problems, they said, could only be resolved once the family had regained a stable home where they felt safe and could resume their farming.

Those people who have been forcibly regrouped feel even more powerless than other displaced persons. Although they find ways to cope, such as opening small shops and travelling to the city for jobs and information, their ability to fend for themselves and provide for others in the community is significantly altered. Once the security situation has improved in Bujumbura Rurale, it is crucial that an in-depth study be conducted to assess the impact of regroupment on communities and individuals. The information gathered from such a study could then be used as the basis on which the international community can advocate against similar practices by governments.

NOTES

1. This is an estimate, as the last census in Burundi was conducted in 1990.
2. The 17th province, Mwaro, was created in 1999 and therefore does not appear on most maps of Burundi.

3. This settlement in new villages has taken place in the province of Gitega in particular. It is mainly for this reason that Gitega was chosen as one of the target provinces for this study.
4. At the time of the Burundian kingdom and during colonial rule, a fourth group was identified. The Ganwa were closely associated with the monarchy. Even though some today claim themselves to be Ganwa, they have generally come to be viewed as part of the Tutsi group.
5. The matrix was elaborated as follows. With the entire community present, participants were asked – for each type of strategy – to decide which category (always comparing categories in pairs) is less vulnerable, or more able to find a solution for themselves. For example: 'Between young women and young men, who is more able to find ways of subsistence?' After each category had been compared with all the others, the team counted the number of times each category was chosen as the least vulnerable. The matrix is therefore the result of open debate and discussion between all those members of the community who wished to participate.

3
The Sudan: The Unique Challenges of Displacement in Khartoum

Karen Jacobsen, Sue Lautze and
Abdal Monim Kheider Osman

In the Sudan, violent social change, gross political and economic inequalities, conflicts over resources, and vulnerability to natural calamities have combined to create one of the world's largest internally displaced populations. According to the UN, there are approximately 4 million internally displaced people in the Sudan. Like many conflict and disaster-affected populations, Sudan's displaced are often beyond the reach of humanitarian agencies and survive almost exclusively through their own coping strategies.

This chapter focuses primarily on the experiences of those who became displaced as a result of war and who are living in Greater Khartoum: the area comprised of the three cities of Khartoum, Khartoum North and Omdurman at the confluence of the White and Blue Niles. This population, the majority of whom are from the south, make up the largest concentration of displaced persons in the Sudan. They are distinct from other vulnerable communities in the Sudan because, we would argue, displacement to Khartoum presents unique challenges.

Displaced persons living in Khartoum originally fled their homes because of war, famine and pressure from the government (and, indirectly, from foreign governments and multinational corporations), which is keen to drill for oil on their lands. These factors have been aggravated by protracted nationwide economic crises and by drought. Over the years, displaced Sudanese from the south, and to a lesser extent, from the west and east of the country, have been attracted to Khartoum's relative security and the expectation of greater opportunities for employment and education there. Extensive social networks have developed among the displaced people in Khartoum, to the extent that many communities have been re-established in internal exile. These communities provide

N

EGYPT

RED SEA

LIBYA

Administered
by Egypt

Administered
by Sudan

Administered
by Sudan

CHAD

NORTHERN

NILE

RED SEA

NORTHERN
DARFUR

KHARTOUM

Khartoum ✪

KASSALA

ERITREA

NORTHERN
KORDOFAN

EL GEZIRA

GEDAREF

WESTERN
DARFUR

S U D A N

WHITE NILE

SENNAR

WESTERN
KORDOFAN

SOUTHERN
KORDOFAN

BLUE NILE

ETHIOPIA

SOUTHERN DARFUR

NORTHERN
BAHR-EL-GHAZAL

WESTERN BAHR-EL-GHAZAL

WAHDA

UPPER NILE

WARAB

EL BUHEYRAT

JONGLEI

CENTRAL AFRICAN
REPUBLIC

WESTERN
EQUATORIA

BAHR-EL-JEBEL

EASTERN
EQUATORIA

Administered
by Kenya

DEMOCRATIC REPUBLIC
OF THE CONGO

UGANDA

KENYA

0   km   500

Map by András Bereznay

Map 3   Sudan

vital information and support to those living displaced in their own country.

In 1998, the UN estimated that, out of Khartoum State's total population of 4.4 million, some 1.8 million were displaced persons. The displaced population is dispersed among four official IDP camps and many other locations throughout Khartoum, particularly in shantytowns and squatter settlements. However, the government of the Sudan has integrated displaced persons into the urban community by systematically demolishing settlements, relocating families and re-allocating land. As a result, the government now officially recognises only 400,000 displaced persons in Khartoum; the rest have been redefined as squatter settlers. Theoretically, this latter group has been given the opportunity to purchase plots of land on which to build houses. But the reality is that war-displaced persons from the south are more likely to be found living in the desperate poverty associated with official relocation camps, while economic migrants, predominantly from the western regions of northern Sudan, live in shanty towns, with greater access to jobs and social services.

Displaced communities in Khartoum differ from displaced communities elsewhere in urban and rural settings throughout north and south Sudan for several reasons:

- the duration of their displacement and associated lack of any obvious 'durable solution' to their displacement
- the lack of a consistent response by the external community (including the international humanitarian and human rights communities, as well as the Western diplomatic community). UN agencies, NGOs and diplomatic missions have had difficulty in developing and implementing coherent short-, medium- and long-term response strategies to meet the needs of the displaced in Khartoum, especially their need for protection and economic self-sufficiency. The international community appears incapable of addressing the overtly political nature of the crisis and has consequently failed to articulate effective strategies in response to the government's oppressive policies against the displaced population.
- continued persecution by the government. Since the late 1980s, displaced persons in Khartoum have suffered a sustained campaign, spearheaded by the Ministry of Housing, to destroy their homes, social services, community networks

and livelihoods. More than 1 million displaced persons have lost their homes – often more than once – to the Ministry's bulldozers. Many displaced persons living in Khartoum have had their land forcibly seized and have been relocated to camps outside Khartoum. These campaigns have been combined with a broader nationwide programme of Arabisation and Islamisation instituted by the government. The displaced populations, particularly those of southern origin, have been effectively excluded from exercising their right to live in the capital.

We argue that the chronic vulnerability of the displaced in Khartoum must be seen in light of the economic, political, military, ethnic and religious ambitions of the northern-dominated government of the Sudan, including both the central government and that of Khartoum state. The strategies employed by the government are designed to keep southerners vulnerable in order to:

- preserve the ethnic/religious identity of Khartoum as an Arab, Muslim capital (as part of a larger Pan-Islamic campaign led, during the 1990s, by the powerful National Islamic Front [NIF])
- generate important revenues for the government at a time of internal fiscal crisis as forcibly seized land is resold to Sudanese expatriates living in the Gulf, or is used to compensate loyal military groups, or to buy the support of some southern leaders
- prevent southern populations from exercising their political rights to be represented and participate in local, state and national government bodies
- maintain a valuable labour pool of impoverished persons willing to work for meagre wages or to be recruited into the national armed forces
- minimise the political backlash against the imposition of increasingly strict Islamic moral codes by creating areas of tolerated social excesses (for example, displaced slums where the brewing of alcohol, prostitution, drugs, etc., are tolerated and informally regulated through routine imprisonment, bribery and fines, especially aimed at women from the southern regions)
- minimise criminal and public health threats by keeping the desperately impoverished southern displaced at a prohibitive distance from Khartoum, where they are regarded as a threat both to public health and public security.

The factors outlined above make the displaced populations in Khartoum, especially the southerners, subjects of a particularly virulent form of oppression. They face discrimination based on ethnicity, religion, socio-economic class, geographic origin and political affiliation.

In reaction, the displaced in Khartoum have devised a complex mix of coping strategies. Some of these responses appear to be counter-intuitive. For example, given the enmity of the government and the problems and oppression experienced by displaced populations in Khartoum, why do southerners continue to seek refuge in the capital city? Why do many southerners voluntarily join the government's army to fight against their brethren in their native homelands? Why do families keep children deliberately malnourished when relief food is available? This chapter outlines and seeks to explain these and other responses by viewing them as costly but essential survival strategies, designed to overcome the particular challenges of being displaced in Khartoum.

BACKGROUND

The war in the Sudan is commonly described as a conflict between the Arab–Muslim north and the Christian and animist south; but over the years, various other factors have fuelled the fighting. Natural disasters, protracted economic crises and, most recently, violent exploitation of natural resources, especially oil have, along with successive civil wars, generated waves of displacement throughout the country. The first civil war lasted from 1956 to 1972 and was followed by a decade of uneasy peace that began with the signing of the Addis Ababa Agreement in 1972. The conflict resumed in 1983, largely because the Sudanese government introduced *sharia* (Islamic law), but also because of southerners' dissatisfaction with progress towards meaningful participation in political processes and concerns over the unequal distribution of development resources in favour of the north.

During the first civil war, southerners fled the conflict between government forces and Anyanya rebel forces to northern towns such as Muglad and El Fula in Kordofan where they were met with verbal and physical abuse. The protection provided by the state, which was never adequate, deteriorated even further. Outright massacres of displaced populations from the south occurred during the first and second phases of the war: in Babanousa, Kordofan in 1965 and then again in Ed Daein, South Darfur in 1987. Such massacres were the culmination of rising tensions between northern residents and displaced populations of southern origin, and reflected the general marginalisation of southerners within the Sudanese political system in the post-colonial era.

From the mid-1980s, raids by government-funded militia (*murhaleen*) forced many southerners, especially Dinka, to flee their homes and nomadic pastoral routes in the southern province of Bahr-el-Ghazal. Most young men fled to Ethiopia to avoid further attacks by northern militia. There they found refuge in the rebel Sudanese People's Liberation Army (SPLA) rear bases that were supported by the Ethiopian government. Women, children and the elderly headed north, often ending their journeys in Khartoum. Drought in the western states of Darfur and Kordofan in the mid-1980s generated further displacement. As a result, the total population of Khartoum doubled between 1983 and 1992.

Oil exploration is inextricably linked to the latest phase of the civil war. Since 1998, the Sudanese government has successfully extracted oil from the south for export through the north. In 2000, Sudanese oil revenues exceeded US$292 million. Displacement has increased markedly as the government seeks to attract international interest in the exploitation of oil fields located in the contested areas of southern Sudan. Clearing the indigenous populations from the land is a prerequisite for establishing the secure environment needed to attract international oil companies. Already, foreign governments, such as China and Malaysia, and multinational corporations, such as Lundin of Sweden and Talisman of Canada, among others, are drilling for oil. Sudan's oil export revenues will increase exponentially in the coming years as the government reaps its share of the oil concessions that have recently been brought into production. In turn, such revenue will continue to underwrite the cost of civil war in the Sudan.

The main groups affected by oil extraction, those who have been forced to abandon their land, are people from the northern areas of southern Sudan. These groups are mainly Panru Dinka from Ruweng province, but also include substantial Nuer, Nuba and Shilluk populations.

METHODOLOGY

In general, it is the Sudan government's policy to prevent or frustrate efforts to collect data on displaced populations because the displaced are perceived as a fundamental political and security threat to the authorities. Therefore, information about places of origin, location, numbers, nutritional status, duration of displacement, religion and gender is very difficult to come by. The data in this chapter are based on existing reports, the professional experience of two of the authors who were in the Sudan in the 1990s, and new data gathered by a local Sudanese research organisation working in collaboration with the Feinstein International Famine Center at Tufts University, Boston, Massachusetts. For security reasons, the name of this organisation is withheld here.

Information on the number of displaced persons and their regional distribution throughout Sudan has long been the source of dispute between the government and the United Nations and international NGOs. This disagreement is based on conflicting estimates related to when displacement occurred, relief strategies and differences in definitions, and is exacerbated by fundamental weaknesses in national census data.

PROFILE OF THE DISPLACED POPULATION

Prior to fleeing their homes in the west and the south, the overwhelming majority of Khartoum's displaced population were pastoral nomads, seasonal fishermen and agro-pastoralists with little, if any, exposure to urban environments. Targeted by northern militia for their cattle wealth or proximity to valued natural resources, the displaced arrived in Khartoum in desperate condition, often severely malnourished, impoverished and humiliated. Their traditional agrarian and pastoral backgrounds did not equip them to deal with the social, political and economic networks of Khartoum. For these once-proud nomads, migration no longer followed the logic of the seasons and pastures, but rather was dictated by repeated, government-imposed forced relocation.

Ten years of displacement to the urban areas of Khartoum have resulted in a fundamental shift in identity, particularly among young people, who consider themselves to be urbanised and have no real desire to return to their rural origins despite their southern ethnicity. We see a split between the generations, where the dwindling older generation still yearns for cattle camps, but the young people see their future in Khartoum. One recent survey of displaced youth born in Khartoum reveals their belief that farming in their home areas will no longer pay enough, and that there are no opportunities for trade and education there. Their hopes lie in Khartoum where there are greater opportunities to acquire skills and jobs. Few are in favour of voluntary repatriation to their original homes.

This attitude is not limited to the youth: as early as 1992, surveys conducted by the government and NGOs indicated that 80 per cent of the displaced in Khartoum wanted to stay there, while only 12 per cent of the southerners wanted to return to the place of their birth.

Displaced communities from western Sudan, such as the Fur and Borgo, have generally fared better than southerners because of their traditional business orientation. Many westerners, the majority of whom arrived in the 1970s and mid-1980s, chose to live in settlements like Soba Arady and became established in businesses. However, poverty is rife among the squatters from the western regions of Kordofan and Darfur.

RELOCATION

Aside from perpetuating the war in the south, the most damaging policy adopted by the government is its programme of relocation and land allocation. This policy is connected with land-title policy, which declares that any and all unregistered land is owned by the state, that is, people may be evicted if the need arises. Removal, relocation and re-planning activities are common.[1] During the past ten years, at least 300,000 shelters and residences for displaced persons have been destroyed. Squatter settlements are sometimes demolished with little prior notice, and often include the destruction of physical infrastructure. For example, in 1992, the removal of 10,000 people from Kurmuta was accompanied by the destruction of a US$2 million water system installed with funds from UNICEF. The official rationale behind relocation is to provide a plot of land for each displaced family and thus re-design the city of Khartoum.

By 1988, 200,000 displaced persons were located in 23 different camps around Greater Khartoum. Many more were scattered in housing construction sites all over the three cities. Of the displaced population 62 per cent came from southern Sudan, mostly Bahr-el-Gazal and the Upper Nile. All of the camps, official and illegal alike, tended to be organised spontaneously along ethnic lines. These attempts at maintaining some kind of community organisation persisted through repeated government programmes of housing demolition, relocation and resettlement, and were an important part of the displaced population's survival strategies.

Massive flooding in Khartoum in 1988 uprooted approximately 20 per cent of the city's displaced population and drew attention to the plight of the displaced living in numerous shantytowns and squatter areas throughout the tri-city area. The government convened a National Conference on Displacement in March 1989. Conference participants recommended:

- returning the displaced to productive agricultural areas near their original homes. This involved relocating them to transitional areas, known as 'peace villages', or government schemes such as the Kenana Sugar Project, one of several large-scale agriculture production areas fed by the waters of the Nile. The Kenana Sugar Project is located in central Sudan.
- moving the displaced to home areas declared safe by the government
- relocating the displaced from Khartoum, Khartoum North and Omdurman to the periphery of the tri-city area.

Following these recommendations and earlier World Bank reports concerning possible re-planning strategies for Khartoum,[2] Khartoum's State Ministry of Housing, led by NIF member Sharaf eldin Banaga, intensified a campaign to demolish camps located in the more urban areas of Khartoum.

This campaign fit into the then NIF-dominated government's pan-Islamic agenda, which sought to 'purify' and preserve Khartoum as an Islamic capital free of alcohol brewing, prostitution and drugs, and included the destruction of churches and church schools.

It is likely, however, that the Ministry's re-planning campaign was more about economics than social engineering: the NIF-dominated construction sector benefited substantially from the policy. Minister Banaga was known to have his own company, which accumulated massive revenues from this project, and Isam el Turabi, son of NIF-leader Hassan Turabi, controlled the cement trade at that time. In addition, the resale of prime urban properties to Sudanese expatriates in the Gulf provided much-needed revenues to the government, and to the Ministry of Housing, in particular.

To say that the government did not solicit the cooperation of the displaced population would be a gross understatement. In the beginning, the displaced population resisted and protested the demolitions, which were supported by the Sudanese armed forces. Some 22 displaced persons living in Khartoum were killed in 1992 during protests over the demolition of the Kurmuta squatter settlement. Over time, however, the displaced realised the futility of protesting and coped with the demolitions by salvaging roofing and other valuable materials before the bulldozers arrived.

By the early 1990s, the government had established four official relocation camps. They were all far from Khartoum proper and were not equipped with shelter and other essential services, including water. Relocation camps on the outskirts of Omdurman were located in particularly inhospitable areas of desert. Sudanese and international humanitarian organisations struggled to deliver adequate supplies of water to the areas. The immediate effect of the relocations was to sever displaced persons' access to casual labour opportunities in Khartoum, reduce their access to social services and disrupt their fragile social networks. In the camps, deepening poverty, poor social services and inadequate housing contributed to the highest malnutrition rates recorded in any peace-time settlement in the world. Every year since 1988, malnutrition rates among Khartoum's displaced have exceeded emergency levels.

Table 3.1   Displaced population in official relocation camps in Greater Khartoum

	1995	1997	1998	2000
Alsalam	65,500	36,000	88,500	114,000
Wad el Bashir	35,000	—	51,000	43,000
Jebel Awlia	56,000	44,500	24,000	21,000
Mayo Farm	28,000	—	36,500	18,000
Total	185,000	—	200,000	196,000

Source: Based on Information from the Humanitarian Affairs Commission and Ministry of Engineering Affairs, Khartoum State; interviews by Partners in Development Research (PDR), Khartoum.

Table 3.1 illustrates the ebbs and flows of intensity with which the government applied its policies of housing destruction, relocation and resettlement. The increases and decreases in the sizes of the official relocation camps correspond to the vigour, or lack thereof, of the re-planning efforts each year.

RECLASSIFICATION AND LAND ALLOCATION

In 1991 and 1992, the government redefined the overwhelming majority of displaced persons as 'urban squatters' and officially recognised only 60,000 households as being displaced. All of these households were to be moved to the official relocation camps. The camps were originally envisioned as providing temporary accommodation; displaced persons sent to them would eventually be allowed to acquire plots of land in other settlement areas in Khartoum. However, the process of acquiring land is cumbersome and expensive. For displaced persons to be eligible to acquire a permanent plot, they must possess:

- a Sudanese nationality certificate, which is obtained through tribal chiefs
- a certificate proving residence in the capital for the past seven years
- family and children certificates
- marriage certificates (with the tribal chief as a witness in case of customary marriage)
- land acquisition fees (Ls65,000[3])
- birth certificates
- a plot survey certificate.

For most of those officially recognised as displaced persons, the dream of permanent land tenure is just that: an unattainable dream.

For squatters – those not officially recognised as displaced – the process is still onerous, but the goal is somewhat more accessible. To qualify and register for permanent land allocation under the planning programme, each resident head-of-household must:

- prove seven years' residence and possess a birth certificate
- wait for the area to be surveyed and household heads registered
- provide a Ls1,000 registration fee for title to a 216-square-metre plot.

As a result of the reclassification of displaced persons in the early 1990s the total number of recognised displaced was arbitrarily reduced by 1 million people and general food distribution was banned throughout Khartoum. Feeding centres for malnourished children and pregnant and lactating women were limited to the official relocation camps and a few other locales in Khartoum.

Reclassification also meant that displaced persons in Khartoum had few settlement options. The vast majority continued to live in illegal squatter camps, or were officially resettled elsewhere within

Khartoum or, to a lesser degree, to the so-called 'peace villages' near productive agricultural areas in western Sudan. A limited number of displaced persons repatriated to southern regions.

As discussed earlier, collecting data on Khartoum's displaced population is a difficult task, particularly so for the more than 1 million people who were reclassified – that is, officially stripped of their displaced status – in 1991. The government has prevented researchers and international assistance agencies from studying or assisting these people.

We do, however, have anecdotal information on a few of the larger relocation camps:

- Kartoon Kassala has a total population of 43,500 (in 2001), is made up mostly of Dinka and Nuba (40 per cent), Shilluk and Fur (35 per cent), and Equatorians and others (25 per cent). As in other camps, some 98 per cent of the women in the camp are illiterate, 30 per cent are divorced and 45 per cent are widowed.

- Wad el Bashir camp, located in Omdurman, has a population of 35,000, according to the government. The ethnic composition of the camp is mainly Dinka, Nuba, Equatorian and some Baggara. The camp is close to the Omdurman industrial area and related employment opportunities. The displaced living there spend more than 80 per cent of their income on food and 10–12 per cent on health care.

- With a population of 18,000, according to the government, Mayo Farm, in Khartoum, is mainly populated by Nuba (75 per cent), southern tribes (20 per cent), Fur and Burgo/Western Sudan (5 per cent). Most of the southerners are Panru Dinka who were displaced by war and by violence associated with oil drilling in their home villages.

SETTLEMENT AND COPING STRATEGIES

Displaced people in Khartoum face repeated destruction of their houses and forced relocation to official camps while enjoying no legal rights, including tenure rights. Such constant threats kill any incentive to invest in houses or neighbourhoods, and make it difficult, if not impossible, to become established in trade or regular employment and to develop long-term relationships of trust that are vital to communities. These dynamics have negative cumulative effects on the physical, economic, social and psychological well-being of the displaced.

The displaced struggle to meet their most basic needs. Food, water, shelter, health care and education costs combine to claim more resources than an average displaced household can muster. Education is particularly difficult to obtain, as many church schools have been demolished. The results are predictable: annually, malnutrition rates exceed internationally established emergency levels; housing is poor, with most houses lacking proper sanitation; morbidity is high; illiteracy is common and school attendance is sporadic.

In response, the displaced living in Khartoum have designed coping strategies that fall into three main patterns:

- New strategies are invented that are unrelated to the experiences, traditions and culture of their pre-displacement lives, and are initiated in direct reaction to displacement-related threats. For example, the displaced have learned to dismantle their houses to preserve movable assets, such as roofs and doors, in advance of government bulldozers.
- Traditional culture is rejected and/or Islamic and Arabic practices are incorporated into their culture. When traditional practices are seen to increase their vulnerability in Khartoum or to hinder their acceptance by the dominant culture, these practices are dropped or hidden. At the same time, the displaced of Khartoum adopt Islamic practices. Thus, there has been a decrease in tribal scarification and an increase in female genital mutilation (FGM), especially among the Nuba, Blue Nile and Fur tribes who did not previously have a tradition of FGM. Among youth, there is widespread demand for formal education, which is seen as their only hope to acquire a secure livelihood. The national syllabus is taught in Arabic and is based on Islamic principles.
- Traditional practices, especially forms of social organisation, are retained as a way to cope with new threats in the urban environment. For example, in response to relocation policies where a mixture of tribes and ethnic groups are indiscriminately dumped on inhospitable stretches of desert, the displaced respond by reorganising and actively re-establishing communities along ethnic lines under the leadership of tribal chiefs.

SUBSISTENCE STRATEGIES

Subsistence strategies are ways to gain access to basic goods and services, such as health care, sanitary conditions, shelter, food and water that are necessary for daily survival in official and unofficial settlement areas. The pressing need for cash has strongly influenced the nature of these coping mechanisms.

Community funds (Sanduk) are revolving funds established by displaced communities and accumulated through regular, small contributions from each member. The funds are disbursed to families who find it difficult to finance school fees, health and medical treatment, and travel expenses, or are offered to support newly arrived displaced persons. In addition, it is a common practice to give in-kind or cash support to individuals within the clan or tribes.

Religious conversion to Islam or Christianity is necessary to gain access to services provided by Islamic NGOs, *Zakat* (the Islamic system for giving alms) or Christian church organisations. Over the past decade, secular international NGOs have found working conditions in government-held areas of the Sudan to be untenable, and their presence has dwindled. The camps for displaced people in Khartoum are tightly controlled by government security forces; work and travel permits are required to gain access to official relocation areas, despite the absence of any war-related security risks in Khartoum. As a result of these policies, the task of assisting the displaced in Khartoum has fallen disproportionately to religious organisations. Many of these organisations, both Christian and Islamic, are providing essential services in the best humanitarian spirit. The politicisation of religion in the Sudan, however, has introduced elements of extremism in both religions.

Access to NGO services, offered by either international or local organisations, requires a variety of strategies through which displaced persons will be recognised as vulnerable and in need of assistance. These strategies include keeping a child malnourished; keeping some family members in camps for registration/rations purposes; and moving from one camp to another to maximise benefits from NGOs. Most alarming, recent studies have documented a practice known locally as 'birth for food', whereby displaced women deliberately become pregnant to qualify for food rations allocated for pregnant and lactating women. These relief rations are often resold to generate much-needed cash. Families send children to schools in camps that are sponsored by organisations like the Sudan Council of Churches or the African Muslim Committees, which distribute free breakfasts and uniforms. Sometimes children leave the school after breakfast.

Engaging in the illicit economy is the most profitable, and most risky, form of 'coping' and includes hidden practices such as brewing and prostitution. The income from brewing can reach up to Ls15,000 (US$10) per day. In contrast, the army pays approximately Ls45,000 (US$30) per month.

Strategies for Obtaining Shelter

The displaced in Khartoum have developed a number of flexible responses to meet housing needs, and as a way of coping with the government's policy of relocation and land re-allocation. Shelter strategies reflect a mix of two of the patterns identified above: new strategies and the use of traditional practices.

For most displaced persons, establishing proper houses is difficult and prohibitively expensive. The use of large, specially made bricks is widespread but the displaced must purchase water to make bricks, a scarce commodity in many camps and squatter areas. Most houses are simple, constructed from locally available and cheap materials, such as waste and by-products from the industrial areas. There is also great demand for the material in which relief goods are packed, such as burlap, oil tins and wooden pallets. Displaced persons use these materials creatively as, for example, fencing and furniture in and around their homes.

Traditional house-building methods are widespread, too. In Kartoon Kassala, the houses are little more than huts that provide shade (*rakuba*), made of wood and straw. They are built in the communal tradition of labour sharing. In Mayo Farm, houses are typically Dinka, made of mud, stick and bamboo. Khartoum's annual rainy season regularly destroys these fragile shelters.

In response to the threat of house destruction, the displaced have learned, the hard way, not to overtly resist the government's repeated bulldozing campaigns. Instead, they anticipate and prepare for the loss of their housing stock by stripping movable assets, such as doors, furniture and roofs, from their shanties when they learn that bulldozing is imminent. The government signals that a bulldozing is planned by painting a large white X on the mud walls of the shanty. The displaced must then calculate how long they have before the bulldozers arrive so they may salvage their housing materials and find a way to transport them to the sites to which they are relocated. Information about pending relocation or bulldozing campaigns is therefore crucial, and the displaced have created strategies to obtain this information. Placing a family member in the police or army may mean less harassment and also increases access to intelligence on the timing of removals, bulldozing or other government campaigns. Families can also use well-placed individuals to try to delay the execution of the plans or get their community prepared and organised to lobby and resist the bulldozing.

Squatting is a common means of obtaining shelter. Some displaced persons stay in buildings under construction in the wealthier parts of Khartoum where they can live with their families and work as guards for these buildings. When the building is completed, they move to another one.

Part of Khartoum's displaced population consists of a large number of undocumented street children. The children devise their own shelter strategies, one of which we might call 'exit and invisibility'. In the early 1990s, these children would often sleep near police stations at night; but in recent years they have been forcibly recruited into the armed forces from the areas around police stations. They are also easy prey for competing Christian and Islamic groups involved in intense 'hearts and minds' campaigns, trying to recruit and convert the children. To avoid these dangers, many of the children must balance strategies of invisibility, such as sleeping in Khartoum's defunct drainage system, with hit-and-run tactics like petty theft and begging. The consequences for children growing up in such conditions are grim.

PROTECTION STRATEGIES

Different groups and individuals within the displaced communities play key roles in developing protection strategies and mediating the relationships among government authorities and displaced communities.

Elders and chiefs represent their communities and intervene with the authorities. They are important interlocutors between the displaced communities and the government, particularly concerning documentation needs (see below). They are also repositories of cultural beliefs that are important for spiritual protection and community harmony in a hostile environment. For example, they provide leadership and resources for the celebration of the seasons. In many communities, there are two sets of chiefs: one that meets with the government and a second that meets with churches and opposition groups. The value of the former is acknowledged by the government in that the government pays the official chiefs for these services.

Community-based organisations are established in and between IDP camps and serve a variety of purposes. For example, joint camp and cross-ethnic interaction committees work to develop mutual benefits and support in the camps. In turn, this increases social interaction and coexistence among different ethnic and religious groups. In the Angola camp, for example, the *Joudia* is a group of community leaders from different tribes. Its role is to resolve conflict, maintain control and keep good relations among people from different tribes in the camp. Similarly, native courts and customary laws are applied to reduce tensions and maintain the integrity of tribal groups.

A widespread strategy to increase protection, and also to increase access to information, is for families to have a member in the army, police force, or the Popular Defence Forces. These forces readily accept all recruits due to the perpetual demands for manpower in the war zones.

One of the main threats facing women is the *Kasha*. This is the public order act based on *sharia* law that calls for the arrest, fining, confiscation of assets and imprisonment of anyone caught brewing alcohol. In response, women established the *Kasha Sanduk*, a revolving fund, to cope with the risk of arrest, related fines and confiscated equipment. The risk of arrest is high and has serious ramifications on children who lose caretakers. Women arrested as part of the *Kasha* campaign are held in Omdurman Prison if they are unable to pay their fines. Strategies of mutual childcare have been developed by the community to care for children left temporarily motherless under these circumstances, but women are sometimes forced out of necessity to take their children to prison with them. Children over two years old are not given food rations in prison. Cells are overcrowded and, increasingly, hold women and men together.

SELF-RELIANCE STRATEGIES

These are strategies that offer or increase opportunities for economic activity.

Child labour. The displaced try to encourage all family members to be productive and so reduce the number of dependents. Children work as water vendors, petty traders and sellers of plastic bags. This activity is common in Souq Libya, a market on the outskirts of

Omdurman. Children make mud bricks, wash cars, polish shoes and do other menial jobs.

Land speculation. In Wad el Bashir, some of those who are legitimately allocated land take advantage of the speculative atmosphere and sell their property, then move to other camps. The sale of land can bring a profit of from Ls100 to Ls200,000 and since those who have to buy land from the popular committee might have to pay around Ls200,000, everyone wins in the deal (Loveless 1999:20).

Inter- and intra-city migration. Those displaced in Khartoum, as well as the urban poor, move from one settlement/camp to another to maximise access to employment, NGO-sponsored vocational training programmes, education and limited micro-credit schemes. These strategies are not cost-free, as settlements closer to urban areas, such as Mayo Farms, have higher rates of prostitution, gambling and criminality but lower rates of NGO-funded public utilities, such as health, water and sanitation services. Camps further away from the urban centres of the three cities have more traditional mechanisms for maintaining social cohesion, but limited employment and other economic opportunities.

Use of repatriation packages. Subsidised return packages consisting of essential resettlement goods (seeds, tools, etc.), food and sometimes cash provided through a variety of organised repatriation programmes, such as that offered by the Sudan Council of Churches, are sometimes exploited by the displaced. Some use the return packages to make 'look-see' visits to their home areas to plan long-term return strategies. Others use the assistance for business purposes, transporting merchandise from Khartoum to the relocation areas and returning to Khartoum after they have sold the goods.

Labour migration. One or two male members of a household may go to agricultural schemes in Gadaref, Damazin and elsewhere, leaving the rest of the family to maintain a base in Khartoum. Income from this work can be quite negligible given the large supply of impoverished workers, many of whom are displaced persons living throughout the Sudan. It is not uncommon that these workers will have nothing to remit to their families, since they earn no more than the bare minimum necessary to purchase food and shelter during the migration season.

For a while, the construction of a thousand-mile oil pipeline from Upper Nile to Port Sudan provided many displaced males in Khartoum with reasonable incomes, even though most of the workers on the pipeline were imported Malaysian and Chinese nationals. The pipeline was completed in 1999.

PUBLIC PARTICIPATION STRATEGIES

These are strategies that improve access to and participation in community, government, and public affairs. They protect the rights of the displaced to organise, associate, vote, etc. In displaced communities further away from urban centres, traditional authority structures and traditional participatory behaviours are evident, providing a powerful response to government policies that threaten to undermine the community.

In camps like Jebel Awlia, 40 kilometres south of Khartoum, chiefs retain much of their traditional authority so community management is more harmonious than elsewhere. In all camps, traditional leaders (*sultans* and *umdas*) lobby for aid from relief agencies and have developed connections and networks with these agencies that advance the causes of their peoples (and themselves: traditional leaders take a cut of all incoming resources).

There are two levels of interaction in the camps: one within each tribal group and one among the different tribes in the settlement. The latter is based on community activities, such as construction of schools, centres, sanitation campaigns, etc. Social relations are maintained among neighbours from different tribes, especially for funerals, marriages and house construction.

DOCUMENTATION NEEDS AND CITIZENSHIP STRATEGIES

Possessing the right documentation is essential for both protection and self-reliance. As part of the de-nationalisation policy directed towards displaced persons, the government is deliberately obstructive when it comes to allowing displaced persons to assert their rights as residents of the city and citizens of the state. Without such documentation, the displaced are highly vulnerable to continued arbitrary demolition of their homes and forced relocation, conscription into the armed forces and punishments under *sharia*.

Three of the main documentation strategies concern:

- acquiring land. The displaced must maintain good relations with tribal chiefs who can certify traditional marriages and thus provide the displaced with a marriage certificate, one of the required documents for obtaining land. This may entail surrendering a portion of relief goods to the chief

- coping with *sharia*. For example, a divorced woman must be able to prove her status as an unmarried woman if she wants to remarry, otherwise she runs the risk of being seen as an adulterer and being punished by the Public Order police
- accessing NGO services. NGOs rely on government-appointed committees to provide figures on the number of displaced persons so they can limit services only to those registered as displaced. Registration often occurs on an *ad hoc* basis with insufficient prior notification. This means that people are compelled to stay at home to ensure they do not miss out on registration. Many displaced persons living outside the camp will return to camp so they don't miss registration, even if that means missing work. Personal relationships with committee members and the integrity of those members thus may determine whether or not individuals have access to the registration process.

CONCLUSION

Civil war, natural disasters and economic stagnation throughout the Sudan have resulted in extensive internal migration and displacement to Khartoum from all regions, and have resulted in the formation of new communities in internal exile. Displaced communities have mobilised in different ways to provide information and support that help the newly displaced to survive. The variety of response strategies discussed above reflects the displaced population's creativity and will to survive. Yet many of the strategies are often only marginally effective, as indicated by persistent and recurrent nutritional crises.

We believe it is important to understand that the government of the Sudan has obstructed not only the displaced population's rights of residence and citizenship, but has sought to prevent efforts by international humanitarian organisations, researchers and human rights advocates to assist the displaced. This strategy has been highly effective: more than one-third of the residents of the country's capital have been rendered invisible to the eyes of the world. It is not only displaced persons who have had to adapt to the government's policies; the international humanitarian community in Khartoum has likewise been forced to make damaging compromises. For example, while the war is being waged hundreds of kilometres away from Khartoum, the UN and NGOs have acquiesced to the government's requirement to obtain travel permits to access the official relocation camps near Khartoum. Likewise, the international community has abandoned efforts to trace, identify and assist the 1 million displaced persons who are not formally recognised by the government.

One consequence of this dearth of information and difficulty of access is that we do not know the long-term effects both of displacement and the consequent coping strategies on the children, communities, and cultures of the southern peoples. As long as the government makes the collection of information on the displaced not only illegal but dangerous, we will never know.

As researchers and members of the international humanitarian community, we worry that the ignorance imposed on us serves to further the government's oppressive policies against the displaced in Khartoum. As long as we call them 'displaced' we reinforce the perception that they are temporary guests in Khartoum who should eventually return to their agrarian roots in the south. By failing to devise longer-term intervention strategies that are oriented to economic support and legal protection, we are abandoning these people to a desperate struggle to meet their own basic needs.

NOTES

1. Such removals are not only common but legal. According to Government Decree no. 941 of 1990, the government may follow 'procedures to contain squatter settlements in planned residential and agricultural land and immediately give land (back) to its rightful owners'.
2. The World Bank, alarmed by the manner in which the government of the Sudan has interpreted World Bank data, has distanced itself from the unpublished reports that were prepared in the wake of the 1988 floods.
3. As of April 2001, one US dollar equalled approximately 2,500 Sudanese pounds or 250 Sudanese dinar.

4
Uganda: The Resilience of Tradition. Displaced Acholi in Kitgum

Ambrose Olaa

Northern Uganda has been ravaged by conflict since 1986. Though the parties to the conflict, their motives and methods have changed through the years, the effect on the local population has remained the same: a slow, steady disintegration of normal life and traditional relationships. Kitgum is the country's largest district; and about one-third of its population of 460,000 have been displaced from their communities and now live in camps set up in areas where their safety could be secured. Those who chose not to settle in the camps live with the threat of imminent displacement in their insecure communities.

Throughout the conflict, the Acholi people of Kitgum district have clung to their tradition, culture and values both as a way to maintain a sense of normalcy in their lives and as a way simply to survive. The Acholi people have coped through years of trauma and displacement by relying on their traditional beliefs and customs, on the power of their clans, and on the support of their extended families. Through the traditional family structure, the most vulnerable members of the community – orphans, widows, young girls who themselves become mothers – all have a network of relations to care for them.

Too often, relief and development interventions fail to recognise the positive influence these relationships have on the individual's ability to cope in a crisis. It is a failure that displaced communities inevitably pay for by becoming dependent on external aid and by adopting socially disruptive behaviour that often stems from the diminished self-esteem that dependency engenders.

This chapter demonstrates that, despite their inability to live their lives as settled communities on their original lands, displaced Acholi do cope with their altered circumstances. It is the responsibility of service providers to understand how they do so and to support these

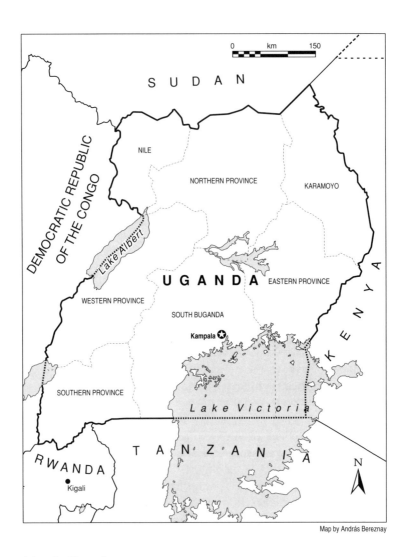

Map 4 Uganda

life-sustaining mechanisms and relationships so these and other communities can survive intact.

BACKGROUND

The Acholi People

The Acholi are a sub-group of the Luo ethnic group, which is spread throughout much of northern and part of eastern Uganda, western Kenya, eastern DRC and southern Sudan. During the eighteenth and nineteenth centuries, drought and other natural disasters continually threatened their livelihoods as farmers and herders. Constant moves in search of better farming and grazing land led to intermittent tribal wars with neighbouring populations. Gradually, Acholi political units, based on military confederacies and alliances, began to emerge. These units formed the basis of clans, the most important social and political unit of the Acholi people.

Clans, named after the people who founded them and helped maintain their stability, are based on the extended family system. In this system, the actions of individuals have consequences for the entire clan. Conversely, the clan is responsible for the welfare of each of its members. In this way, social order is maintained.

The solidarity of the clan is reinforced through communal work. Digging, harvesting and consuming produce are all shared activities. It was common to find a homestead of ten or more households in which cooking was done separately, but at mealtime, the food was consolidated and all the households ate together. People of similar age and gender ate from a single, common dish. This approach ensured that the most vulnerable individuals of the homestead, such as orphans and widows, as well as any visitors, did not go hungry. The produce of the community was shared among the entire community, regardless of any individual's particular social status.

Not only was it difficult to identify distinct categories of disadvantaged persons within the Acholi community; it was also difficult to determine exact relationships among family members. Children referred to their parents' brothers as father, not uncle; their parents' sisters as mother, not aunt; and their cousins as brothers and sisters. When officials from the District Disaster Relief Committee tried to determine how many people were living displaced in Kitgum district, it took several attempts to understand the actual relationships among people who all referred to themselves as brother and sisters or sons and daughters. Yet this lack of differentiation reinforced the perception that all individuals had a place in the community and were entitled to an equal share of the community's resources.

Women played an important role as custodians of community welfare and household budgets; they also managed food production. Every child had a mother whose role and responsibilities were recognised, respected and supported by the community. Men who tried to interfere with women's authority on these matters were held in low regard, as they were seen to be violating the prescribed norms of the community.

From the colonial era onward, the political power of the clans has been gradually sapped, while economic, social and cultural traditions of the Acholi have been undermined. Under the colonialists, new institutions, such as district commissioners and county chiefs, were set up as parallel administrative units; new leaders were installed, while traditional chiefs were either forced to submit or forced into exile. Post-independence governments maintained this power arrangement and added elective posts at all levels of government. As a result, traditional institutions lost substantial control over the management of their people's lives. Their roles were reduced to conducting cultural ceremonies like cleansings, traditional marriages and solving feuds and inter- and intra-clan disputes. In turn, the people began to lose touch with their traditions, their culture, and their identity.

The Insurgency

The conflict in Acholiland began in 1986 as a rebellion against the government of the National Resistance Army/Movement (NRA/M), which had overthrown the Acholi-dominated military regime of General Tito Okello. Since then, the objectives, targets and operations of the conflict have changed many times.

Long-term population displacement was rare before 1991. At that time, civilians were not targets of the war; they largely supported the rebels and often collaborated with them against the government. Also, the rebels' violent activities were not perpetrated across the entire district but, rather, were concentrated in scattered pockets of fighting.

After 1991, many rebels of the Uganda People's Democratic Army that was fighting the government responded to a peace proposal and surrendered. A small band of rebels, however, remained. The group was weak and did not hold territory, but it operated in small, highly mobile units that began to target the civilian population. Their intermittent attacks against local populations were driven by their need for food, medicines and manpower.

Whenever fighting intensified in their part of the district, villagers left their homes to sleep in the nearby bush at night, then returned in the morning. The bush was considered safe because the rebels normally used village paths and they were most active late at night, when the Uganda Peoples Defence Forces (UPDF) and other para-military units had returned to barracks.

Other villagers 'commuted' to trading centres and towns and slept on shop verandas, in schools and in other public buildings. No matter where they found a place to sleep, they were always crowded in with others. Often, people could not sleep in the same place two nights in a row because of overcrowding.

During this period, many families began to move out to safer areas near trading centres and towns for longer periods of time, but they maintained contact with their homes and returned when conditions permitted. Some wealthier families moved to Masindi district, south of Kitgum district and across the Nile where there was no insurgency. But these displacements early in the conflict were sporadic and relatively short-term. Since people could still tend their crops and move about relatively freely, there was no official proposal to set up camps for the displaced.

Despite the surrender and defeat of many of the rebel groups, a few elements of the rebel forces remained operational. In an attempt to renew support for the rebellion, they developed a fanatical ideology based on belief in both traditional African spirits and Christian fundamentalism. This manufactured 'cause' was alien to both sides of the original rebellion, and it signalled an ominous change in the nature of the conflict.

The Holy Spirit Movement and the Lord's Resistance Movement

During the early and mid-1990s, Alice Lakwena's Holy Spirit Movement/Army and Joseph Kony's Lord's Resistance Movement/Army, both quasi-religious rebel groups, terrorised Kitgum district. Their target was the civilian population. They looted and burned homes, abducted and tortured inhabitants, laid landmines along villages paths, in fields and near wells, and ambushed civilian commercial traffic. Thousands of civilians were killed and maimed during their reign of terror.

The government tried to stop them, but the rebels proved elusive and effective. The terrain of Kitgum, large tracts of uninhabited land with vast forests, favoured the rebels, especially since they travelled in small, lightly armed units of between five and seven persons. These small groups were highly motivated by their own sense of power and their ability to get whatever they wanted or needed by looting. Traumatised villagers felt powerless against the rebels.

Children were not spared the rebels' rampages; indeed, they were specifically targeted. They were maimed and tortured along with their parents; but they were also abducted and forcibly recruited. The rebels set their sights on children for several reasons:

- Adults were no longer willing to join and support the rebels.
- Children were easily indoctrinated.
- Children were more susceptible to terror tactics through which the rebels exacted the children's unwavering compliance.
- Large numbers of children could be abducted at once, either from schools or as they were on their way to or from school.
- Children were a more reliable labour force because they never escaped.
- Girls were taken to become rebels' wives. Sometimes, they were exchanged for guns in the Sudan.

Based on an oral testimony given to an assistant community development officer working in the Kitgum District Psychosocial Support Programme (second names and places of residence are withheld here for confidentiality):

Okot, son of Okello and Marinana of B ward, NKN Parish, is 19 years old. He was abducted on 16 December 1998 with his eldest brother, Okidi, from their home in Bombay ward. They were abducted at around two o'clock at night. He stayed in the bush for one and a half weeks and Uganda People's Democratic Force soldiers rescued him.

Okot said that when he was in the bush, he was forced to kill people by beating. He said he remembered killing at least three people by beating. He said he also participated in burying six people in a mass grave. He said he has frequent nightmares and bad dreams of that past experience. He has also become very aggressive and violent to the rest of his family. He does not want his parents to talk to him.

These quasi-religious rebel movements, shunned by the community and pressed by government forces, were all but routed by 1993. But the government of neighbouring Sudan claimed that Uganda was supporting the rebel Sudan People's Liberation Movement/Army that was active in southern Sudan and, in retaliation, the Sudan offered sanctuary and arms to the Ugandan rebels. From 1994 on, rebels launched their intermittent attacks on the Acholi people from the Sudan and returned to the Sudan with their loot and their captives.

Table 4.1   Abductions in Kitgum district, 1990–2000

Children (under 18 years)

	Male	Female	Total
Not returned	1,526	527	2,053
Returned	2,134	704	2,838
Total	3,660	1,271	4,931

Adults

	Male	Female	Total
Not returned	2,430	254	2,684
Returned	3,208	949	4,157
Total	5,638	1,203	6,841

Note: 'Not returned' individuals are those who remain unaccounted for. They are either dead or still in captivity. Given the reported conditions in captivity – the prevalence of combat, torture and disease – it is estimated that up to 60 per cent of those listed as missing are dead.

Source: Based on information from the Abducted Children Database, Kitgum district/UNICEF.

In January 1997, a band of some 600 rebels of the Lord's Resistance Army entered the Kitgum district from their bases in the Sudan. In three days, they killed 412 people and wounded another 221, burned 1,252 huts and 823 granaries, and raped more than 30 women. People were hacked to death with machetes, battered with axes and hand-hoes, burned in their houses and hunted down in their hiding places in the bush. The bush was set alight with the intention of burning anyone who sought safety there.

The scale of the carnage and devastation wiped out any hopes that villagers could continue living safely on their own land, in their own houses. Granaries were destroyed; and gaining access to fields and water wells was a dangerous business, as the rebels roamed freely everywhere. Even the bush was no longer safe.

People began moving to trading centres and to Kitgum town where food, water and medical services were available. Some people from the Lokung and Agoro sub-counties sought safety in the mountains in those areas. But there was no clear policy, at either the local or the national level, on how to assist the displaced persons. Nor was there any legal framework in place to guarantee that the rights of displaced persons would be protected or to guide decisions on how to allocate land to the displaced, and on what terms.

CREATING CAMPS

The first camps for the displaced were established in 1997. Initially, people moved spontaneously to safer areas, such as trading centres or towns where the army could provide security. Traditionally, the Acholi owned land communally, through the clans. It was also common practice to offer land to others, especially those seeking refuge. So when displaced persons began establishing new settlements on uninhabited land, there was little objection among the local population, especially if there were relatives of the displaced persons among the host community.

But the newly displaced usually had no access to water, sanitation or health care and, at the time, there were no established aid agencies in these areas. In response, the government relocated the displaced communities within the same area, but on larger tracts of land. The displaced were asked to build better shelters for themselves and the government mobilised aid from agencies based elsewhere in the country. Members of the same village settled together and built their own huts using grass, mud and wattle. Villages were then clustered according to their original parishes. The camp thus became the new parish. The displaced population elected village leaders, parish leaders and camp leaders and their executives. Later, camp leaders became the representatives of their respective camps in the District Disaster Relief Committee.

In January 2000, the Kitgum district local council established the District Disaster Relief Committee to oversee assistance to the seven IDP camps then in existence. Several sub-committees were also organised to focus on specific aspects of camp life including: documentation and administration; the provision of food and non-food assistance; education; water, sanitation and health services; and security.

Table 4.2   Camp population statistics, Kitgum district, 2000

Camp	Female	Male	Population
Agoro	1,275	1,128	2,403
Padibe	11,553	9,865	21,418
Lokung	7,871	8,035	15,906
Palabek Kal	10,023	7,030	17,053
Palabek Gem	4,436	4,089	8,525
Patika A&B	2,986	2,689	5,675
Atanga	6,780	4,885	11,665
Total	44,924	37,721	82,645

Source: Based on Information Collected by the Kitgum District Disaster Relief Committee.

Women and the Camp Economy

Before 1986, Kitgum's inhabitants subsisted on their land and livestock. The conflict brought an increase in cattle rustling, and the communities thus lost a major source of income as well as a food source. As the conflict spread and villagers became displaced, their access to their crops was limited or cut off completely.

Since rebel activities were usually concentrated in just a small part of the district at any one time, men who were living in displaced camps with their families were sometimes able to return home to tend their fields. In addition to harvesting cassava and potatoes, they grew crops of sesame, sorghum, beans and maize to supplement the food rations they received in the camps. The District Disaster Relief Committee encouraged the displaced population to tend their lands by providing families with tools and seeds. The value of maintaining a degree of self-sufficiency was clear: when food rations at the camps were cut by 30 per cent in September 1997 because of low stocks, there was no significant decline in the community's health.

Since men were often out working their fields or exchanging their labour for cash in the host communities, women began to assume a greater number of responsibilities in the camps. One or two women would remain in the camp to look after children and prepare food while others sought additional food or income. Women exchanged firewood for food or cash, brewed alcohol, made and sold handicrafts and engaged in small-scale trade. Small markets, with names that reflected camp conditions, like *loyo nono* ('better than nothing') and *nywal pe* ('no reproducing'), began to sprout.

Spending most of their time together and pressured to provide for the family, some women started a revolving fund, or *kalulu*. Every week, each woman in a small group paid a certain amount of money into a pool. Each week, one member of the group would receive all but a certain percentage of that money. The percentage not paid out to a group member was set aside for the benefit of the group. If a member needed more capital to start a venture, she could borrow the group savings and pay back the loan, plus a small, pre-agreed interest fee, later.

Before displacement, a cash income was unnecessary, as families produced their own food and bartered for items they didn't have. Thus, the increase in economic activity among women in the camps became a source of tension in families, especially as any income the men earned was often squandered on excessive drinking. Domestic violence erupted as men fought for control over the women's earnings when their own cash ran out. Men felt their authority over the family was undermined by the women's new economic clout.

During a discussion on gender relations with women in Padibe camp, one woman said:

I do not know what is happening to my man nowadays. He gets up early in the morning and goes for *leja-leja* (causal labour) in the centre. He stays there until night. When he comes back, he demands food, which he expects to get at all cost. So I have to work very hard to get food. One time, my second-born son was sick, so I took him to the health centre. This was the day there was immunisation, so I stayed longer and did not have the time to look around for firewood, because when I returned home there very little firewood left. I decided just to make porridge. My husband came back as usual and asked for food. I told him I just had porridge. He couldn't believe that [taking the sick child to the health centre] had taken most of my time in the day. He slapped me twice in the face. I had no alternative but to fight back. Because he was drunk, I overpowered him and managed to break away and run to my mother-in-law's hut and slept there. Since then, he has tried to stop me from coming to these meetings and even from meeting with other women. He claims I don't listen to him, yet he is the owner of the home. I am just a woman who was married and paid for with bride's wealth.

When this woman was asked when her husband began to behave like that, she said:

My husband was a very responsible man when we were in the village. For about three months after we came to the camp we could share some responsibility. After that, he changed suddenly. He started drinking heavily and caring less about the family. It was so strange. Up to now, I cannot tell what went wrong. From that time, I knew I had to use my brains to make my children survive.

The Power of Spirits

Most Acholi maintain a deeply rooted belief in their traditions, which, they believe, can protect their community. Some believe that by applying traditional institutions and conflict-resolution mechanisms, the ongoing conflict could be resolved and peace could be restored. One ceremony that could produce such a result involves eliciting the intervention of ancestors through prayer and animal sacrifice. Another involves casting a bad spell on those who perpetrate evil against the community. A third is to nurture a process of reconciliation (*mato Oput*).

Acholi culture and tradition is rich with mechanisms for solving problems within the community. Cleansing rituals, mediated by good spirits, are employed to restore normalcy after any misfortune, including displacement. The Acholi believe that people who have been victims of abduction, torture, rape and other assaults have been dehumanised and have become alienated from good spirits. In these instances, traditional religious practitioners use a cleansing ceremony to restore the individual's relationship with the good spirit and the individual's relationship with the rest of the community. But the capacity to conduct these activities effectively has been degraded by the continuing conflict.

In October 1996, when Oryem was 12 years old, he went to visit his grandmother in a village 14 kilometres from town where he lived with his parents. One night while he was there, rebels attacked.

I had slept with four other children in a hut. When I heard a lot of noise outside, I knew we had been attacked by the rebels, because earlier we had been told that they had been seen about 10 kilometres away. They banged on our door and ordered us to open the door. When we opened the door, they flashed torches at us and saw that we were all children. They ordered us to get out and join many other people who had been captured. I realised that many of them were children just like me. My grandmother began pleading with the rebels, who numbered about 14. They grabbed her and told her not to disturb them. They got a cane and beat her and tied her up and threw her back into the hut. We were tied at the waist in groups of five and there were three groups. We were ordered to march to the next village.

When we reached the next village we were told to sit down. I took advantage and untied the rope because I was tied at the end of the rope. I left the loose rope attached to my waist and asked to take a short call. We were escorted to a nearby bush. Fortunately, we were escorted only by a small boy of nearly my age. I burst into a run with the intention of knocking down the youth, which I did, because he fell down. My colleagues also managed to run away. I ran back to my grandmother's place. I found her still tied. I untied her and helped her to sit up. My cousins were not that fortunate because they remained in captivity.

In the morning, my grandmother went into the bush, collected some herbs, pounded them, came and rubbed some on my forehead, the back of my hands and legs. Some was rubbed on the entrance to the compound ... This was meant to cast out the misfortune that could have befallen the home and to make sure that no such thing would happen again.

In July 2000, a band of rebels attacked Palabek Gem camp. They burned down 87 huts and killed one person. According to Acholi tradition, when a house is burned, a sacrifice has to be made to cleanse the people; if not, an epidemic would spread throughout the community. When a team from the Kitgum District Psychosocial Support Programme visited the camp to assist the victims, the displaced persons asked to have a sacrifice performed so normalcy could be restored to the camp. At the time, a cough was rampant in the camp. Although health care was provided free to the displaced community, no one went to the clinic because people believed the cough was the natural result of leaving the community uncleansed. The team of social workers consulted a council of elders in the sub-county who prescribed sacrificing a goat. The goat, they said, should be killed with a spear and its blood and the contents of its bowels should be sprinkled over the camp to cast out the bad spirits. After this was done, the people in the camp no longer resisted going to the health centre since they knew that any future ailments could not be blamed on those bad spirits.

Maintaining a System of Justice

The Acholi's traditional justice system, based on reconciliation rather than punishment, was used in the camps to settle many disputes. The crowded conditions in the camps and the idleness induced by dependency resulted in increased rates of criminal and social offences. Sex-related offences, like adultery and sexual abuse, became more frequent, as did instances of petty theft and family brawls. With the absence of an effective judicial system (the nearest courts were, on average, more than 30 kilometres away in Kitgum town), the displaced were compelled to devise their own means of exacting justice. The outcome was a mix of modern penal codes, camp laws established by the displaced, and traditional laws.

Camp leaders had the administrative authority to demand the compliance of individuals who resisted participating in communal activities, such as building pit latrines and maintaining water sources. They also dealt with petty brawls and inter-family feuds. Most social offences and disputes were handled by elders of the community, the traditional leaders, in the presence of locally elected officials, such as camp leaders and local council members.

Family Relationships Undermined

Although many of the Acholi's traditions survived with them in the camps, the same cannot be said of some of the basic relationships that held families and villages together before displacement. The lack of land and livestock meant families could not afford dowries, so there were fewer marriages. Alcoholism, adultery and physical abuse began to tear married couples apart. The loss of livelihoods led to a disinclination to work and a despondency and dependency that, in turn, led to the loss of self-esteem and feelings of inadequacy.

Displacement made the most noticeable impact on children. Although displaced children had access to local schools, those facilities could not accommodate the influx of new students. The District Disaster Relief Committee established temporary schools in the camps, but many children still did not attend because of their families' pressing social and economic problems. Although the government provides free universal primary education, most displaced parents could not afford the pens, books, uniforms and other items that were required. In many cases, education was simply not a priority. Instead, many children spent their days looking for food or doing manual labour, such as carrying baggage, digging, and cleaning houses, to earn money; some sold alcohol.

As family structures broke down, children began to lose respect for their parents. They increasingly turned to their peers for companionship and guidance. Many of the young children in the camps said they felt more comfortable with their friends because they had time to play and talk about some of their problems. They saw the peer group as a new support structure. These groups have not yet had a detrimental effect on the social cohesion of the displaced population: since the extended family structure still exists, there are always relatives around to intercede when any serious problem arises among the youth.

Female children in the camp have become most vulnerable. To many parents, girls are seen as a source of income. Although Acholi culture does not sanction child marriages and prohibits elopement, parents no longer prevent their under-age daughters from eloping and marrying because the girls receive a dowry or an 'elopement fee', a sum that used to be paid as punishment for a social transgression. Since marriage is an expensive proposition, elopement has become a desirable alternative, since a girl will receive a fee from every man with whom she lives, no matter how long the co-habitation lasts. Sometimes, a girl will exchange sexual favours with a man, such as a soldier or a teacher, who can provide her with material goods like sugar, salt, meat and clothes. Her parents generally will not object to the arrangement, especially if some of those goods are shared with the extended family.

With so many families desperate for income, child prostitution is a growing phenomenon among the displaced. Before displacement, the Acholi social system was so strong and the extended family so tightly knit, that this kind of behaviour was non-existent. That the ongoing conflict has shaken the foundations of Acholi society is clear from the emergence of these harmful practices.

CONCLUSION

The insurgency in Kitgum district has scarred all the people of the area. The daily patterns of people's lives have been disrupted, the economic foundation of the communities has been shattered; some of the relationships that sustained the communities have been undermined or sundered. Yet, the strength, depth and resilience of the Acholi's tradition and culture have helped displaced persons cope with their desperate situation. It is clear that, had the displaced not been able, or not been allowed, to continue to practice their traditional cleansing rituals, had they not been able to work their land (or new land) and, most important, had they not been able to rely on the essential support provided by their extended families, their already desperate lives in the camps would have been intolerable.

Asia

5
Afghanistan: Displaced in a Devastated Country

Grant Farr

In the autumn of 2000, the forces of the Taliban government in Afghanistan made yet another military push into the heart of the Tajik area in the north of the country. In their campaign to capture the city of Talaqan, one of the last cities to remain outside Taliban control, government forces destroyed homes, burned fields, blocked irrigation canals and bombed civilian areas. When Talaqan finally fell to the Taliban in September, over 70,000 people fled their homes rather than live under Taliban rule. These displaced persons sought refuge either in the surrounding mountains or further north, with the hope of crossing into Tajikistan. Russian soldiers who feared that the Afghan civil war would spill into Tajikistan turned back those who made it to the border. As of December 2000, as many as 10,000 displaced Afghans were stranded on small, barren islands in the middle of the Pyandj River that is one of the borders with Tajikistan (USAID 2000).

BACKGROUND

Afghanistan is a Central Asian country with a population of approximately 25 million people. Iran lies to its west, Pakistan to the east and south, and the newly independent republics of Turkmenistan, Uzbekistan, and Tajikistan to its north. The country also shares a 76-kilometre border with China. Afghanistan has seen almost continuous civil strife since the fall of the monarchy of Mohammed Zaher Shah in 1973. Since then, a series of unstable governments has been unable to bring peace and security to the country. Because these governments have been perceived as favouring one ethnic group over another, their rule has provoked violent ethnic uprisings.

A poor country before this period of turmoil began, Afghanistan is now economically and socially devastated. During the past 25 years, over 5 million Afghans fled to neighbouring Pakistan and Iran, and over 1 million have been displaced internally. Although some of the refugees have returned to their homes, over half remain abroad.

117

Map by András Bereznay

Map 5   Afghanistan

Some of those displaced internally have also returned to their homes, but since the fighting continues, others have not been able to return and displacement continues.

A Profile of the Country and its People

Afghanistan, which gained its independence from Iran in 1747, is one of the oldest countries in Central Asia. Both its rugged geography and its ethnic diversity have played a part in the country's history. The mountains of the Hindu Kush (Hindu Kush means 'Indian Killer' in Persian) bisect the country east to west, the high plains of the Amy Darya, sometimes called the Oxus river, stretch across the north, and deserts lie in the south.

Although a united country for most of its existence, Afghanistan is made up of several ethnic, linguistic, religious and racial groups. The major ethnic groups are the Pushtun (also called Pukhtun), who comprise approximately 40 per cent of the population; the Tajiks (approximately 25 per cent of the population); the Hazara (approximately 20 per cent population); and the Uzbeks (approximately 6 per cent of the population). Persian speakers live in the eastern and central areas, Central Asian Turkic groups stretch across the north of the country, and South Asians reside on the south-eastern border.

Ethnic, tribal, and sectarian rivalries, sometimes violent, have dominated Afghan politics and social life since the founding of the country. For most of Afghanistan's history, the Pushtun have dominated Afghan politics. All of Afghanistan's shahs, or kings, most of the commanders who led the war of resistance against the Soviets during the 1980s, and most of the present Taliban leaders have been or are Pushtun.

Pushtun dominance in Afghan society is partly explained by the fact that the Pushtun are the largest ethnic group in the country. More significant, however, is the fact that they are organised in hierarchic tribal structures based on male lineage. This flexible structure allows the Pushtun to maintain very large tribal confederations involving hundreds of thousands of people, or smaller tribal units, sub-tribal units and extended family clan groups. Most other ethnic groups live as settled subsistence farmers in isolated villages and do not have similar networks of clans and tribes.

Pushtun tribal culture is built on strong codes of behaviour that call for bravery, revenge, justice and nationalism. The Pushtun are also strongly patriarchal: women are viewed as male property and their purity and protection is related to male honour.

The Tajiks exist largely as settled farmers in the valleys of the northern slope of the Hindu Kush, although over the past century, some have migrated to the Shamali Plain just north of Kabul. They have been active in both the guerrilla war against the Soviet army and the present struggle against the Taliban. Although the Tajiks have cooperated with Pushtun groups at different times and have acquiesced to Pushtun-dominated governments in Kabul, there remains great animosity between the Tajiks and the Pushtun.

The Uzbek population in Afghanistan is culturally similar to the Tajik population, though the two groups speak different languages.

Meanwhile, the Hazara live in the central mountains. Of Central Asian descent, they speak Hazaragi, a Persian dialect, and are Shi'a Moslems, indicating that they were once part of a former Persian Empire. They are an oppressed and persecuted minority in Afghanistan, in part because of their religion. Historically, they hold the most menial jobs in Afghanistan and are the butt of cruel jokes. The Hazara exist largely on subsistence farming and herding. During the recent fighting, Afghan government forces have systematically

Table 5.1   Ethnic groups in Afghanistan

Ethnic group	Population	Location	Religion	Language
Pushtun	9.5 million	Eastern and southern area	Sunni Moslem	Pushtun
Tajik	6.25 million	North-east	Sunni Moslem	Tajik (Persian dialect)
Uzbek	1.5 million	North-west	Sunni Moslem	Uzbek (Turkic language)
Hazara	5 million	Central mountains	Shi'ah Moslem	Hazaragi (Persian dialect)
Other Groups Aimaks Balooch Nuristani Turkmen	2.75 million	All areas	Shi'ah and Sunni Moslem	A variety of languages

Source: the author.

killed the Hazara; yet the conflict has also heightened Hazara nationalism and spurred this oppressed group to political and military action.

A History of Conflict

Although its history is marked by international wars and internal conflict, Afghanistan was a united and relatively peaceful country until 1973. Governed by a constitutional monarchy, Afghanistan, while among the world's poorest nations, has been since the Second World War the site of large projects funded by the United States Agency for International Development (USAID), Soviet foreign aid assistance, and other development projects that seemed to be propelling the country slowly forward. By the early 1970s, a small middle class of largely Western-educated intellectuals and professionals emerged to assume leadership positions and push for social and political change. The influence of this segment of Afghan society was, however, confined primarily to the capital, Kabul.

This period ended in 1973 when Mohammed Daoud Khan, a cousin of Afghan ruler Zaher Shah, overthrew the monarchy and created a national republic. The rise of Daoud Khan's government in 1973 marked the end of the post-war era of stability and the beginning of almost three decades of violence.

The Republic survived only five years. In 1978, a small group of Marxists seized power, but its ideology was not well received in Afghanistan, particularly among tribal leaders and the Islamic clergy. Armed resistance erupted in many rural areas as local traditional leaders rejected the Marxist call for such changes as land reform and the emancipation of women.

By 1979, much of Afghanistan was in open revolt and the collapse of the Marxist government appeared imminent. But in late December 1979, the Soviet army entered Afghanistan to support the government. Afghanistan exploded in revolt. What had been a civil war became a war against foreign occupation. From 1980 to 1989, Afghanistan was plunged into a full-scale resistance war against some 100,000 Soviet troops. The resistance was led by various fundamentalist Islamic organisations based in Pakistan and generously financed by Islamic nations and the West, including the United States.

During this period, over 5 million Afghans fled to Pakistan or Iran, creating the largest refugee population in the world at that time. These refugees included pastoral nomads, peasant farmers and much of the new middle class. Over a million men were killed in the fighting, creating a large population of widows and female-headed households.

When the Marxist government fell in 1992, the Islamic resistance groups swept triumphantly into Kabul and other major cities. They attempted to create a national government in Kabul based on a loose and unworkable pact among the resistance parties. Afghanistan was ruled for one year by a compromise president, Sheikh Mujadidi, a progressive but ineffectual resistance leader. In 1993, Professor Burhanuddin Rabbani was selected to lead the country in what was supposed to be a revolving presidency among the various militia commanders. The presidency, however, never revolved; Professor Rabbani, a Tajik, ruled until the Taliban threw him out in 1996. President Rabbani's control of Afghanistan was tenuous and at times did not even include all of the capital itself, let alone the rest of the country.

Outside of Kabul, militia warlords carved much of Afghanistan into private fiefdoms based largely on traditional ethnic and tribal divisions. The militias that had fought together against the Soviet army now turned on each other. Pushtun commanders threatened Kabul from the south; Hazara resistance groups held parts of Kabul itself, including the area around the university; and Kabul was bombed more than once by Uzbek groups in the north. The country was again mired in sectarian conflict.

Refugees began returning to Afghanistan from Pakistan and Iran in 1992. Both asylum countries exerted strong pressure on the refugees to return since, as far as they were concerned, the war that had created the refugees was over. In addition, a change in government in Pakistan led to increased pressure on Islamabad to end the 'refugee problem' in Pakistan. Pakistan closed camps, offered incentives to the Afghan refugees to return to Afghanistan, and tried several times to close the border to Afghans seeking entry into Pakistan. But since fighting erupted again, repatriation was largely unsuccessful; many of those who tried to return were forced to leave again as the fighting intensified.

By the mid-1990s, a large internally displaced population had developed. Relief agencies opened several camps for the displaced in the Jalalabad area. Other camps were opened in the area around Mazar-i-Sharif in the north and in Herat in the west, near the Iranian border. These camps housed over 400,000 displaced persons.

Out of this political chaos, a new ultra-conservative Islamic movement began to assert control. Called the Taliban, meaning religious students, a group of *madrasa* (Islamic school) teachers and their students seized the southern city of Kandahar and the surrounding provinces in October 1994 (Rubin 1999). The Taliban appeared to offer Afghanistan a new Islamic movement, free of the corruption and infighting found in the so-called Islamic government at that time. But their unstated goal was to return Afghanistan to Pushtun rule: most of the Taliban leaders are Pushtun and their movement received much of its support from Pushtun leaders in the Pakistani government.

In the beginning, most non-Pushtun areas of the country resisted the Taliban movement; but by 1998, the Taliban had gained control of most of Afghanistan, including Kabul, and seized control of the government. In the Taliban's push to power, thousands of combatants and civilians were killed. Only small areas in the north and the central mountains remained outside of Taliban control in late 2000.

THE DISPLACED

The location of the fighting and the attitudes of the surrounding countries have prevented most Afghans from leaving the country entirely. The fighting that created the large refugee population in the 1980s was largely in the eastern and south-eastern areas of Afghanistan near the Pakistani border. It was thus relatively easy for Afghans to cross the border into Pakistan. In addition, the governments of Pakistan and, to a lesser degree, Iran were sympathetic to the Afghan cause at the time and accepted the refugees willingly.

Today, the fighting is concentrated in the central and north-eastern areas of the country, far from Pakistan or any other friendly governments. Neighbouring countries are now much less willing to receive and house refugees. The government of Pakistan has changed several times in the past two decades and now regards the Afghan refugee population as a potentially destabilising presence. Likewise, the governments of Uzbekistan and Tajikistan are fearful that the Afghan civil war will spill into their countries. Both have tried to block refugees from crossing their borders.

The UNHCR estimated that there were 315,000 displaced persons living in Afghanistan at the end of 1998. Although some returned home, another 350,000 people were displaced in the fighting between the Taliban government and the United Front in the Hazarajat, in the Shamali plain north of Kabul, and in battle for Talaqan, the provincial capital of Takhar province in the northern part of the country. It is estimated that perhaps half of this group returned home, but many were uprooted again by renewed fighting in 2000. It is now estimated that there are between 500,000 and 750,000 displaced persons in the country, although some estimate that over 1 million people are displaced (USCR 2000). Perhaps as many as 75,000 displaced persons live in Kabul, more than 20,000 of whom are in the former Soviet embassy compound (UNICEF 2001).

The pattern of displacement follows the pattern of fighting. In the early 1990s, after the Marxist government fell and the resistance militias returned to Afghanistan, those who feared reprisal from these groups, largely because of complicity or suspicion of

Table 5.2   Number of displaced by year, reason for displacement, place and origin

Period of displacement	Reason for displacement	Number of displaced	Displace- ment site	Place of origin
1992–93	Fear of reprisal from Islamic militias	400,000	Mazar-i- Sharif and Jalalabad	Kabul
1992–93	Combat	200,000	Kabul	surrounding provinces
1995	Flight from the Taliban	180,000	Kabul and northern Afghanistan	southern areas
1997	Fighting in the provinces near Kabul and in the north	600,000	Kabul and Mazar-i- Sharif	Areas near Kabul and in the northern provinces
1998	Fighting in and around Mazar-i- Sharif	50,000	Mountainous areas in the north	Uzbeks and Hazaras living in Mazar-i- Sharif
Summer 1999	Fighting north of Kabul in the Shomali plain	100,000	Panjshir valley	Tajiks from Shomali plain
Autumn 1999	Fighting in the Shomali plain	12,995	Kabul, ex- Soviet embassy compound	Tajiks from Shomali plain
Autumn 1999	Fighting in the Panjshir valley	100,000	northern provinces	Tajiks from Panjshir valley
Autumn 1999	Fighting around Talaqan in Takhar province (a Tajik stronghold)	16,000	Areas around Faizabad	Tajiks from the Talaqan area
Winter 2000	Fighting in the Hazarajat	60,000	Near Behsud or Pul-i- Khumri	Hazaras and Tajiks from Bamiyan area

Table 5.2   continued

Period of displacement	Reason for displacement	Number of displaced	Displace-ment site	Place of origin
Summer 2000	Fighting in Panjshir valley and Shomali plain	50,000	Kabul and Panjshir valley	Tajiks from the Shomali plain and the Panjshir valley
Summer 2000	Fighting around Talaqan in Takhar province	15,000	Badakhsan area	Tajiks from Talaqan area

Sources: USCR (2000); United Nations Resident Coordinator Office (UNRCO 2000); Bashir/Agence France-Presse (AFP) (2000).

complicity with the Marxist government, fled the capital. With the Pakistani border closed, many who were displaced from Kabul went north to the area around Mazar-i-Sharif or south to Jalalabad, where large camps were set up for the displaced (USCR 1995). During this period, many people from the provinces who feared retribution flooded into Kabul.

By the mid-1990s, when the Taliban movement began to expand out of the Kandahar area, displaced people moved north, fleeing the Taliban advance. As the Taliban forces approached Kabul in 1995, people again fled the capital, only to return shortly thereafter when the Taliban forces were temporarily defeated (USCR 1996). But in September 1996, the Taliban captured Jalalabad, a principal city and the site of two large camps for the displaced. Most of these people were forced to move again. In the following weeks, the Taliban pushed into Kabul. The capital, and thus the government of Afghanistan, fell to Taliban control on 27 September 1996 and a mass exodus out of the capital ensued (USCR 1997).

Those who fled Kabul in the autumn of 1996 were largely non-Pushtun minorities who feared retribution from the Pushtun-based Taliban. With the southern and eastern parts of Afghanistan under Taliban control, many of those fleeing Kabul moved north into the Tajik areas or to the Uzbek area around the northern city of Mazar-i-Sharif.

After capturing Kabul, the Taliban forces continued to press north creating another wave of displacement. Displaced persons, now mostly Tajiks, were forced to continue to flee north, although some sought refuge in Kabul itself. By July 1998, the Taliban forces took the city of Mazar-i-Sharif.

The capture of Mazar-i-Sharif had great strategic and symbolic importance. The city had become the headquarters of the Taliban opposition and was an important stronghold for non-Pushtun groups. Its capture meant that Taliban forces controlled almost all of Afghanistan. After Mazar-i-Sharif was captured, Taliban forces massacred thousands of civilians, including many displaced persons, who were members of the Hazara ethnic group (USCR 1999; HRW 1998).

The displaced populations in Afghanistan now have very few options. The main escape routes to the south and east are under Taliban control and the borders into Pakistan, Uzbekistan and Tajikistan are closed. Although some have fled west to the city of Herat, that city is also under Taliban control. Some have voluntarily moved to Kabul to live with relatives; others have been forcibly relocated, by the Taliban, to compounds in the capital. The few areas not under Taliban control are the Tajik areas in the north-east and in the high central mountains of the Hazarajat. Yet even in these areas, the Taliban are slowly gaining control.

LIVING CONDITIONS

Internally displaced persons live in desperately poor conditions. Their immediate concerns are safety and access to food and shelter; health care and sanitation are non-existent. Access to education, civil rights, and personal liberty are of profound importance, but are relative luxuries considering that most displaced persons are just struggling to survive.

In addition to the hardships and devastation caused by the conflict, recent earthquakes and an ongoing drought are taking their toll on the economy, in general, and on the displaced, in particular. The desperation of the displaced is only exacerbated by the fact that relief agencies have had a difficult time operating in Afghanistan. The Taliban government has harassed relief groups, particularly on issues dealing with women. This has made it nearly impossible for relief organisations to employ female staff and, therefore, to provide assistance for women's health and safety.

After three UN staff workers were killed in August 1998, the UN temporarily closed its offices (AFP 1999, Section 4). Since then, the UN has had an on-again, off-again operation in Afghanistan. An IDP Task Force was set up in Kabul and Jalalabad composed of the ICRC, the UNOCHA, the World Food Programme (WFP) and various NGOs to monitor and assist displaced persons (USCR 1998). But the difficulties and dangers in working in the country have severely limited the Task Force's effectiveness.

Panjshir Valley

The Panjshir valley is a narrow strip of land along the Panjshir river, whose mouth lies less than 100 kilometres north of Kabul and which runs near the major north–south highway. There are now thought to be between 30,000 and 40,000 displaced persons in the valley, most from the Shomali plain north of Kabul.

The situation in the Panjshir is grave. Some of the displaced are housed in the area's few public buildings, such as mosques and schools, but most have no shelter at all (UNDPI 1999). Most of the displaced had fled their homes quickly, too quickly to gather food or possessions. In March 2000, an estimated 50 to 70 per cent of the displaced in the valley had no food. A small number had food supplies to last for up to three weeks, but none had reserves beyond three weeks (UNGA 1999).

Hazarajat

The Hazarajat, the home area of the Hazara people, is in the highest mountains of central Afghanistan. There is limited access by roads at the best of times; in winter, the area is covered with snow and largely inaccessible. The people of the area live mostly as subsistence farmers and herders. The growing season is short and the standard of living low.

Because of its remoteness, and to some degree because of the active resistance of Hazara militias, some parts of the Hazarajat have remained outside of Taliban control and have thus become a refuge for displaced people fleeing the Taliban government. The fighting in Kabul in the period between 1992 and 1994 drove many of the Hazara who had migrated to Kabul back into the Hazarajat, including a small, educated elite. Beginning in 1999, Taliban forces began to move into the Hazarajat and fighting erupted around the major towns, especially Bamiyan, Yakawland and Dar-e-Souf. It is estimated that over 50,000 persons have been displaced and have either moved to safer areas within the region or fled into nearby mountains to escape the fighting (UNRCO 2000).

Many of the displaced left with few, if any, possessions; and since they lost their crops and homes in the fighting, many have neither food nor shelter. Disease and chronic conditions related to poverty and extreme cold are pervasive among the elderly and the young. Cholera epidemics have broken out, too, as the displaced are forced to use water from open irrigation canals that also serve as waste runoff ditches (Doctors Without Borders 1999).

Kabul

The third largest concentration of internally displaced persons lives in the city of Kabul. The UNHCR estimates that some 55,000 to 60,000 displaced persons are dispersed around the city, most staying with relatives. Another large group are encamped in the grounds of the former Soviet embassy. Most of the displaced are ethnic Tajiks who were forcefully relocated during the fighting in Shomali plain over the past two years. Those living in the bombed-out compound are a group of women, children and elderly men who were separated from their male relatives by the Taliban during the fighting. As villages were captured, the men were either conscripted into the Taliban military or killed. The women, children and elderly were first sent to an IDP camp near Jalalabad where they were held as prisoners. Because of the terrible conditions at the camp, the Taliban moved them to the compound.

The displaced families have been living in the compound for more than 18 months. The living areas, both inside and outside, are cramped. International agencies have delivered some food to the displaced population there, but malnutrition is prevalent (UNOCHA 1999). There are no sanitation facilities and fresh water is limited. Women are restricted in their ability to move out of the compound because of strict Islamic laws (US Department of State 1999). With no source of income, many survive by begging.

Of the compound's displaced population 65 per cent are children. Collapsed buildings and debris make the compound dangerous for them, especially as there is no play area; overcrowding exposes the children to infectious diseases; their diet is limited. The children there display behaviours associated with anxiety, no doubt because they feel deeply the loss of their community and the male members of their families (WFP 1999).

COPING STRATEGIES

Ethnicity, Tribalism and Survival

When people are displaced within their ethnic homelands, such as displaced Tajiks in the Panjshir valley, or displaced Hazara in the Hazarajat, they are more apt to receive aid and assistance, or at least sympathy, from the local population. In contrast, those who are displaced in regions of other, especially antagonistic, ethnic groups are often not well received and certainly not offered assistance or comfort. This is true of the displaced in Kabul, both those in the former Soviet embassy compound and those dispersed around the city. They are mostly Tajiks and Hazara in a city that is predominantly Pushtun, and they are not treated well.

In addition, different ethnic groups have different social structures and therefore differing abilities to support ethnic solidarity. The groups that are organised into kin-based tribal structures are more likely to identify with and assist fellow tribesmen because of tribal codes of hospitality and stronger ethnic bonds. These are largely the Pushtun, who have been, and in some cases still are, pastoral nomads.

Other ethnic groups, particularly the northern groups, live in semi-feudal, land-based social and economic systems. These societies form primary allegiances around land or location, as opposed to kin relations, and are therefore less likely to identify with and aid others of the same ethnicity who might be from another region. These groups include the Tajiks, Uzbeks and Hazara who live as settled farmers. For example, Tajik farmers have only a weak notion of being part of a larger Tajik nation, but identify themselves by their local sub-region. As a result, displaced Tajiks in other parts of the Tajik ethnic area may not be welcomed because they are seen as people from another valley or region.

People seldom flee as individuals or as nuclear family units; they often flee in clan groups or as whole villages. The decision to leave their homes is usually made by village or tribal elders, who may be in contact with local commanders. This fact is often lost on relief agency officials who are unaware that displaced individuals do not make decisions outside of their traditional social network.

Food and Shelter

For their immediate needs of food and shelter, displaced persons tend to turn to kin or ethnic relations, local commanders or, when possible, international relief agencies. They find temporary shelter in public buildings or stay with local families, sometimes paying rent to do so. Local people may share or sell food to displaced persons for cash or barter or help people find food by loaning them money or animals. However, since local Afghans are often also impoverished, these options are limited.

An important coping strategy among subsistence farmers is to try to retain major assets, such as livestock and land. Most displaced persons try to take their animals with them. Among the displaced in the embassy compound, one-third brought livestock with them, mostly sheep, goats or cattle and, in some cases, chickens. Most prefer to use their animals for milk or eggs or to slaughter the animal for meat, rather than sell it. At times, however, they must sell or barter an animal to obtain other food items, such as rice or bread. The displaced are also sometimes forced to sell animals because they can no longer feed or house them. By some UN estimates, the sale of an animal provides a displaced family with up to two months' worth of resources. The long-term problem is, however, that once used or sold, that asset is gone forever.

Many of the displaced also try to continue farming, despite their displacement. Some males may stay behind to tend the family farms and protect family property, hiding when necessary. However, this strategy is risky since young men arouse suspicion from military groups. Reports indicate that most men who try to stay behind are eventually caught and either conscripted into the military or killed.

Another strategy is for the males of displaced families to return to their villages during lulls in the fighting to check on their property and continue farming. The ability to return in this way is dependent on the existence of a safe corridor between the place of refuge and the area from which they were displaced. These safe routes are sometimes negotiated by international relief agencies or are 'opened' by the warring parties during temporary truces. Displaced persons in Kabul from the Shomali plain just north of the capital report that unless the roads are closed by either the Taliban or the Tajik resistance groups, they can travel back and forth from Kabul to their villages to farm. The danger of getting caught up in the fighting is obvious; but in addition, the Taliban have been known to detain Tajik men at roadblocks and forcibly recruit them. More often, the displaced return to their villages clandestinely, travelling at night or by circuitous, concealed routes.

Still, the difficulty in obtaining adequate food supplies cannot be overstated. Of the population of Afghanistan 90 per cent are farmers, herdsmen or a combination of both. Even in normal times, the average Afghan farmer or herdsman does not have a large supply of extra food or savings; he must produce a crop each year to survive. With natural disasters, such as the current drought, and the man-made conflict that has destroyed most of the country's infrastructure, the production of food is becoming almost impossible.

IDP families who have depleted their food stores turn to the government, international relief agencies or to more desperate methods, such as begging. Interviews with some displaced families in Kabul indicate that the number of young children dying of mal-nutrition-related diseases has increased dramatically in the last five years. According to UNICEF, about 268,000 Afghan children under the age of five die each year from easily treatable illnesses such as diarrhoea and pulmonary conditions (UNICEF 2001).

Displaced and starving Afghans may also try to reach the Pakistani border where they hope to find food and shelter. Although the border with Pakistan is officially closed, some Afghans are able to get into Pakistan by crossing the border in remote areas. During winter 2001, many Afghans desperate to cross into Pakistan congregated at the border town of Torkham where they waited in horrendous conditions. Desperately poor with nothing to keep them in Afghanistan, many chose to risk the trek over perilous mountain passes to slip into Pakistan, even though they knew they would not be welcome there.

PROTECTION STRATEGIES

In the last 25 years of fighting, over 2 million people have been killed in Afghanistan, most of them civilians. There are few sources of protection for displaced persons. There is no responsible government to which the displaced can appeal and the presence of international agencies is limited. Those agencies that have been able to operate in Kabul have called upon the Taliban government to protect internally displaced persons, but those calls have, in general, been poorly received. The Taliban are not the only threat to security, however. Guerrilla groups have also been involved in killing and harassing Afghan citizens.

Since the displaced are largely unarmed civilians, they must either rely on hiding or fleeing, or seek protection with sympathetic resistance commanders. By agreeing to side with either the Taliban government or one of the various resistance groups, the displaced can win some measure of protection. To some degree, a displaced person's choice of protective political group depends on his ethnic background. The Pushtun have generally sided with the Taliban, and the non-Pushtun groups – the Tajik, Uzbeks and Hazara – have sided with groups hostile to the Taliban. Many non-Pushtun groups have also joined the Taliban, but it is unclear whether this choice was made freely or not.

PERSONAL RIGHTS AND FREEDOMS

Bibi is an ethnic Tajik about 40 years old. Her husband was killed in the fighting some years ago and she lived in the rural area north of Kabul with her two sons of 15 and 18, in the village of Donsghipaya. She and her sons had been surviving on a small plot of land inherited from her husband, raising grapes. When the Taliban moved into the area she lost everything:

> We lost our house, our property, and our belongings and ran away to Kabul, with nothing but our bare hands and feet, into the mountains. We now live in a small place with the help of other people. The Taliban and some of the war groups forced women and the older men to go to Jalalabad. Youngsters ran away and the groups killed many of them.

When they returned later to Kabul, Bibi added:

> I lived here with the help of donations from others. I had no shoes to wear in the winter. I cleaned other people's homes and did chores for them and lived with the meagre income of that. My mother and two other families live in the Russian Embassy and we live with the help of the UN. Even God does not help us. We are wandering here and there, sometimes at different people's homes. Now we live in the countryside of Afghanistan. We live a bad life.

The Taliban government has imposed a strict version of *sharia*, Islamic law, on the country, prohibiting a wide range of public activities. Many of these prohibitions are particularly designed to restrict the freedoms and rights of women. Under this interpretation of Islamic law, women are prohibited from most jobs, often from going to school and, in some cases, from leaving the home. Women who violate these restrictions can be punished severely and their families held responsible for their behaviour. Women must be veiled in public and must restrict their movements outside their homes.

Photo 2   A family and a widowed woman are forced to leave their village north of Kabul, Afghanistan (UNHCR, R. LeMoyne 1996)

Displaced women who have no shelter in which to maintain their privacy are doubly disadvantaged.

Even before *sharia* was imposed, the patriarchal society of Afghanistan required that women depended on close male relatives to survive. Now, women are not allowed to appear in public with men who are not close relatives (UNCHR 1999). This restriction has created particularly severe problems for widows who have no male family members to help or protect them. Since women are defined by their relationship to a male member of their family, displaced females who have no male relative present, either because the men stayed behind, were arrested, or were killed, are particularly vulnerable. A widow's brother or close male relative of her deceased husband will often protect her by marrying her, as men are permitted four wives under Islamic law. This form of protection has increased among the displaced population and among Afghan refugees, though it is by no means a complete solution to women's considerable problems.

The Taliban also interpret Islamic Law to forbid unrelated men and women from being in close proximity. This has led to problems with males trying to help displaced women. In 1998, three women and their three children, all suffering severe malnutrition, were attempting to drive to a feeding centre where they could receive food. Their van was stopped at a Taliban checkpoint and the male driver was taken and badly beaten for having allowed one of the mothers to sit in the front seat. The mothers and their children were forced from the vehicle. They never reached the feeding centre (Shorish-Shamley 2001).

In an effort to help themselves, women gather informally in groups, or cooperatives. These groups are modelled on the traditional living arrangements in Afghan society, where women live much of their lives apart from men in groups related by birth or marriage. In the traditional household compounds, sisters, sisters-in-law, mothers, grandmothers, daughters and, in some cases, multiple wives form tight bonds and develop informal networks outside the home.

Displaced women in desperate situations form similar bonds. In these groups of unrelated women, food and other resources are shared and labour is divided: some women look after children while other women search, or beg, for food. Since women beyond their childbearing years are somewhat freer to move around in public, they represent the group in society. Some groups number only a few women; others can include more than two dozen people, including children.

These groupings can, however, be the source of new problems: traditional Afghan society views unattached women, especially those living together, as sinful. They are assumed to be prostitutes. Why else, the traditional thinking goes, would they have no men with them? While there have been reports of prostitution among displaced women, evidence suggests that it is a rare occurrence.

EDUCATION

Even before the recent fighting, the education system in Afghanistan was a shambles. Kabul University has been closed for almost a decade and most secondary and elementary schools were closed for most of the 1990s. Those schools that operate do so on a very limited basis, teaching mostly Islamic subjects and serving mostly men. Various international relief agencies have tried to re-introduce schools into the country, including education for girls, but with limited success. Educational opportunities for displaced children are virtually non-existent in most areas.

The one exception has been the introduction of a school programme for displaced children in the former Soviet embassy compound. In July 2000, UNICEF and Save the Children introduced a primary school for displaced children there. Over 2,500 children, 40 per cent of them girls, attend the school (UNOCHA 2000). The school was created and is run with the permission of the Taliban government, which insists on approving the teachers and the curriculum. The Taliban allow girls to attend school under certain conditions: that they are pre-pubescent; that the curriculum is censored to exclude material that could be offensive to strict Moslems; that the teachers are only women; and that the girls and boys are separated. Besides providing a much needed education, school imposes a welcome structure on the displaced children's days.

It is not true, however, that the absence of formal schooling means that displaced children receive no education. Even before they became displaced, these children probably did not attend school. In much of Afghanistan, education is still provided by the extended family and the local Islamic clergy, village priests who teach the children to recite the Koran. Although this traditional education is mostly experiential, or, in the case of religious training, a product of rote memory, and much more limited in scope than school-based education, it does teach each new generation the basic skills and information it needs to survive. In the traditional village, grand-parents often teach young children the family genealogy, local customs and traditions, and traditional legends and folklore. Girls learn to sew and cook and boys learn the art of farming and tending flocks.

Since displaced children are often separated from their extended families and from the male members of the family, even such traditional education is not available. As a result, a generation of Afghan youth has grown up without even a traditional education. The results are seen among the youth who roam the major cities, working in menial jobs or begging, many at very young ages. Without an extended family to care for them, they join militias or become the foot soldiers of the Taliban movement. One often sees young teenagers with submachine guns manning checkpoints for government or opposition groups.

The displaced have few options for educating their young. Even when public education is available, the displaced can usually only send the youngest children. After children reach the age of ten years or so, they are expected to contribute to the survival of the family. Girls care for the sick or the younger children; boys go out to find food by begging or taking menial jobs. Some boys join militia groups as soon as they are old enough, not because they are eager to fight but because they may receive food and protection and, in some cases, a small amount of money that they can then use to help their family.

CONCLUSION

More than two decades of internal turmoil and ethnic conflict have left Afghanistan, already one of the world's poorest countries, eco-nomically and socially devastated. The fighting, which began as a war against a foreign occupier then devolved into civil war, has displaced as many as 1 million people, most of whom would have fled the country entirely had the borders of neighbouring Pakistan and Tajikistan not been closed. The displaced are largely members of the northern ethnic groups, the Tajiks, Uzbeks and Hazara, who have been forced out of their villages by the advance of the largely Pushtun Taliban government in Kabul.

In many cases, people were forced to move quickly and took few possessions with them. Food and shelter in the areas of refuge they now occupy is limited, international aid workers have difficulty in reaching them, and the Kabul government offers little or no assistance. Their coping strategies are also limited: they seek shelter and food from local residents; they try to secure their physical safety by hiding or seeking the protection of one of the local militias. Some were fortunate enough to have brought livestock with them; some continue to farm, either by leaving male members of the family behind or by risking the danger involved in returning to their villages periodically.

For the most part, the displaced do not have access to health services or to education for their children, except in the few places where international relief agencies have been able to establish schools. The social and economic restrictions on women imposed by the fundamentalist Islamic government make displaced women's lives even more desperate.

More often than not, the displaced population's most valuable coping resource, the extended family, has been shattered. Although families often flee together, in most cases, the male members of the family have either been killed or forcibly recruited, leaving women and children to fend for themselves in a hostile social climate. To protect themselves, women often gather into groups that resemble indigenous communes. For the displaced in Afghanistan, education, civil rights and political participation are concepts that have little relation to their reality. Their immediate concern is finding food and shelter; they are simply trying to survive.

6
Burma: Displaced Karens. Like Water on the *Khu* Leaf

Chris Cusano

War disrupts the normal relationship between people and place. Displaced by war, people must adapt to survive, both physically and socially. When people are displaced for a long time, these adaptations become normal; thus displacement starts as an aberration but becomes a constant way of life. In eastern Burma, 'normal' displacement has led to significant changes in the political, cultural and economic relationships between Karen people and their 'place' – both the physical space they occupy and their position in society. Those changes, and particularly the Karens' own revised perceptions of their place in the world, provide insights into how they, and others in Burma, cope with displacement.

In Burma,[1] population displacement is widespread, though little understood. Armed conflict, disputes over land and natural resources, and poverty drive people from their homes; but there has been little research on displacement's effect on people's lives.[2] Many internally displaced persons live in remote areas that are also theatres of war; and the government of Burma denies permission to researchers or aid workers hoping to visit these contested regions. Furthermore, until a few years ago, Burma's displaced population attracted little international attention. Few, apart from a handful of Thailand-based aid organisations, knew about conditions in the war zones. By the late 1990s, however, the world became more aware of conditions inside Burma, thanks to reports of displacement, increasing numbers of would-be refugees seeking asylum in Thailand, the controversial repatriation of Burmese refugees from Bangladesh, deteriorating tolerance for refugees in Thailand, and the burgeoning influence of Burma's democracy movement.

The portrait of displaced Karens presented here is a composite drawn from dozens of documents, interviews, conversations, and observations culled by the author, who worked with Karen refugees in Thailand for seven years in the 1990s, and by his colleagues and friends, many of whom are displaced Karens. Almost all the

De facto frontier
(claimed by India)

Frontier claimed
by China

0   km   300

BHUTAN

INDIA

BANGLADESH

KACHIN

CHINA

SAGAING

**M Y A N M A R
(B U R M A)**

CHIN

SHAN

MANDALAY

ARAKAN (RAKHINE)

MAGWE

KAYAH
(KARENNI)

LAOS

BAGO
(PEGU)

KAWTHULEI (KAREN)

*Bay of
Bengal*

IRRAWADDY

⭐ Yangon

YANGON
(RANGOON)

MON

THAILAND

N

TENNASSERIM

● Bangkok

A N D A M A N

INDIA

S E A

*Gulf of
Thailand*

Map by András Bereznay

Map 6   Burma

statements reported here were originally recorded for other purposes, mostly for documentation of human rights abuses, and are credited to their original sources. Though only relatively few people around the world are involved with human rights in Burma, a large body of documentation exists detailing the plight of displaced Karens and other peoples of Burma. Yet there have been few attempts to understand what displacement means to the people who live it: what effects it has on their economic, political, cultural and moral life. This chapter examines how Karens in eastern Burma respond when displaced by the ongoing war between the Burmese government and the Karen National Union (KNU).

The war in Burma has caused three main kinds of internal displacement:

- *jungle displacement*, in which people in remote rural areas flee their homes and hide in the hills and forests
- *forced relocation*, in which rural villagers are evicted then moved to sites under close state supervision
- *social dislocation*, in which persons leave their homes and try to survive on the social and economic fringes of existing communities.[3]

These three categories do not represent all varieties of displacement in Burma; they are simply a handy way to compare the circumstances in which one ethnic and social group finds itself. Forced relocation and social dislocation are omitted from this chapter with the caveat that various displacement experiences, such as hiding in the jungle, fleeing to a refugee camp, migrating to the city, or finding a job abroad, are not always distinct routes, but steps along a single path.

BACKGROUND

Karen Diversity and Distribution

'Karen' is a blanket term that covers several peoples inhabiting a large area of mainland South-east Asia between Burma's Irrawaddy river and Thailand's Chao Phraya. Today, Karens live around the Irrawaddy river delta and along the Sittang, Salween and Tennasserim rivers in Burma, and along the Moei, Ping and Kwae Noi rivers in Thailand. Karens inhabit much of the Burma–Thailand border area, from the northern boundary between Kayah state and Mae Hong Son province to the southern tip of the border at Burma's

Victoria Point and Thailand's Ranong province. Many Karens live in major Burmese cities, including the capital, Yangon (Rangoon), and the Irrawaddy delta towns of Bassein and Myaungmya, and on the outskirts of major Thai cities, such as Chiang Mai, Lampang, Tak and Kanchanaburi.

No one knows how many Karens live in Burma. A 1931 census, considered by some to be Burma's last proper population count, recorded 1.3 million Karens; a 1947 census counted 5 million; in 1971, the government counted 3.2 million Karens; and a 1983 census counted 2.12 million (BERG 1998:7–8). The disparity could be the result of a failure to include remote villages, of problems of classification (who, exactly, is Karen?), or of a political intention to reduce the official number of Karens, and thereby emphasise their minority status. Using fertility rates to project population, the government, in 1992, estimated that there were 6.2 million Karens. The Karen National Union, which has not taken a census, claims 7 million Karens throughout Burma. If there were 6 million Karens in Burma today, they would comprise about 12 per cent of the total population. Approximately half of them live in eastern Burma, including Karen state, parts of Mon state, Tennasserim division and the eastern extreme of Pegu division.

As this broad distribution suggests, there is no single homogeneous Karen cultural group. Significant cultural, economic, linguistic and religious differences exist among people who call themselves Karen, and significant similarities exist between Karens and non-Karens.[4] The degree to which Karens absorb Burmese national culture also varies. Nevertheless, a rough description of major sociological differences helps define who displaced Karens are. Although it is customary to divide Karens into Pwo and S'gaw sub-groups, this division is only relevant as a way of noting that Karens usually speak either a Pwo or S'gaw dialect, and that eastern Pwo Karens tend to be Buddhists and S'gaw Karens tend to be Christians or animists.

There are important distinctions between highland and lowland Karens. Living in the mountains, highland Karens are largely removed from the national culture. They often speak their native Karen dialect only, not Burmese (Walker 1981:89); and their lives are less influenced by popular culture as conveyed in print, radio, and television. In contrast, lowland Karens are more likely to interact with other non-Karen peoples, and may share more characteristics with the majority culture. They may have attended Burmese schools and speak Burmese anywhere from 'market-level' proficiency to native fluency. Some may not speak Karen at all. They may adopt Burmese or western dress, or mix these with Karen costume.

Highland Karens are chiefly involved in subsistence agriculture. Like other mountain peoples, they practice shifting cultivation of 'dry rice', meaning rice not grown in flooded paddies, and they grow vegetables and raise livestock. Exceptions to the subsistence-only economy include training and hiring out elephants for logging, and trading livestock, highland crops or forest products with the lowland populations. Lowland Karens grow 'wet rice' in paddies, and are more likely to sell or trade their surplus produce and participate in a cash economy. They often hold non-agricultural jobs, including owning small businesses, working as teachers and civil servants, serving in the military, or being employed in any of the myriad occupations cosmopolitan life has to offer.

Religion also differs among Karens. While followers of traditional animism almost always live in mountains or deep forests, the highland/lowland description is less useful in identifying the territories of Buddhists and Christians. Both Buddhists and Christians live in the Irrawaddy delta. American and British Protestant missionaries began converting Karens in Burma from the first half of the nineteenth century, and today Christianity is practised by perhaps one-third of the Karen population. Missionaries were active in the mountains as well, and many Christians can be found throughout the eastern highlands. With Protestantism came education, and many mountain Karens were taught in local mission schools.

Differences among Karens may also arise depending on whether or not they are affiliated with the KNU. The KNU considers itself the single valid national political organisation representing all Karens. From this point of view, all Karens are affiliated with the organisation. In reality, however, some choose to participate in the KNU, some choose not to, and others participate nominally by paying taxes, accommodating Karen National Liberation Army (KNLA) soldiers, and not running afoul of the organisation. Many families have proud traditions of voluntary service in KNU. As soldiers, teachers, medics, administrators or representatives of the KNU bureaucracy, Karens in this category tend to benefit from whatever perquisites and exemptions KNU might offer. Decidedly non-aligned Karens and nominal participants may enjoy few such benefits. For example, KNU often requires households under its administration to contribute one member to 'the revolution'. Houses that do not or cannot provide members may be taxed more heavily or conscripted for porter duty, and are less likely to benefit from certain kinds of KNU activities.

Taken together, these distinctions produce several rough portraits of Karens in Burma today. One portrait depicts Karens as highland living, subsistence farming, predominantly S'gaw speaking, animist or Christian, and culturally distinct from mainstream Burmese society. Many Karen civilians displaced by combat in the mountains of eastern Burma belong to this group. Another group of Karens can be described as lowland living, paddy farming, agriculturally diversified, Karen and Burmese speaking, Buddhist or Christian, and more integrated into Burmese society. Many Karens in this category also number among the displaced. In addition, there is an elite of Karen society: they are urban dwelling, middle class, educated, economically diverse, primarily Burmese speaking, possibly English speaking and often not Karen speaking, and usually Christian. Contrary to expectations, members of this group are also among the displaced people in eastern Burma.

Over the course of a 50-year civil war, these three population types have met and mixed, despite their geographical and cultural differences. Starting in the 1950s, the centre of KNU power gradually shifted from central Burma to the east. As the eastward retreat into the Dawna mountains and towards the Thai border hastened during the 1960s and 1970s, lowland and urban Karens from the Irrawaddy delta, Yangon and Insein began moving to the new 'liberated' areas. Serving the KNU's mountain strongholds, the lowland Karens married local highlanders, producing a generation of culturally, linguistically and religiously diverse Karens who personify the socio-demographic impact of the KNU's eastward migration. As war in the mountains intensified, the KNU recruited more of the traditionally insular highlanders, and the fate of migrant KNU insurgents and local Karen civilians became inextricably linked.

These dynamics created the great variety one sees among displaced Karens today: former Buddhist monks trained at Burmese monasteries; Baptist mission school graduates from the delta; and animists brought up with local spirit traditions. Among the displaced are teachers who followed the KNU east, college students who fled cities after the 1988 military coup, and indigenous farmers, hunters and healers. There are Karens who can hold a conversation more easily in English than in Karen, those to whom English and Burmese are foreign tongues, and eastern and western Karens for whom Burmese is the common language.

For many lowland migrants, displacement began 20 or 30 years ago when, voluntarily or not, they left their homes and moved eastward. Although war is responsible for their displacement today, the ultimate resolution to their problems will involve land, politics and economics far from where they started. Highland Karens, displaced from their villages, may also have migrated several times. Their original homes may have already been taken over by others, degraded by logging, or seriously altered by development projects. Karens affiliated with KNU recognise that displacement is only one of their problems. Unless some political settlement reduces conflict with the government, they will risk displacement no matter where they stay.

History of the Conflict

Nothing is more contentious than a fact. Even if history, in some simple, idealised sense, is merely a sequence of facts, then the history of civil war in Burma is, at best, a battleground of facts, opinions and interpretations. The facts are deceptively straightforward. Until the mid-nineteenth century, dozens of racial groups occupied the territory of mainland South-east Asia, now known as Burma (or Myanmar), without much in the way of distinct national boundaries. Various kingdoms, including the Siamese, Burman, Mon, Khmer and Rakhine, waxed and waned, while many peoples lived under smaller-scale polities. England fought two wars with the Burman dynasty, and towards the end of the nineteenth century annexed, or colonised, the traditional seats of Burman influence in Lower and Upper Burma. The colonial regime also set out to oversee nearby peoples remote from the traditional locus of political power. These became the 'ethnic minorities' in the new Burmese province of British India. Britain drew borders around Burma and maintained a semi-benevolent, semi-oppressive relationship with its subjects until 1948 when, in the wake of India's independence, it also handed over this newly constructed state to a shaky coalition of national leaders.

To some people at some moments, ethnic conflict in Burma is a colonial legacy: the many races of Burma co-existed peacefully until the British landed and used their infamous 'divide-and-rule' strategy to play formerly amicable peoples against one another. In this inter-pretation, having deposed the Burmese king and unceremoniously ended the dynasty, the British made enemies of the Burman people while extending favour to minorities such as Karens and Kachins. This unequal treatment lasted until Burmese independence, in 1948, when hostility erupted between those who had been 'vanquished' and those who had been 'liberated' by colonial rule.

But to others, Karens and Burmans have been enemies since time immemorial. According to this interpretation, aggression by Burmans and retreat by Karens was constant throughout history. Burman kings dominated, abused and enslaved the Karens; while modern Burman rulers perpetrated genocide against the Karens. In response, modern Karen nationalists displayed indomitable political and military resistance.

Shortly after independence, Karen and Burman leaders began quarrelling over autonomy for the Karen people, and an armed rebellion broke out. Well-educated Karens who had served in the British colonial army and civilian administration quickly organised this revolt, built a national revolutionary organisation with military and administrative branches, and began pursuing national independence. Despite several attempts at negotiation, the war between the KNU and the Government of Burma continued throughout the 1950s. In 1962, a Burmese General, Ne Win, overthrew the government in a coup, introduced a socialist economy, and cut Burma off from most of the rest of the world. Inside the country the war intensified, and the KNU found itself steadily losing ground in south-central Burma, in the Irrawaddy river delta districts west of the capital city, Yangon. Karens began migrating eastward towards 'Kawthoolei', the new seat of KNU power named after the legendary Karen homeland, near Burma's mountainous, forested border with Thailand. After another military coup in 1988, the Burmese army committed itself and its resources to eliminating ethnic nationalist movements and insurgencies. Karens were one group among many that sought autonomy or independence.

INTERNAL DISPLACEMENT AND KAREN NATIONALISM

Displacement of Karens rarely surfaced in media coverage or debate on Burma until the KNU suffered substantial military losses in the mid-1990s. A strong KNU had once prevented the Burmese army from penetrating deeply or permanently into insurgent areas, so many Karens lived behind the KNU 'front line'. When the KNU held significant territory between the Thai border and the plains west of the Dawna mountains, Karens displaced or disturbed by military action could relocate deeper into the mountains, that is, deeper into KNU territory, and establish new villages or integrate with existing ones. KNU military centres, such as Kawmoora (lost in battle in

1984) and Kyon Doe (1997), and military–political centres like Three
Pagodas Pass (1992), Manerplaw (1995) and Htee Kee (1997), offered
sanctuary to Karens who relocated from precarious frontline areas.
They survived either by participating in the local economy or by
joining the KNU. While people suffered the immediate effects of displacement, such as insecurity, hunger and homelessness, these were
likely to be temporary conditions that would change when the army
retreated or when Karens fled to secure areas nearby. An aid worker
whose organisation provides emergency assistance to displaced
Karens observed, 'It's not that internal displacement has just begun
happening. I think it's been going on for years, but [displaced people
and Karen authorities] had their own mechanisms to deal with it'
(AHRC 1999:80).

Shifts in the military strategies both of the KNU and the Burmese
army have increased the incidence of internal displacement. Once,
civilians were accidental victims of combat; or the Burmese army
targeted persons with known links to the KNU or communities
known to provide the KNU with supplies and recruits. While these
standard anti-insurgency tactics undeniably caused much suffering,
in theory they distinguished between civilians and combatants. But
during the 1990s, the Burmese army seemed to have abandoned
these distinctions in preference for a less discriminating strategy.
'The big issue,' the aid worker said, 'is that before, people were
dislocated due to fighting between the Burmese army and the ethnic
insurgencies, and the villagers were caught in the middle, so they
had to flee. Now, it's not because of any offensives that they have to
move; it's directly because of military activities against civilian
villages. The Burmese army specifically orders civilians to clear out
of areas they have lived in throughout their lives. The army marks
off an area and sends the orders to clear it.'

Human rights investigators have found that Burmese army field
commanders confirm this tactical shift. For example, the Karen
Human Rights Group (KHRG) reports that in November 1999 a
battalion commander explained to a meeting of village heads that
the army views Karen civilians and insurgents as one:

In a pool, we can't leave some fish to catch, so we have to catch
them all ... Right now, I do not fight [KNU]. I am fighting the
civilians. If the people dare to shoot one bullet at me, it is
enough. I will shoot into the village. I have no relatives there.
(KHRG 2000:1)

One villager extended the officer's metaphor: 'They plan to make the resistance disappear. For example, they say the fish are in the pond, but there are a few fish they can't catch. So they drain the water to catch the fish.' A decade of human rights abuse reporting also testifies to the Burmese army's impatience with distinguishing between civilians and insurgents in the civil war zones.

Another major factor affecting Karen displacement over the past decade has been the Karen nationalist movement's split into two competing factions. In 1994, the Democratic Karen Buddhist Organisation (DKBO), known by its armed wing, the Democratic Karen Buddhist Army (DKBA), challenged the KNU's exclusive claim to Karen nationalism. The group organised Buddhist Karens in the KNU rank and file and, with support from the Burmese army, drove the KNU from many of its strongholds along the Thai border. By cooperating with the Burmese army, the DKBA flouted the dominant mode of Karen nationalism, which was Christian-led, S'gaw speaking, partially westernised, and essentially separatist in its attitude towards the Burmese state. Posing the first powerful alternative to the KNU, the DKBA has enhanced the political status of Pwo-speaking Buddhist Karens of eastern Burma. Indeed, the DKBA has brought to light the complicated relations between Karen civilians and militant nationalists.

The advent of the DKBA changed several aspects of how Karens become displaced and cope with their displacement. Because the DKBA is composed of Karens from former KNU areas and, like the KNU, is sustained by Karen communities in eastern Burma, it is a powerful agent in depriving the KNU of civilian support. With intimate knowledge of local terrain, political history and economy, the DKBA has been able to pinpoint and challenge KNU bastions. For example, in Pa'an, Hlaingbwe, Kawkareik and Myawaddy townships, the DKBA has relocated villages, confiscated rice and controlled rice distribution. The DKBA controls several key transportation routes leading to the Thai border, and has the power to stop would-be refugees from reaching camps in Thailand. The DKBA controls many border villages that once provided personnel and succor to the KNU. The group tries to woo KNU members and sympathisers from refugee camps, promising a better deal under the DKBA if they return – and threatening retribution if they don't. By attacking KNU-controlled refugee camps in Thailand, DKBA has influenced displaced Karens' choices about where and how to flee.

It is difficult to count displaced Karens. Armed conflict only exacerbates the technical and political obstacles to conducting a census, and problems of classification blur the distinction between who is and is not displaced. The only known attempt to count displaced Karens, undertaken in 1997, subtracted the number of refugees registered in Thai camps from the total number of people believed to have been displaced, then estimated how many of the remainder may be internally displaced. Using this method, researchers suggested that approximately 30 per cent, or 480,000, of the rural Karen population of eastern Burma was displaced at that time. In addition to the 91,000 Karen in refugee camps in Thailand, 100,000–200,000 were displaced internally (BERG 1998:35). Since then, fighting and forced relocation have continued, and it has become more difficult to enter Thailand. It is likely that some 200,000 Karen men, women and children live displaced in the jungles of eastern Burma.

PHASES OF DISPLACEMENT

Some displaced Karen today trace the origins of their displacement to Burma's post-war land reform, particularly the nationalisation of agricultural land in the 1960s and 1970s. The failing socialist economy and what some perceive as the racially biased redistribution of farmland coincided with the KNU's eastward move. Karens moved east from the Irrawaddy delta looking for a better social, political and economic future, and were imbued with pioneer spirit as well as revolutionary spirit. They maintained contact with their homes and retained the wish to return. But in the ensuing years they moved farther eastward and gradually lost contact with their homes. In some cases, families and neighbours followed them east. The government, relatives or settlers may have claimed the land once held by the migrants. Throughout these years, eastern Karens also began to move. By the 1970s, Karen state and other areas of active rebellion were upheaved by displacement linked to the counter-insurgency. Anecdotal reports suggest that since then, eastern Karens have been hiding in the jungles, living in relocation centres, wandering in and out of cities and across borders in growing numbers.

Though people may ultimately flee in a sudden, violent moment, they probably anticipated that they would leave, but didn't know when. The Burmese army's counter-insurgency tactics usually follow a pattern: after targeting an area for depopulation, the army orders villagers to move by issuing a written notice, convening a meeting of village headmen or visiting the village themselves. According to field reports, notification seldom results in quick and orderly compliance. Unless or until the army comes back to move or scatter the villagers, people assume a subtly defiant wait-and-see attitude. They may attempt to negotiate with the local military command but, more often, they will ignore the first notice and go about their business. The army sometimes reacts to uncooperative villages by sending a detachment of soldiers to emphasise the order. This may result in the first instance of serious human rights abuse, and may include detention, torture, summary execution, looting and destruction of homes, property and livestock. Knowing that farmers are reluctant to leave their land, the army may also burn or confiscate crops, food and farm implements. This is when jungle displacement begins.

However, the army does not always notify in advance. Areas with heavy insurgent activity (those in designated 'black zones'), remote villages that orders may not have reached, and villages that have flouted army demands for provisions and labour may suffer a rapid attack from which people also flee into the jungles. But even without prior notice, Karen villagers are aware of the army's movements and potential for violence, and of their community's standing in the political struggle among rival military powers. They choose to stay on their land until combat, human rights abuses or hunger finally force them off.

After fleeing, displaced Karens seek the first opportunity to return home. Though they lose their houses and possessions, they still manage to return to their fields. Temporary displacement may be a frequent, even routine, way of life in the war zones. For example, in 1998, villagers in Mone township reported:

This year we ran from the army four times, and three times in September they really reached our place. The first time they took all our possessions. The second time they destroyed all our crops. The third time, they pulled all the paddy stalks from the ground and burned down the field hut. (AHRC 1999:19)

At best, villagers may flee with ample warning, stay hidden in the jungle for only a few hours or overnight, and return to an intact village, perhaps because the soldiers changed course or, for other reasons, did not enter the village and moved off to a safe distance. More often, however, people flee with little warning and must wait out the troops' stay and the inevitable looting of food and valuables. Soldiers may make the village a temporary base, or may stay until the villagers come out of hiding and return.

At worst, displaced people see no chance of returning home. Interviewed in 1998, this displaced Karen villager from Palaw township, in South-eastern Burma, had been living in the jungle for three years:

> Twice the Burmese army ordered villagers to relocate to Palawgon, first during the harvest in 1996, again during the 1998 harvest.[5] My family did not move; we fled to [a place] two hours' walk from our village. There were nine families ... 43 persons. So I left my village three years ago, even before the relocation began. I left my plantation, my house, all of my livestock. I could carry nothing. I left everything behind. Now I have no income. (Eh Na 1998:20)

Life in the jungle is harsh, and becomes even harsher the longer people stay. Not only is food in short supply, but so are medicines, clothing, blankets, clean water, pots and pans, knives and other essential instruments of survival. People often construct temporary shelters, perhaps with no floor or walls, only a roof made out of leaves. But if alerted to approaching danger, persons living displaced in the jungle may abandon these temporary homes at a moment's notice and move on in search of safer ground, usually staying along the banks of small streams and rivers.

To avert total destruction of the village, or to avoid having soldiers hunt for people in the forest, people sometimes choose to return and 'surrender' themselves to military rule. This was the decision made by Naw Ble and other residents of a village in Dawei in southern Burma:

> After wandering in the jungle, we felt that there were no more places to go. Some people suggested that going back would be better than being caught in the jungle. So one day when there were no soldiers in the village, we re-entered. We saw all our possessions scattered, and no cock crowed, no dog barked, no cat cried and no cattle wandered about the place. Everything was quiet. The next day, [soldiers came and] started to dig trenches by our houses. They did not harm us, but would climb our trees and take fruit. They ordered us not to leave the village without

permission. To go out cost 15 kyat per day, and we had to be back before dark. (AHRC 1999:31)

This sense of alienation from a familiar place demonstrates the cultural nature of displacement: it is a social and psychological state as well as a physical dislocation. Superficially, Naw Ble and her neighbours seem to have entered a 'resettlement' phase; but more accurately, displacement profoundly changed the relationship between her people and their place.

PLACE, DISPLACEMENT AND KAREN IDENTITY

Displaced Karens are known for their tenacity. They can survive for years, even decades, without sufficient food or medicine. They endure the gravest human rights abuses. They resist the safety and sustenance found in towns, lowland villages and refugee camps. Why would people insist on staying where they can barely grow a crop, where they could be killed by landmines or shot on sight, and where fear and despair seem to rule their lives? The only way to understand what jungle displacement means to Karens, and how they respond to it, is to explore their beliefs and attitudes about land, displacement and cultural identity. Karens' understanding of their origins, their arrival in their current homes and their 'correct place' in the world colours their perception of history and helps explain their current political and economic hardship. Displacement, alienation and racial conflict are recurrent themes in Karen mythology, tradition and world view.[6]

Myth, History and Alienation

Displacement and dispossession are themes found in Karen creation and migration myths. Several slightly different versions of the migration story have been recorded since the nineteenth century, but they all agree on the main points. Karens recall that they came south from China or Mongolia under the leadership of the first Karen patriarch, Boar Tusk. The Karens were accidentally separated from their leader in the jungle, and had to complete the journey by themselves. Although a new leader found suitable land along the Ping river, by the time the Karens arrived Thais had already taken the land and the Karens were forced to settle in the surrounding mountains and jungles. Another story tells how, in even more ancient times, Karens were put at a social and intellectual disadvantage to other races by their own carelessness. When God handed out sacred books to various races, the Karens accidentally burned theirs and lost the chance to become a sophisticated civilisation.

Almost all Karens know these stories and their themes of dislocation, loss and homelessness. According to one student of Karen history, Karens describes themselves as a disenfranchised people:

> As the Thais and Caucasians grew robustly, the Karens were forced to endure a life of poverty, toil and adversity in the jungle ... Karens believe they lost the best valley land to other groups. Whether they lost it through carelessness or others' dishonesty, both stories conclude that they did forfeit land they once possessed. Karens believe that ... they lost a position of pre-eminence when these peoples forced the aboriginal Karens of Thailand and Burma into the uplands ... and the southernmost marshes of the Burma Delta. Both stories, above all, tell that Karens feel they are orphans who lost the chance to be an advanced, powerful people. (Renard 1980:2–3)

Displaced Karens explain their current status in similar terms. In one parable, they lived idyllically in the fertile plains of lower Burma. One day, a Karen returned to his favourite spot on the river to find a strange fishing pole, belonging to a Mon, planted in the ground next to his own. He returned another day to find yet another pole beside the second, this one belonging to a Burman. Sensing trouble, he went home, packed up his house and family, and fled lower Burma for the eastern mountain ranges.[7] This story intimates the troubles Karens expect when what they perceive as racially incompatible peoples live too close together.

Racial incompatibility is an important element in Karens' views on displacement. Local histories describe how the encroachments of incompatible races inevitably drove Karens from their places. For example, a Karen village near Kyauk Kyi township lay just outside the Burmese army's operation zone, and therefore enjoyed a degree of stability that attracted settlers from the plains. As more Burmans arrived, communal tensions arose. The Burmans built fences around their houses and considered everything that wandered into their space, including neighbours' stray chickens, as their own property. They did not trim bamboo to allow new shoots to grow, so the village bamboo supplies dwindled. The Karens felt that the Burmans were forcing them off their land by making it uninhabitable, and so they began moving into the remote mountains of the east.[8]

Karen accounts of losing land to foreign encroachers contain economic factors as well. In 1999, a local correspondent explained the history of a village tract in Pegu Division's Kyauk Kyi township:

> Before World War II, the first village was Pawpeet'der, named after the founder Phu Pawpeet, who lit beacons at night along the roadside using coconut oil for fuel. The people set up plantations and gardens for growing tomato, eggplant, coconut, durian and mango. They hired Shan and Burman labourers who settled around the village. Burmans named the place Meetaingtaw, after the beacons, and called their own village Lower Meetaingtaw. Over time, these settlers bought up the Karens' land. After Karens built a church, Burmans called the original village by a new name, Kyaungsu. Lower Meetaingtaw became just plain Meetaingtaw within our current generation. This situation is reminiscent of the proverb told by our ancestors, 'The dog covers the pig's tracks.' Before World War II, these were all Karen places, but now other races outnumber the Karen. (Kweh Klo 1999:6)

Ultimately, this Karen quarter was known not for the founder or his landmarks, but for a church, which in Buddhist Burma is something of a foreign structure. According to this story, the Karens were transformed from indigenous people to strangers on their own land within 50 years. Such experiences, coupled with the Burmese army's indiscriminate counter-insurgency strategy, contribute to perceptions that the Burman race is waging a war of ethnic hatred against the Karen.

Place, Displacement and Karen Nationalism

The KNU also applies themes of place and displacement to its historical analyses and political programme. Displacement from traditional land is a fact of history that justifies KNU political ambitions. By raising the hope of reuniting Karens with Kawthoolei, their promised land, the KNU exhorts Karens to rally to its cause. Nationalists contend that Karens have proprietary land rights to much of Burma, since they were the country's first inhabitants and were forcefully evicted by 'foreign' settlers. The significant innovation of Karen nationalism is to propose that united, Karens can create or reclaim Kawthoolei, a pure Karen homeland. The KNU's vow to establish Kawthoolei appeals to the dispossessed: through KNU, Karens can redress their separation with Boar Tusk, their squandering of the 'book of knowledge', and their subjugation by alien races.

Place, Identity and Subsistence Agriculture

Most Karens are farmers and, perhaps like all farmers, feel a close identification with the land they work. Two important features of traditional rural economy create this close connection between people and their place: free land and communal labour. Normally, highland Karen farmers do not buy, sell or own land. Because the land is sparsely populated and fertile, farmers simply appropriate what land they need. Communities or households do not own this land, but act as stewards responsible for both exploiting and protecting it.

Communal labour also fixes Karens' identity to their place. While a farmer is theoretically free to claim as much land as he wants, he relies on his neighbours' labour, and must likewise contribute time and energy to their farms. Agricultural labour benefits the entire community, not just the individual land-tending household. Therefore, survival depends not only on the availability of land, but also on the stability of the community workforce.

COPING WITH DISPLACEMENT

Displacement changes life so drastically that, in a sense, everything displaced people do is a response to their circumstances. I have sorted these responses into five categories: subsistence; protection; access to education; public participation; and religion, language and identity. Naturally, these categories overlap, forming an overall system of adaptation. For example, protection and subsistence are interdependent. The ways and means by which displaced people obtain food, shelter and health care are constantly subject to the need to maintain security. Conversely, security can never be total, because survival demands that people venture from their hiding places, and risk detection, to search for food.

Before considering each aspect of adaptation, it may be useful to get an overview of displacement and survival from a displaced Karen. At the time of this interview, in 1997, Saw Htoo K'baw was a 36-year-old teacher and father of five who had migrated to Karen state from the delta, and finally fled to a refugee camp in Thailand:

I arrived in Papun in 1981. I went to help, and as a high school graduate I was given a job teaching in the KNU high school. Before 1992, conditions weren't too tough. But in January 1992, the Burmese army began to battle the KNU. Our area had been pretty stable; people from other places fled there to escape the fighting. Population pressure increased over time. When I left earlier this year the village had more than 200 houses, compared to the typical village size of only 30. Originally, apart from growing rice, people had no problems – fishing, breeding livestock, growing and foraging for vegetables, cutting timber and trading. But over time it became harder to live by agriculture. Land should lie fallow for at least three or four years, but nowadays it's two years at most. The land is totally exhausted.

After 1992, I, too, grew my own rice. I planted three to four baskets of seed the first year. Because the soldiers were patrolling and the soil was poor I didn't harvest enough to feed my family, only five baskets. After school closed in January, I planned to trade in biscuits, *Ajinomoto* [a powdered seasoning], and clothing. But the soldiers were patrolling and would stop people on the road or shoot at them. I tried it once, in 1992. As I was going home in a group of five people, soldiers beside the path saw us and shot. We dropped our stuff and ran for our lives. So, I lost all my valuables and was discouraged from trading.

By 1994, more villagers had come, the village was getting crowded and dirty, and people were getting sick. Most young children were ill. One illness was 'yellow eyes'. Apart from yellow eyes and face, children's livers were swollen. One-fifth of the children under five died. At first, people didn't think too much of it and used traditional medicines. When that didn't work, the people tried to get help from outside, but it was too late.

My neighbour lost a two-month-old baby. He went for a KNU medic, but the child had already been sick for three or four days. Anyway, the medic had nothing, only paracetamol and quinine. Pu Ta Thoo had no money; intravenous drips from Thailand cost a lot, and medicine from Burma is unreliable. So the child died. The mother was also ill, weak with fever and headache. My family got sick, too, and what's more, we had to flee the army and stay at the bottom of a river valley. We didn't have spare clothing or mosquito nets, so the children suffered chills.

Work became harder. The soil was becoming barren. Soldiers patrolled at harvest time, crops were destroyed and went bad.

Starting from September 1994, my family had to eat rice porridge. Sometimes I had to go without food to feed my family. Sometimes all we had to eat were boiled bamboo shoots and roots.

In 1995, because of constant Burmese army movement, we had to be ready all the time. In the hot season I worked odd jobs. The school committee couldn't take care of teachers anymore. We couldn't buy clothes, and had only one set each. Some newer arrivals risked their lives and returned to their old villages. My children were coughing terribly, but I had no money for medicine. I searched far and wide for money, but couldn't earn enough. I just made certain that I boiled the drinking water.

In September, I planted two baskets of rice seed. It was almost harvest time when we fled to where there was no food. Since we had not brought much, we ate porridge. For two or three months we hid, and our fields were trampled by livestock and destroyed by the soldiers. I would forego food so my children could eat. I would go around and beg for rice. Some people would take pity and give me a cup or two – mostly hill people who were coping better than the rest of us. People suffered differently. Recent migrants who had been farming or fishing were doing badly. Traders and the traditional hill people were better. We only cooked one small pot of rice per meal. We had one pot, but no plates, bowls or cutlery, so we ate from bamboo. In 1996, things became so tough that we couldn't even get salt, which used to come in from Papun. All roads had been cut. No one dared travel, afraid to be shot along the way.

Villages on the other side of the river received little warning when the soldiers came. They suffered constant harassment, and they never had enough food. In spite of all this they didn't want to move. From June to August of 1996 they ate porridge and bamboo shoots, and from September to November they ate roots. My family ate like this until the December harvest. That year, I planted three baskets and reaped 15.

In early November 1996, my uncle was killed. He was about 47 years old and had four children. The troops approached as he prepared to flee, but he didn't know how close they were. His wife left and he followed, but he took the wrong path. His wife heard gunfire. After a couple of days, she understood what happened. Everyone was terrified, and for over a week none of them went back.

Around April, it rained very heavily for about a week. Our house collapsed into the river and was totally destroyed. We were left with nothing, no food and no place to stay, so we fled and hid. The children were sick, and a KNU administrator gave me some grain. I thought about the situation, and thought that as we had lost our house and possessions we wouldn't stay there anymore, and so we came to this refugee camp step by step. By 1997, it was easy to flee; we had nothing left anyway. We had lost, sold or exchanged all our meagre possessions over time in order to get food. We never had much, but before 1992–93, we had four or five items of clothing each, enough blankets, mosquito nets, plates and spoons to go around. By 1997, my wife, our three oldest children and I had exactly one set of clothes each, and our youngest two children we simply wrapped in rags, and carried them on our backs when we fled. A machete, a pot and a bamboo bowl, some rice, two blankets and one mosquito net were the sum total of our possessions. Under such conditions, money is not spent on clothes and such; you only think about getting food. (AHRC 1999:88).

SUBSISTENCE STRATEGIES

Hiding Rice

The most common subsistence strategy for people displaced in the jungle is hiding rice, other foods and personal belongings. Since it is impractical to run carrying a large basket of rice, and because rice left unattended in villages is in danger of being destroyed or confiscated, Karens often stash rice in well-concealed locations in the jungle. Each harvest season, which usually coincides with an increase in military activity, farmers rush to get their rice from the fields and begin stashing it away. This strategy is not without its problems. According to a 1996 report from the war zones of Mone township:

When the army columns come into the mountains, they destroy any house they find, shoot whomever they see, and take or burn all possessions. If they come to a village they don't see any people because everyone has run into the forest already. If they find rice stored in the jungle, they take or burn it, or sometimes lay mines around it. Many villagers have been killed, maimed and blinded by this tactic. We always look for a safe place in the jungle to hide our food. These hiding places may be safe from soldiers, but not from the wildlife. Bears, rats and insects can find and eat the food we hide. Bears sometimes eat the food, sometimes destroy it and sometimes carry it away. The bears are very clever and can sort through the food to pick what they like. But the rats are really terrible: they not only eat the rice but they nest in it. If we use an old metal locker, only the insects can get in, but if we only have a basket wrapped in leaves or plastic, there's a good chance the other animals will get to it. The wildlife is just as destructive as the enemy. If there were no military activity, we wouldn't have to hide our food in the jungle; we could build food stores in the village and take care of our rice. (Kweh Say 1996:7)

With experience comes greater caution. When people have the time and inclination to prepare themselves for long stays in the jungle, they divide their rice and belongings into smaller stashes to hide in several locations. This way, the people don't risk losing everything at once.

Hunting, Foraging and Sharing

In addition to hiding rice, displaced people survive by foraging for food in the jungle. In fact, this is a normal part of life for rural people; Karens are used to searching for fruit, plants, roots and animals to supplement their diet. However, displacement makes this foraging more crucial and more difficult. The displaced must always be alert to the location and movement of soldiers. Many executions, rapes and beatings occur during chance encounters between people looking for food and small military units on patrol. In addition, it is often too dangerous to hunt with rifles, as Karens normally do, because the sound of gunshots may draw attention and lead the army to a jungle hideout. While all displaced people confront these difficulties, new settlers to the highlands may have more problems because they are less familiar with local plants, animals and survival skills than are natives. Lowland settlers who are unaccustomed to the rigours of jungle displacement are more likely to cross the border into Thailand and live either as refugees or migrant workers.

Another important coping strategy is rationing and sharing food. There is no organised system for food rationing; it just seems to be a natural part of communal life. People displaced in the jungle also commonly report that they feed as much available food as possible to children, while the adults fast, eat only what they can forage, or consume reduced rations. Nevertheless, not everyone benefits from sharing. According to one man whose village was displaced into the jungle three times in 1996:

> Each time we had no food. In the forest, relationships varied. Some shared food with others then left to look for roots together; others did not. I saw one family close to utter starvation, the two small children crying from hunger. The mother pitifully fed them roots which hadn't been boiled long enough; she probably didn't know what else to do. After that they suffered nausea, vomiting and diarrhoea. They had absolutely no possessions whatsoever, other than one pot, a machete and a small blanket. (AHRC 1999:24)

Covert Agriculture and Trade

Producing food is another tactic. Displaced people may either surreptitiously return to their fields or attempt to cultivate small plots of land hidden in dense jungle. People report that this covert farming is dangerous and not terribly productive, though necessary to provide at least some food. The same wildlife that threatens hidden rice stores also menaces untended crops; wild boar are particularly destructive. Since jungle farms are usually not protected by bamboo fences, which might be spotted from afar, displaced farmers have little chance of keeping animals away from their plants. Migrants from the lowlands, if they farmed before, are accustomed to wet rice cultivation, and find it difficult to learn a new technique under the pressures of displacement.

In many places, people in the jungle maintain some trade with villages, relocation centres or mobile traders inside government-controlled areas. In Tennasserim, for example, forced relocation split communities into those who fled to the jungle and those who complied and remained. Despite the dangers, necessity compelled them to maintain contact:

> Other food such as salt and fish paste, which they cannot produce themselves and is part of their main diet, is another problem for the IDPs. They try to sneak into the nearest relocated village to buy these foods. Many die along the way when they get caught in the middle of ambushes. There are no easy routes, because these areas have been declared free-fire zones, and the relocation sites

are fenced in and watched by the People's Militia or Burma army. Villagers at the relocation sites have their movements severely restricted. However, the IDPs and villagers at relocation sites have secret deals for selling and buying food. Villagers at relocation sites sneak out and bring things to sell to the IDPs. This business is very dangerous, and they cannot do it every time. (Eh Na 1998:7)

People in the relocation centres will take advantage of what little freedom they enjoy to return to their fields and, perhaps, arrange secret rendezvous with their displaced neighbours. In northern Karen state, and probably throughout eastern Burma, some traders specialise in sneaking rice and provisions into the mountains.

Seeking Aid

The final strategy is to seek support from international aid organisations, either by relocating to refugee camps in Thailand or by trying to have aid delivered *in situ*. Most displaced people consider the Thai refugee camps to be a poor and unhappy alternative, and try to survive close to their homes for as long as possible. Throughout the 1990s, crossing the Thailand–Burma border became increasingly difficult, with the Burmese army attempting to seal the border on one side, and a growing unwillingness from Thai officials to allow entry on the other. In partnership with two KNU-related welfare organisations, the Karen Organisation for Relief and Development (KORD) and the Committee for Internally Displaced Karen People (CIDKP), aid agencies have managed to supply rice, or cash to buy rice from lowland Burma, to displaced communities deep inside Burma's civil war zones. Such aid, however, is only available in some situations, depending on the people's location, condition and ability to communicate their needs to the intermediate organisation. Furthermore, to send either significant quantities of rice or money through the mountains from Thailand is a complicated and dangerous logistical feat.

Karens use the same techniques – foraging, trading with the lowlands, and seeking aid – to obtain health care. Malaria, diarrhoea, malnutrition, respiratory infections, obstetric emergencies, and injuries are the major health problems of displaced persons (Beyrer 1999:4). Karen healers apply their knowledge of herbal medicine and Burmese traditional medicine with varying success; though by all accounts there is a dearth of adequate health care, and modern medicine is expensive and hard to find. While the KNU once maintained clinics in its territory, by the end of the 1990s, mobile medical teams supported by aid agencies in Thailand had become a more practical alternative.

Although people living in relocation sites fall outside the category of jungle displacement, they also struggle with basic subsistence. Describing their predicament here may help shed light on why Karens might choose to stay in the jungle rather than accept relocation. The army chooses relocation sites for strategic advantage in government population control. Access to arable land, good water and work do not seem to be major concerns. Relatively little is known about conditions inside relocation camps; most information comes from those who have left the camps and come to the Thailand–Burma border. One priority for relocated people is to maintain contact with their former land, often complying with a system by which they pay to leave the camp each morning, walk up to 10 kilometres to reach their fields, work for the day, then walk back to the camp before nightfall. This arrangement is only available when villages have been relocated or consolidated within a reasonable distance from their homes. Even so, rice farming is labour-intensive work for which, even in stable villages, people often choose to sleep in small, temporary field huts. Many farmers consider it nearly impossible to work this way, and either flee the relocation centre to live displaced in the countryside close to their fields, or abandon farming altogether.

Relocation centres seem to offer few occupations apart from farming. Although the concentration of many people into a small space should create good opportunities for commerce, often by the time people reach relocation sites they have little disposable income. In some cases, a black market economy exists. Western medicines, for example, are in great demand, but may be considered contraband by local authorities, who fear they will be smuggled to rebels in the jungle. Batteries for portable radios and cassette players may be banned for the same reasons, since they could power the rebels' walkie-talkies. The dangerous business of supplying such items does not make people rich, but it does circulate cash.

PROTECTION STRATEGIES

Flight and Evasion

The main evasion tactics, fleeing and hiding, sound less like coping strategies than simply reactions to danger. But displaced people determined to stay near their land have evaded danger for so many years that fleeing and hiding have become well-known routines. The key to successful flight is preparation. Displaced persons in the highlands of Mone township, says one resident, prepare to run every day:

> When we wake up in the morning, we fold up our blankets, cook, eat and put everything back in our carrying baskets so we will be ready to run if the soldiers come. If we don't do this, we risk losing our possessions. (Kweh Say 1996:7)

One sure sign of a village accustomed to jungle displacement is the prevalence of carrying baskets, rucksacks and plastic bags packed and ready to go, and usually kept under the house or close to the door. While a bamboo house is a temporary shelter that must be modified and rebuilt every few years, durable goods such as enamelled plates, teapots, warm clothes, blankets, knives, books and radios are not easily replaced. Karens consider such possessions to be more valuable than a bamboo house; that is why, if they anticipate displacement, they keep their valuables bundled and ready to move at a moment's notice.

Under such conditions the simplest of materials attain importance: a good backpack or an intact plastic tarpaulin can make the difference between saving or sacrificing one's food and possessions. The same is true for certain valuables that cannot be easily transported, including livestock. When possible, people will trade for more portable currency, especially small amounts of gold and silver jewellery or Thai currency.

There is little documentation of how individuals flee when the time comes. If given ample warning and enough time to prepare, for example, if approaching soldiers are more than an hour's walk away, villagers may discuss how to divide into groups and plan their rendezvous. If there is little or no warning, that is, when gunshots signal the army's arrival, planning may be impossible. But people know which routes to follow and where in the forest they might hide. Apart from the material hardships of hiding – finding food, staying dry, coping with disease – displaced persons are always at risk of being discovered. One account relates the problems of hiding:

> The villagers of Nwar Lay Khoh knew that troops were approaching, so they began to evacuate their houses. They fled

into the scrub, dangerously close. They had to kill roosters and geese, because their cries travel far and might reveal the hideout. For security, dogs too were beaten to death: there is a lot in the jungle to bark at. (AHRC 1999:19)

Once in the jungle, however, Karens disperse into small groups. It is safer to live in many small enclaves scattered through the mountains than in one large group. In 1998, in South-eastern Burma's Palaw township, Karen villagers resisted a relocation effort:

Many villagers fled the relocation programme and are hiding in the jungle watershed. They are hiding at a distance from each other, not like when they stayed together in the village. Two or three families hide together by one stream, and a few others hide by the next. They grow crops at the hiding places in order to survive. They have built small huts to hide their paddy, food supplies and other materials. They hide in heavily forested valleys, where it is harder to find them. They do not make clear footpaths to their hiding places, and they are careful whom they show their places to. According to the KNU, there are 660 households currently displaced. (Eh Na 1998:6)

Accommodating the Army

In and out of the jungle, one way Karen displaced protect themselves is to submit to the demands placed on them. To provide the required food, money, labour, information and other services required is neither easy nor pleasant; nor does it guarantee safety. Nevertheless, it is often the best response available, a tactic for negotiating survival based on the calculation that complying is less dangerous than resisting or avoiding the army altogether.

While some demands are dangerous, many others are simply onerous. The latter type includes providing food, cash, wood and bamboo for construction, and some forms of routine labour. When there is little threat of violence, the real drawback to helping the army is that the time and expense involved make it even more difficult for displaced people to survive. Villagers must decide whether the advantages of staying on their land outweigh the poverty they endure.

The army's most dangerous demands include carrying loads for combat troops, guarding and maintaining strategic roads, which may be mined, and, for women, the added chores of working as servants and masseuses in army barracks, which may result in sexual abuse.

Apart from poverty and the threat of physical harm, accommodating the army creates political pressure. While the Burmese army does not normally conscript soldiers from among displaced Karens, tha KNU and DKBA do. Displaced people must negotiate the conflicting demands of different military powers:

> The DKBA are intimidating villagers to provide recruits. If we don't, they said they'd ring our village with one thousand landmines until we wouldn't dare to set foot on our own land. We were going to get the recruits, but the KNU didn't like it, so we were caught in the middle, neither here nor there, and we have had to flee to other places. We don't know what will happen in the future. (Htoh Lwi War 1999:15)

Accommodation, however, does not always mean submission. Appearing to comply, villagers find subtle ways to resist military control. For example, a villager in Thaton interviewed in 1999 reported:

> Each day, three women must go to the army camp for 'patrol'. The patrol women have to report to the camp commander about whether or not any KNLA have come to the village. Most of the time the women lie. Sometimes the KNLA comes but the women say they didn't come. If only two or three KNLA come it is no problem, the patrol women don't tell them; but if 70 or 80 come then the women must inform them about where they're headed. If the KNLA are headed to L— they tell him that they are headed to T—, and if they are headed to P— the villagers tell him they were headed to H—. If the Burmese say that they didn't see them there, the women say, 'We can't help it if you didn't see them. We saw them pass our village and watched them until they disappeared, but we dared not follow them so we can't say exactly where they went.' Sometimes they tell him that the KNLA have come and headed someplace and that there are 200 or 300 of them, when really there were only none to 80 of them. Sometimes people tell them but they don't give chase, they just say to the women, 'Let them go, let them go.' Most of the time he says, 'It's enough to inform us about it, as long as we know, it's no

problem.' The camp commander is kind, but still his heart is crooked because he is a Burman. (KHRG 1999)

Joining the Armed Struggle

People in civil war zones almost always have the chance to join an armed faction if they so choose. After displacement, unaffiliated civilians who try to align themselves with the KNU, the DKBA or some other faction are clearly trying to cope with their new circumstances. While they may be radicalised by the trauma of displacement and may resent the Burmese army, often they are simply hoping to obtain a weapon or receive warnings to defend themselves and others from further harassment.

Yet in some places there is barely a distinction between protecting the interests of civilians and those of the rebels. They do not necessarily share a political ideology, but they need each other to survive. Especially in the highlands of northern Karen state, local rebels may be protecting their own home villages and displaced families. Where the KNU has lost substantial ground, communication and supply routes, its soldiers are just as displaced as civilians and the two groups often band together for survival. Explained one native of Mone township, when the Burmese approach, every Karen man becomes a soldier simply to stay alive.

Among the displaced, affiliation with an armed group is ultimately a pragmatic reaction to desperate circumstances. A farmer from T'Nay Char township in Pa'an explained:

> I am ordinarily able to grow 100 baskets of paddy every year, but this year, as there was no rain, I have only been able to get more than 20 baskets. So I have had to sell all my livestock, and the rice grain I gave some to Burmese soldiers, some to the DKBA and the rest I sold to pay off debts. I have nothing left. Therefore, to avoid being taken as a porter, I have been fleeing into the scrub every night. When they came to collect porter fees I had nothing left. So I plan to join the KNLA, and if that's not possible, then the DKBA. (Htoh Lwi War 1999:13)

Religious Affiliation

Another example of pragmatism in the face of desperation is when male villagers become Buddhist monks. In some communities facing continual military harassment, Buddhist monasteries are comparatively stable environments where the danger of being levied, conscripted or forced to serve the army are greatly reduced. Monks may enjoy greater freedom of movement and more respectful treatment by soldiers, but they are not necessarily above suspicion. There is no evidence that women cope with displacement by becoming Buddhist nuns.

Some displaced Christian Karens have missionary contacts that might help them obtain schooling in Burma or in refugee camps. One Baptist family that had lived displaced on and off since the mid-1970s sent the daughters to mission schools in Yangon and the sons to refugee camp schools in Thailand.

Political Negotiation

Villagers may promise the Burmese army that they will have no contact with the rebels, will supply materials and labour as asked, and will not flee when the army approaches. In return, the army vows not to burn down or punish the entire village, but keeps a close eye on suspected rebel sympathisers and may punish them individually.

Some villages may reach temporary agreements with local army units that wish to avoid battles with the rebels. The army won't enter the village or harass the people there, even when there is evidence of rebel activity. But these arrangements are less common today than they were in the mid-1990s, and they rely on the army's unwillingness to pursue Karen insurgents.

EDUCATION

Many Karens value education highly. Displaced Karens regard formal schooling as a refuge from the hardships of the jungle and as the foundation for a better life. As war gradually permeated the Karen state, many local schools under KNU administration suffered. Education for displaced children is now available only in schools in more stable areas of Burma or in refugee camps in Thailand. Christian Karens with missionary contacts may attend religious schools inside Burma, and boys from Buddhist families may seek to study at monasteries in towns or stable villages. Despite the hazards of travel, it is common for displaced families to send their children across the border to study at refugee camp schools. While camp schools provide basic education, they also introduce rural Karens to a more urban, modern setting, albeit on the outskirts of Thai society. The prospect of further education, the hope of earning cash, and the appeal of modern technology combine to draw children from displaced families out of the jungle into the lowest strata of Thai society and, with luck, to international refugee status, third-country resettlement and western education (Tun 1998:9).

When displaced communities enjoy a degree of stability, they may try to set up schools, either independently or supported by the KNU (the DKBA is not yet known to have sponsored schools). Teachers may be educated members of the community or, fairly often, Karen missionaries or KNU sympathisers who migrated from the lowlands. KNU schools offer a nationalist curriculum, which, along with basic literacy and numeracy, inculcates traditional views of Karen identity, including all the themes of loss, displacement and racial incompatibility between Karens and Burmans.

One controversial issue in education is the extent to which Karens should study Burmese. Because Karen nationalism adamantly distinguishes between Burman and Karen culture[9] and fears that the Karen language will disappear, leaders and educators emphasize S'gaw Karen as the primary language of education. Many Karens feel that accepting Burmese as the national language puts non-native speakers at a disadvantage and fails to recognise the cultural rights of linguistic minorities. This is a politically sensitive issue: to point out the practical advantage of Burmese language education – that it equips people to integrate and cope in Burmese society – is to suggest that Karen nationalism will not succeed.

RELIGION, COMMUNITY, LANGUAGE AND IDENTITY

Religious Movements

Displaced Karens sometimes adapt their religious beliefs to explain and rationalise their plight. Millenarian movements or apocalyptic trends can be found in Christian, Buddhist and traditional beliefs among displaced Karens in eastern Burma. Throughout the 1990s, evangelical Baptists expressed concern, and relief, that the world would end in the year 2000. Missionary efforts accelerated, including a Year 2000 campaign to baptise as many Karens in eastern Burma as possible.[10] In the late 1990s, Christian refugees asked to comment on their political problems declined to speculate, saying that Judgement Day was just a few years away and that all would be resolved by God. While less is known about the DKBA, its militant nationalism is also believed to include messianic elements related to the popular belief that a powerful Buddhist political figure will arrive to prepare the world for the advent of Maitreya, the future Buddha.[11]

Most recently, God's Army, a nationalist-messianic movement in southern Burma, has posited divine intercession in displaced Karens' opposition to Burma army offensives. As responses to displacement, all such beliefs sustain the hope that powerful moral intercession will alleviate Karens' suffering.

Isolation

Traditional distrust of outsiders becomes an important response to displacement. Scattering into small groups and keeping a distance from others has already been described as a protection tactic, but it is an act of defining and preserving cultural identity as well. Although the war between Burma's government and the KNU is sometimes described as a national struggle, many displaced Karens are not interested in either side's claim to political legitimacy. Speaking their own dialect, managing their own affairs, surviving in their own domain, highlanders and forest-dwelling Karens wish, above all, to preserve their independence and stay on their land. If they were traditionally taciturn and distrustful of 'foreigners', then the rigours of war have made them militant in resisting outsiders, including other Karens.

Language

One way Karens respond to displacement is by talking about it, and in their descriptions one recognises efforts to cope with the problems they face. Displaced people compare their experiences to their natural environment and agrarian way of life. They say they are like 'drops of water on the *khu* leaf, never settling down and always in danger of being shaken off'; or like 'chickens sleeping at night, never resting and always on edge'; or their predicament makes them like fish: 'swimming upstream, we are caught in a trap; swimming downstream we are caught in a net'.

PUBLIC PARTICIPATION

Given the dismal state of civil and political rights for all people in Burma, it is no surprise that displaced Karens enjoy little or no representation or participation in public affairs. Within their own villages, people might have a say in decisions that affect the whole group, although the degree of participation depends on the structure of the village. In small, isolated communities consensus is an important element of village politics; but in larger lowland villages that interact with outside political forces, more power accrues to the village headman as the community's representative. He is saddled with the burden of fulfilling the armies' demand for supplies, labour and recruits. Village heads who represent displaced communities often suffer the twin pressures of defending the people's best interests and satisfying soldiers' needs; they risk detention, beatings or worse if the village fails to comply. One way of coping with this burden has been to transform the office of village head from a permanent post to a rotating one, so several villagers will take turns negotiating with the army.

Another response to the changing role of Karen village leaders has been an increase in women holding the post. Perhaps because few men want the job, or maybe because women have been more successful in managing the twin burdens of leadership, there has been a trend towards middle-aged Karen women negotiating with the army on behalf of displaced rural communities. It is difficult to determine why this is occurring. One theory is that young Burmese army field officers, raised in a culture where sons show respect and devotion to their mothers, perceive women leaders as surrogate mother figures and are reluctant to harm them. Officers may feel that women leaders are less duplicitous, less inclined to support the KNU behind the army's back. Perhaps because older displaced Karen women have endured for years under the harshest conditions, they have developed the shrewd skills needed to survive. Women sometimes even scold soldiers for their rude and violent behaviour, cautioning that their mothers would not be proud of them.

CONCLUSION

For thousands of Karens in eastern Burma, displacement has a profound impact on survival, culture and identity. To some, displacement heightens a sense of loss over their stable and prosperous past and contributes to a belief in racial incompatibility. For them, displacement is the inevitable result of innate antagonism between the Karen and his chief foe, the Burman. Karen nationalism recalls better days and advocates that Karens reclaim their birthright by establishing a racially and morally pure homeland, Kawthoolei. Despite nationalist dreams of an autonomous Kawthoolei, it appears that most displaced Karens simply wish to be left alone.

Displaced Karen civilians cope with their plight by surviving on or near their land, appeasing the nearest military force or, if necessary, affiliating themselves with it. How people survive, protect themselves, and otherwise adapt to displacement are all closely related to the relationship between people and place. Hiding in the forest, foraging for food, and defining community ties are all adaptations that evolve from the close relationship between Karens and their land. There is little evidence that displaced Karens cope better by migrating to cities or becoming entrepreneurs.

Observers agree that the only sustainable solution to the plight of displaced persons is ending Burma's civil war. But achieving peace will require cultural, as well as political, accommodations. Karens must build relationships with the peoples and polities around them; they must forge new identities as members of a pluralistic society, and acquire the skills and confidence needed to thrive among other cultures. Until political and legal reforms make this possible, the need for emergency relief, such as protection, food and health care, is obvious – as are the political obstacles that now block this aid.

ACKNOWLEDGEMENTS

A great many friends and colleagues have educated me about war, peace and displacement in Burma. Without holding them responsible for my opinions, I thank them for their insight, openness and perseverance. Special thanks go out to Saw Kweh Say, Th'ra Hsar Say, Th'ra Paw Moo, Saw Hsar K'Baw, Saw Dee Gay Htoo, Htilowar, Mahn Kwa Ee, Naw Kai Kyote, Naw Gey Ray Paw, Naw Hser Ku, Mahn Robert Zan, Saw Kaw Htoo, Th'ra Nick, Saya San Min Min, Graham, Max, Basil Fernando, and Th'ra Lawrence Po. Each of these remarkable lives deserves a book of its own. This chapter is dedicated to Ma Pein and Saw Min Min, who are in my thoughts every day.

NOTES

1. This text uses both the old style translation of Burmese place names, such as *Burma* rather than *Myanmar*, and the new, as in the use of *Yangon* rather than *Rangoon*.
2. BERG's 1998 report on Karen internally displaced persons attempted to quantify and describe international displacement; its 2000 report treats displacement among another Burmese minority group, the Karenni.
3. BERG's recent study of displacement also defines three types of internal displacement: involuntary relocation and consolidation of villages; transient displacement, relocation, landlessness and movement in and out of relocation sites and concealed villages; voluntary migration, temporary or permanent, for work or trade (2000:48).
4. See Renard (1980) and Keyes (1979) for discussions on the anthropological problems of defining Karen ethnicity.

5. Military activity, including relocation programmes, usually increase during the cool months of October–February, coinciding with the rice harvest.

6. To speak of a dominant Karen culture is to commit a broad and loose generalisation. Here, I mean those social and economic practices that Karens describe as unique to traditional Karen rural life.

7. As told to me by a delta Karen in Mae Sot, Thailand, in 1996.

8. Comments by a Karen highlander made in Mae Sot, September 1996.

9 According to *Karen History in the KNU Narrative*: 'The Karens are much more than a national minority. We are a nation with a population of 7 million, having all the essential qualities of a nation. We have our own history, our own language, our own culture, our own land of settlement and our own economic system to live.'

10. The importance of millenarian beliefs should be neither exaggerated nor dismissed; such beliefs are features of a broader religious landscape. For example, one Baptist missionary who participated in the campaign told me that he didn't really expect the world to end, but the year 2000 was a good slogan for evangelical work and was a target date by which to measure the campaign's success.

11. For a description of chiliastic Karen Buddhism, see Stern (1968); for a description of millenarian Buddhism in Burma, see Spiro (1967; 1982:162–86).

7

Sri Lanka: Developing New Livelihoods in the Shadow of War. Displaced, Relocated and Resettled Muslims

Birgitte Refslund Sorensen

This chapter presents the strategies adopted by some of the 100,000[1] displaced Muslims after they were suddenly and forcibly expelled from their homes in October 1990 by the Liberation Tigers of Tamil Eelam (LTTE). In an attempt to better reflect the heterogeneity of the displaced population and the complexity of their situation, the study includes Muslims of different socio-economic backgrounds, such as farmers, fishermen and smallbusiness people, and of different gender and age. The study also includes people who live in welfare centres (the official term for IDP camps in Sri Lanka) as displaced persons and people who have either relocated to new village settlements or have returned to and resettled in their home village. The latter are included, because although they are no longer physically displaced, they may still be socially, culturally and economically displaced. Especially when parts of the country are still at war, as is the case in present-day Sri Lanka (see also Sorensen 1996), re-establishing livelihoods is a difficult, long-term process.

BACKGROUND

The armed conflict between the Sri Lankan army and the LTTE began in July 1983 when the LTTE killed 13 Sinhalese soldiers in an ambush. The incident triggered organised violence against Tamil residents in the south, followed by island-wide communal violence between the Sinhalese majority, who represent 74 per cent of the population, and the Tamil minority, who represent 18 per cent. The fighting displaced some 200,000 Tamils, half of whom remained in the country, further polarised the two ethnic communities, and prompted a more militant mobilisation of the Tamil community to achieve its goal of a separate state, Tamil Eelam.

Map 7   Sri Lanka

However important the 1983 incident was in provoking ethnic clashes, it, alone, does not explain the conflict. Since the mid-1950s there have been a number of skirmishes between the Tamils and the Sinhalese. These were caused by growing competition for recognition and influence and a contest of philosophies over the direction of post-colonial Sri Lanka.

During the period immediately following independence, large portions of the Tamil population responded to these attacks on their positions and integrity through democratic means. But in the 1970s, which was marked by a period of economic decline, dissatisfaction with both the national government and the Tamil political elite grew, especially among Tamil youth. Out of this dissatisfaction grew a new Tamil militant agenda, which saw a separate Tamil state as the only solution to the Tamils' problems.

The armed struggle for Tamil Eelam is generally divided into three different phases. Eelam War I lasted from 1983 to 1990. Apart from the confrontations between army forces and the Tamil militants and an escalation in arbitrary and retaliatory killings of Tamil civilians, this was a period that was marked by brutal internal power struggles among the many different Tamil organisations that had emerged. The LTTE ultimately emerged the victor and became the dominant voice for Tamil Eelam.

Eelam War II quickly devolved into a 'dirty war' that affected the civilian population more than ever before. It is estimated that between June and September 1990, more than 1 million people were displaced by the fighting in the north-east (Seneviratne and Stavropoulou 1998:370). Only after the 1994 election of a new president, Bandaranayake Kumaratunga, was 'peace' once again put on the political agenda. The new government agreed to a cease-fire with the LTTE to start negotiations. But dissatisfied with the results of talks, the LTTE soon withdrew from the negotiations and took up arms again. Thus began Eelam War III.

This time the government adopted a new strategy called 'War for Peace'. While the government repeatedly stressed that the conflict could only be solved politically, it also argued that it was necessary to weaken the LTTE and dislodge the rebels from their stronghold in Jaffna, the capital of the Tamil homelands. From mid-1995 until late 1999, the government launched a series of military operations to achieve this end. As a result, hundreds of thousands of people, mainly Tamils, were forced to flee their home villages and seek refuge outside the battle zone, either in more peaceful areas within

Tamil-dominated regions (the so-called 'uncleared' areas) or in government-held territory ('cleared' areas).

Table 7.1   Displaced people by district

District	No. of welfare centres	No. of people in centres	No. of persons outside centres	No. of economically affected	Total displaced
Jaffna	58	6,191	253,680	9,390	269,261
Vanni	148	98,604	143,394	9,545	251,543
Eastern	26	10,313	46,643	—	56,956
Border	157	53,856	27,005	—	80,861
Other	20	1,572	17,152	3,541	24,645
Total	409	172,816	487,874	22,576	683,266

Source: Commissioner General of Essential Services, June 1999. Reproduced from WFP (1999).

Throughout most of 1999, the government claimed control over increasing amounts of territory, creating new opportunities for return and resettlement of displaced people. An end to the war was in sight. But these dreams were shattered in November that year when the LTTE launched a series of surprise attacks on several army camps along the main north–south supply route, ending the army's northbound clearing operation. This was followed by an attempted assassination of the president on 18 December, and a fierce battle on the Jaffna peninsula and around Jaffna town. The ongoing battle in Jaffna added more names to the lists of civilians displaced or otherwise affected by the war. The UNHCR estimates that as of 2000, approximately 800,000 people were displaced in the north and east of the country, of which close to 200,000 were living in about 400 welfare centres. An estimated 500,000 more persons were living outside Sri Lanka in India or in the West as refugees (UNHCR 2000:3).

The Conflict and Sri Lanka's Muslims

Initially, the Tamil militants declared that Tamil Eelam was for all Tamil speakers, including Muslims; but the Muslims never fully identified with and supported the 'Tamil cause'. Instead, they tried to maintain a neutral position, but were inevitably caught between the polarised Sinhalese and Tamil communities.

The Muslim minority comprises 8 per cent of the total population. As a social group, the Muslims are as heterogeneous as the Sinhalese and the Tamils. The two primary 'communities' of Muslims are those who live in the urban areas of the Sinhalese south and whose main occupation is trade, especially in gems, and business, and those Muslims who live in the Tamil north-west and north-east and who are mainly agriculturalists, fishermen or small-scale businessmen (Mauroof 1972:68–9; Ismail 1995). Unlike the Tamil and Sinhalese groups, the Muslims do not have their own language. Even though they speak Arabic in religious and cultural contexts, the Muslims mainly speak Tamil for all other purposes. In southern areas, where they live among Sinhalese people, many Muslims are bilingual.

Most studies of the Muslim minority emphasise that Muslims have traditionally relied on an accommodationist strategy, so there is now a vast difference between the Muslims living in urban areas in the south and those living in Tamil areas in the north and east.[2] This also partly explains why Muslims have tried to remain neutral in the conflict between the Sinhalese and Tamil groups.

However, they have not fully succeeded in remaining neutral. The first sign that the Muslims' friendly relationship with the Tamils was deteriorating came in the mid-1980s, when a number of Muslims were attacked and killed by Tamil militants. In the summer of 1990, the LTTE again carried out several massacres against Muslims in the multi-ethnic east, among them the brutal killings of 140 Muslims at prayer (Schrijvers 1998:17; McGilvray 1999:219). In response to the rise in violence, the government established Muslim Home Guards to help protect local (Muslim) villages threatened by Tamil Tigers. But this action only ignited more clashes between the Muslims and Tamil militants, who widely believed that the Muslims acted as informers for the government. In addition, the Muslims' growing self-perception as a distinct ethnic group with legitimate claims for influence in the Tamil homelands was perceived by the LTTE as a threat to Tamil Eelam and to their own claim of being the sole and rightful representatives of the Tamil population in these areas.

The deterioration of relations sunk to a nadir at the end of October 1990 when Muslims were expelled *en masse* from the north. The LTTE ordered all Muslims to leave their communities within 24–48 hours and to bring no more than one shopping bag containing their personal belongings with them. All valuables were to be handed over to the LTTE before leaving.[3] The displacement affected between 70,000 and 100,000 people, most of whom moved to locations in the belt from Puttalam[4] to Anuradhapura and Kurunegala, where there were already small Muslim populations, and which lie outside the war zone.

RESEARCH METHODOLOGY

This study is primarily based on information collected during 1999–2000, when I worked for the Danish Refugee Council (DRC) as a Training and Programme Advisor. My role as an advisor brought me into contact with most of the other actors who also attempted to assist and protect displaced people, including UNHCR, the Government Agent's Office in relevant districts, a number of local NGOs in northern Sri Lanka (cleared areas) and, of course, the Tamil, Sinhalese and Muslim people that had been displaced because of the war. Frequent interaction and discussions with these actors regarding displacement and its short- and long-term solutions contributed greatly to my understanding of the complexity of war-related displacement and resettlement issues in Sri Lanka and more generally.[5] This information provides a critical context for this study that helps put the individual accounts in perspective.

To understand more fully the kinds of response strategies, and their long-term consequences, that had been developed by Muslims who were displaced in October 1990, I decided to conduct more focused field research in selected communities. This research was carried out with some local DRC staff and staff of the Rural Development Foundation (RDF), a local Muslim NGO that has worked with these communities over the past ten years and knows them well.[6]

The methodology we applied was a combination of PRA techniques and group and individual open-ended interviews. In most cases, the participants were asked to draw a timeline dating back to their first displacement and including all major moves or shifts in their livelihoods that they had experienced until the present. The timeline naturally led to a discussion of what they had done in each situation and of any other important changes that had had a positive or negative impact on that particular aspect of their lives. We did not in any way direct the interviews more than this, but only asked additional questions for clarification. To facilitate cross-checking with other members of the community and to generate a more critical and reflexive discussion around the issues that arose, we summarised all points and pieces of information on cards that were displayed for all participants to see and comment on.

I have chosen to present the individual narratives more or less as they were told to us in the field, without any comments or major restructuring.[7] I believe this is the best way to illustrate both the complexity of the problems that the displaced Muslims face and the often creative ways in which they deal with those problems. My interpretations and comments follow the accounts from the field.

In a local war, where the conventional two antagonists have been replaced by a plethora of ever-changing players, positions and perspectives, and where many actions occur in an emergency setting, speaking out about one's experiences and thoughts of the situation can be dangerous. This is especially true when one is dependent on the support and protection of many different actors, as the displaced Muslims are. So even when our informants seemed to trust us, they were careful about what they told us; in some cases, they were hesitant to elaborate on issues that had come up in the discussion. To minimise the risk that any of the people who were kind enough to participate in this study come to any harm because of their cooperation, the real names of communities and individuals are not disclosed here.

DISPLACEMENT AND AFTER: FOUR CASE STUDIES

In a New Village Settlement

The settlement village was established only a few years ago and is now home to some 160 families. It is located on a narrow stretch of land between the Indian Ocean and the main road leading from Puttalam to Chilaw. Most of the houses are made of plastered clay, but there are also a few brick houses. All of them have *cadjan* (palm leaves) roofs that must be replaced once or twice a year. The houses and gardens are fenced with palmyra palm leaves that shield against the gaze of strangers and protect against stray animals. Most of the inhabitants of the settlement are or used to be farmers with paddy as their main crop.

We met some members of the community on the shaded porch in front of the community mosque, the only place available for large meetings. The porch was also used for pre-school and Koran classes. Since women are not allowed to enter the mosque, no women attended the meeting.

The dozen or so men with whom we spoke began by explaining that they came from a large village of 400 families in the Musali Division in Mannar district where they earned their livelihoods in agriculture. Most of them had owned land that they cultivated and gave assistance to each other when needed. Since they were practically all relatives, there had been strong social cohesion in the village. Their relations with the surrounding Tamil communities had been good and collaborative; indeed, the Muslim and Tamil populations relied on each other economically, to some extent.

Even though the villagers were aware of the terrible incidents that had occurred in the east, the LTTE announcement in 1990 that all Muslims must leave their villages within 24 hours came as a terrible shock. Many said they were still puzzled about what happened back then, but, at the time, they saw no option but to pack a few belongings immediately and prepare for their departure. They also handed over all their valuables, including water pumps and jewellery, to the LTTE, as demanded.

The villagers left together as a group. They first went to an army camp nearby, as they believed that their displacement would be temporary. But after some time the army told them that they should move on because they could not stay, nor would they be able to return. When they moved this second time, the village community split into smaller groups, as people had different views on where it would be safest and where they could most easily find temporary accommodation. Households, however, remained intact. Some went to the coast to take a boat to Kalpitiya; others began walking towards Kurunegala in the interior of the country.

The approximately 350 families who headed for Kurunegala first settled temporarily in a Sinhalese village, where they were given shelter and some basic assistance. According to our informants, the army and government had spoken with the villagers beforehand and had helped them prepare to receive the displaced Muslims. It was difficult for the village to accommodate such a large number of displaced persons, but the local school building was temporarily transformed into a hostel for the displaced and the government provided dry rations for the new arrivals.

According to our informants, their brief stay in the Sinhalese community had not created any major problems with the host community, and they all appreciated the way the Sinhalese villagers had received and supported them. However, it was clear to everyone that they could not remain indefinitely in this village, so the local government divided them into three smaller groups and encouraged them to travel to different areas with a larger existing Muslim population.

For many, the next destination was the Puttalam area on the western coast. The displaced had heard that education facilities were better there, and they were all concerned that their children had missed several months of school.

When they first arrived in Puttalam, they found shelter in a school building where they crowded together with many other families in a small room. Since there was no privacy in this arrangement, they soon began looking for other accommodation. After some time, they found some land owned by a member of the local Mosque Trustee Board (MTB) who was willing to let them build houses on his land. But after a few years living on this land, the displaced were keen to re-establish their own community again and started looking for another place to live. They wanted a place where all the members of their home village who wished to do so could come and live together again, including those who had resettled elsewhere.[8] At that time, there were many villagers living in other settlements, but also some 60 families who were living in camps.

The villagers looked for land for many years, and on some occasions were close to buying property. Finally in 1998, after eight years of searching, they found the right location for their new home.[9] The land was owned by the government and was given to them on a long-term lease contract. In addition to the land, the community also received the 'resettlement package'[10] that the government gives to internally displaced people upon relocation or resettlement.

While they were searching for a place to re-establish their community, the displaced were also looking for ways to earn an income and to support their families. Most qualified for and received relief assistance (dry rations) from the government, but the supplies were irregular and not sufficient to meet their needs. Accepting assistance, however, underscored their dependence upon others, which many found humiliating, especially those who came from better social and economic backgrounds.

In the initial phase of displacement, they had relied on casual labour to earn money. Opportunities for such labour were found on large paddies in the Sinhalese areas; but since the displaced did not speak Sinhalese, it had been difficult for them to contact Sinhalese landowners and they did not feel comfortable in Sinhalese areas.

There were few alternatives, however, and gradually several of them had learned sufficient Sinhalese to be able to negotiate decent labour contracts. Contracts were usually given on an individual basis, but our informants told us that if possible, they would work in groups and divide the money among themselves. But work for Sinhalese landowners often required migrating to other regions in the peak seasons and leaving families behind, sometimes for several weeks.

Other displaced persons stayed in the area and worked on the local commercial prawn farms. As with agricultural work, the contracts were generally short-term: in the prawn trade, usually between three and 30 days during each of the two to three cycles per year.

The displaced found it difficult to plan household budgets, given that their income was now both more uncertain and spread out over the entire year instead of being concentrated within a relatively short time span, as it used to be. It was particularly difficult to amass capital for larger expenditures, such as repairs on their houses, investments in business or agriculture, and payments needed for festivals and ceremonies. Many families did not have any savings and they found it difficult to get bank loans because of their status as displaced.

In response, the community re-established a traditional Muslim system in which all capable community members voluntarily contributed to a fund to assist others in need. Interestingly, the term 'community' had been redefined to include the few Hindu Tamil families that had also settled in the area. This inclusion was made on grounds of their common experience of displacement and their shared vulnerability.

In addition to their work as labourers in the fields and in others' businesses, some of the displaced tried to build up their own businesses in the hopes of earning larger profits and gaining more independence. A few men, for example, invested some money in commercial onion production, but their lack of experience with this crop resulted in large losses for the investors.

Others began trading local products, such as *rottis*, a kind of bread, snacks, baskets and mats, throughout a large area, including Vavuniya, Colombo, Mannar and even Jaffna. The woven baskets, mats and shopping bags were usually made by women, sometimes with the help of children. Most women already knew how to weave mats, but they had learned other techniques and how to use other materials during their stay in the Sinhalese community shortly after they were displaced. Some bags are made from plastic wires, which the women buy from outside the community; others are made from palmyra leaves, which are available locally in the neighbouring community.

According to our informants, they had always been allowed to collect the palmyra leaves from the neighbouring village, but a conflict had recently erupted between the Muslims and their neighbours and the Muslims were no longer welcome. The men did not discuss this dispute with us. According to the women with whom we spoke later, the men feel ashamed of or refuse to recognise the women's economic contribution to their households. But according to the women, the situation was serious: they could not continue their activities and they feared that their neighbours were sending away interested customers and business contacts. The women said their neighbours were jealous of the extra assistance the displaced received. The women hoped that, in time, relations would improve.

The Role of the MTB

According to the informants, the Mosque Trustee Board (MTB)[11] had played and continued to play a central role in community development. The MTB collects and distributes money to the community or to individuals facing a crisis, such as a death in the family. The fund is financed through monthly contributions (usually about Rs30–50 per family) and *ad hoc* collections. The MTB also decides who is vulnerable and needs support – a role that extends beyond decisions concerning the distribution of its own funds to include decisions regarding who should receive external emergency relief. When the government wants to distribute assistance, it contacts the MTB for information about community members.

Our informants stressed that the MTB acts as a bridge between the community and the outside world. They reported that few organisations are interested in assisting and investing in Puttalam. They rather concentrate on, say Mannar, which is closer to the war zone. Therefore, the community relies on the MTB to seek out assistance and establish appropriate contacts.

The MTB had negotiated a contact with a wealthy Muslim businessman in Colombo to fund improvements in the community's pre-school. While in Mannar, most community members had not put much emphasis on education, since they were fully dependent on their land. But the Sinhalese host community valued education, and their attitude prompted a change among the displaced population. Most of the informants said that they were well aware that even if peace was restored and the obstacles against their return were removed, few of their children would be able to go back to Mannar and run efficient farms there. Since they had spent most of their lives in Puttalam, they had not learned the necessary agricultural skills. So for the displaced youth, education had become an investment in the future. The displaced came to realise that, unlike their material assets, education 'could never be lost', even if they were to be displaced again. So members of the community set up a voluntary organisation that supports children's education. Members contribute Rs100–500 to enable youths to go to schools in Puttalam or Colombo. Anyone who contributes money can become a member of the organisation.

The partial reliance on external contributions for community development (the well outside the mosque was constructed with the assistance of the Saudi Arabian embassy in Colombo) was reflected in a conscious change in the profile of MTB members. Earlier, members had all been elderly men who enjoyed the respect of the community, partly because of their seniority and insight into religious matters. However, the community now gave priority to qualifications, such as fluency in Sinhalese or in English, so that board members would be better able to communicate with government officials and representatives of relief and development organisations, and the ability to write project proposals for funding. Mobility and independence were also stressed, since board members are expected to travel and make contacts in the donor community. These new criteria favoured younger male members of the community.

Although the displaced Muslims had tried to rebuild their livelihoods and become integrated into the local community, they complained that they were still seen and stigmatised as 'refugees' and 'outsiders' by the local population, a view supported by the women's conflict with their neighbours. The local population continues to refer to their new settlement as a 'refugee camp', even though they own the land on which they live. When asked what they would do if there were peace, there was no agreement among the informants. Some wanted to stay, but others said, 'We have to go back in order to get rid of the refugee label.'[12]

The Women's Meeting

Since we could not speak with women at the first meeting, we set up a separate meeting with them to see if they shared the men's perspectives and experiences or if they had other concerns. We met with about 30 women in a private home.

Apart from the conflict with their neighbours mentioned above, the main problem the women raised focused on their children. The women were concerned that their teenage daughters had become 'lazy and expensive'. They believed this change was a direct result of displacement. Girls and most women, they explained, had nothing to do in the new settlement, while in their villages in Mannar everyone played a role in agricultural production and house-keeping. In addition, their new proximity to urban areas presented an array of temptations – clothes, music cassettes, movies – that the young people found difficult to resist, but that their parents could not afford.

The women were also worried about their daughters' futures. In Mannar, they explained, a bride's parents paid a dowry – in reality, the daughter's inheritance – to their new son-in-law, usually some land and cattle, and maybe, in wealthier families, some cash. After they were displaced from Mannar and became reliant on casual labour and dry rations for their livelihoods, families no longer possessed any of the assets that would constitute the bulk of a dowry. Instead, dowries were paid in cash only. But this was also a problem, because families no longer earned enough. From the women's perspective, it had thus become difficult to find money for their daughters' weddings or, to put it another way, to get their daughters properly married. And since many young men were now acquiring better educations or had become socially more attractive because they had spent time abroad, the sum expected as dowry was increasing.[13]

When asked what could be done to solve this problem, the women reported that, in some families, young women were sent to the Middle East as migrant labourers,[14] either to earn money for their own dowry or to acquire a higher social status so that they would be able to marry a man of at least equal standing who would, in turn, be able to help the whole family.

In a Welfare Centre

The selected camp[15] is located at the outskirts of Kalpitiya town on the tip of the peninsula that stretches from Puttalam towards Mannar, some 60 kilometres away. This area was the first destination of many Muslims who escaped Mannar by boat and it continues to be the home of many displaced people. The camp is situated on

Photo 3   Internally displaced persons, Sri Lanka
(UNHCR, M. Kobayashi)

sandy land, making it inhospitable when strong winds blow and rendering it unsuitable for agriculture and home gardening.[16] Most of the people here used to or continue to live off fishing and related activities.

The camp houses nearly 80 families and is surrounded by a number of other camps that are located so close to each other that it is almost impossible to discern the boundaries of each. Apart from a few public buildings, such as the central school, which is a permanent brick structure, the residential houses are mostly made of wood, palmyra and cadjan leaves and are surrounded by a palmyra or wooden fence.

We met with members of the community at the pre-school, a wooden building with a cement floor and corrugated iron roof. More than 30 men and women participated in the meeting. We had a common discussion followed by talks among smaller groups of men and women.

One of the men, who represented the community, said that they had all come from the same small coastal village in a remote part of southern Mannar district. When the LTTE told them to leave, they immediately packed their belongings and fled by boat, together, to Kalpitiya. They first settled in a camp where there were many other displaced persons, mainly from Mannar. They lived in that camp, which was closer to Puttalam town, for several years. After a fire destroyed large parts of the camp, they were forced to leave again and found their present camp.

In Mannar, most of them had owned their own fishing boats and gear; those who did not, worked for the others. Since all were relatives, everyone had a support network. When they were displaced, they lost all their equipment to the LTTE. So once they arrived in the camp, they had to look for alternative sources of income and build new livelihoods from almost nothing.

Although the displacement had been a major blow, they did not recall the first years as being particularly difficult. Since the camp where they first found refuge and this camp were both located in urban areas, there had been many opportunities to find work with local landowners, business people or fishermen. Even though many activities were new to them, they had adjusted.

Now, however, they feel that these opportunities are diminishing or, rather, that the opportunities do not allow for any socio-economic upward mobility. Many of them work for local *mudalalies* (businessmen), and have done so for years; but given the kinds of jobs and contracts they get, they can only earn a small income. No matter how hard they work they cannot save enough to be able to invest in their own equipment and build up their own businesses. Instead, many are forced to take loans from the *mudalalies* to cover their expenses during periods when they don't earn enough. With interest rates as high as 20 per cent per month, this soon makes them completely dependent on their employers.

To secure an extra income or be able to repay loans, some of the women also began working for the *mudalalies*. Many found work in the large onion fields, but most eventually stopped working because the pittance they earned made little difference to their household budgets. The landowners paid them less than they paid local women (Rs70, as opposed to Rs100 per day). In addition, the women had to pay for transport and food, and they had to find someone to look after their children during the day.

Although there was a steady demand for labour, more women than men were hired, primarily because they were cheaper to employ. This had severe repercussions on the social organisation of the community and the family. Whereas men used to be the bread-winners and women stayed at home to tend to domestic affairs, the roles had reversed. In some families, the man had become responsible for taking care of the children while the wife was at work. In others, the woman ended up with a double burden and, often, a frustrated husband, as well.

The consumption patterns of the displaced began to change too. No longer able to produce most of the food they ate, they now had to purchase their food in the market. The temptations of urban life lured some children away from school to work, instead, for local fishermen so they could earn money. While some parents encouraged their children to work so they could contribute to the family income, many children did not remit the money back to the family, but spent it, instead, on things for themselves.

The community recognised the danger in allowing capital to flow from the village to the town. One woman told how she had tried to set up a small garment business in the camp, but it had not been profitable because, according to her, there was little money around and too much competition from the town. She felt that it was necessary to find a way of generating and keeping capital within the community so women could stay at home and look after their children.

Plunged into poverty, families were undergoing radical changes. According to some of the informants, it was not uncommon for girls as young as 12 and boys as young as 14 to marry. They told us that early marriages were a recent phenomenon directly linked to their displacement. Many couples marry young so they can become independent of their parents who cannot afford to support them, anyway. The dowry, when it is paid, is their start-up capital. But most parents now find it difficult to raise the dowry, and this leads to family conflicts. In an attempt to remedy this situation, the local MTB has advised against giving dowries, which, it says, is not part of Muslim tradition; but the displaced seem to ignore the advice.

In this community, the MTB's work focuses on religious matters, although the board also addresses emerging community problems. But according to several of the informants, their mosque and the board members do not play a significant role in promoting community development. In fact, some women criticised the board for ignoring their problems. They had heard that the MTB in other Muslim settlements had been instrumental in securing funds for community projects, and they were disappointed that their board did not assume a similar role.

The women also complained about the attitude of many of the men in the community who, they said, did not take enough interest in the development of the community. When some of the women tried to build a business, the men not only did not support them, they created obstacles; some responded with outright hostility. Moreover, the women cited many instances of sexual abuse and harassment. While some felt the community's problems were related to gender conflicts, others cited low educational levels and their rural backgrounds as reasons for the lack of community development.

One young woman who had worked as a volunteer with one of the international humanitarian organisations and who had many suggestions about how to help the most vulnerable groups said that the community was not very understanding or supportive of those kinds of initiatives. Everyone is concerned only about him- or herself, she said, and there is a lack of good leadership, which makes it difficult for the community to approach others for help. Some of the women had contacted local NGOs to ask for assistance in income-generating projects. One NGO provided them with sewing machines and a sewing course. But after some time, the organisation stopped supporting them. The women were too shy to ask why, and none of the male members of the community or community leaders followed up on the matter, either.

The Businessmen

The camp in which the interviewed businessmen live houses around 800 families and is located near Puttalam town. Because of its size, it is divided into a number of separate administrative sectors. A number of well-established shops (a bicycle repair, a grocery, a butcher) are located at the entrance to the camp. Inside the camp, there are more enterprises such as telecommunication shops with IDD lines for phones, e-mail and Internet access, a transportation business with heavy lorries, and several small hotels. There are also a health clinic and a pre-school. The residential houses differ in size and quality, including both relatively simple houses made of plastered clay and more permanent brick houses with tile roofs.

We first met with a large group of inhabitants, but unlike in other camps we visited, we felt no sense of community. People originated from many different places and only shared the destiny of having been displaced and temporarily settled in this camp. We therefore changed our research strategy and held a number of individual interviews with people previously or presently involved in business activities.

Our first informant, a man in his thirties, who is married and has two small children, is involved in the garment sector. He had a permanent house and owned many appliances, such as a gas cooker, an electric water pump and a toilet, which are rare among displaced populations living in camps. His wife was adorned with gold jewellery, another display of his relative success.

Our informant told us that he came from a wealthy, semi-urban community on Mannar Island with very good facilities, including a good school. When the Muslims were forced to leave in 1990, he did not join the others who went to the camps, but instead went straight to Puttalam, where he stayed with friends. Determined to make the most of his new situation, he immediately invested his savings of Rs3,000 in a jewellery business patronised by mainly Sinhalese customers.

The business world was not new to him since his father had been involved in trade between Sri Lanka and India.[17] He had visited India with his father and had many contacts both in India and in Colombo through his father. After a while, he shifted from the jewellery to the garment trade, and this, he said, is still his main occupation. He travels occasionally to India where he buys a load of garments at a low price. He then resells his stock to clothing shops in Colombo for a small profit. Even though there is a large garment industry in Sri Lanka, he still makes money from the trade, he said.

As the conversation proceeded, it soon emerged that neither his trade in jewellery nor in garments had been as profitable as he had expected: he still could not save much money. But it also became clear that his main problem is not the little profit he earns, but rather the extent of his obligations. Since he was displaced, he has had to pay dowry for his two sisters. His wife, whom he married in 1995, has seven sisters, all of whom expect some assistance from him, as well. Coming from a wealthy family in Mannar, he also has high expectations for his own standard of living. So he has now become involved in trade involving US dollars and gold. The trade is both illegal and risky, but he accepted the risks for the chance of making huge profits. A wealthy businessman in Colombo runs the business; our informant's role is to bring the goods to and from India. His trading experience and current garment business provide a cover for these illegal activities.

The motivation behind his high-risk strategy, he said, is to be able to move one day to a new settlement that was established three or four years ago along the main road from Puttalam to Colombo. This settlement, he said, was mostly populated by wealthy people, many of whom came from his home community. Through his business contacts, he has already obtained some land there and if he is successful in his business activities, he believes he will be able to build a house there in a couple of years. He told us he has no intention of moving back to Mannar because the situation there is not stable enough, and most of his relatives are now living in the Colombo area.

Our second informant, a middle-aged married man with grown children, comes from Jaffna, where he had a large tea wholesale business and a large house. Today, he lives in a medium-sized plastered clay house with his family, including two of his sisters and one of his wife's sisters. Although the house is not of very high quality, the family owns wooden furniture and other items such as a stereo, a television set, a wall clock and an iron.

Our informant told us that he was first displaced in 1987. At that time, he went to Mannar and lived there for four months before returning to Jaffna. His second displacement, in 1990, had been far more disruptive. He estimated that he had lost several hundred thousand rupees when he was forced to leave then, even though some Tamil business friends had helped him and his family by bringing some of his valuables and savings to Mannar, his first destination. But when fighting between the army and LTTE escalated in 1990, the family realised that Mannar was not safe and that they would have to leave. Like many others, they decided to go to Puttalam and ended up in one of the reception centres there.

In Puttalam, the family settled in a camp together with many other displaced Muslim families from the north. The experience of being in a camp and being dependent on dry rations was a bitter surprise, and soon our informant tried to re-establish his tea business from Jaffna. But the business did not fare well in Puttalam. According to him, the local people tried to prevent displaced persons from becoming too influential in local business. Also, the price of tea had dropped considerably, and there was more competition in Puttalam than in Jaffna, where the distance to tea plantations was longer and there were fewer people engaged in the trade. In addition, the population in Puttalam, a large part of which is Muslim, consumes less tea than the Hindu Tamils, who predominate in Jaffna.

He also said his lack of success was the result of the loss of access to his usual business network. He did not know the whereabouts of many of the people with whom he used to do business, and he has not been able to establish a similar network in Puttalam.

When he realised that he was not able to support his family from the tea trade alone, he tried to include various other products, such as coffee and homemade soap, in his business. That brought in more money, but not enough to cover his growing expenses. So he was forced to take some loans from one of the local moneylenders and was now struggling with debts. When we met the family, they expressed deep despair because they could not see a way out of their situation. The memories of what they had lost and whom they used to be made it even more difficult to accept their present circumstances.

Informant number three was a man in his forties from Jaffna who owns a small restaurant in a brick house on one of the main roads in the camp. He lives there with his wife and two small children. In Jaffna, he mainly traded textiles between Vavuniya and Colombo. He left Jaffna in 1987 because of the fighting and settled in Mannar, where he continued his business. In 1990, he was displaced from Mannar to Puttalam. He repeatedly told us how bewildered he was by the forced displacement because the Tamils and the Muslims had enjoyed such good relations in the past.

Like many others, he left Mannar by boat and arrived in Puttalam. He wanted to build his own business again, but did not have the necessary capital. For two years he worked as a casual labourer for local landowners and tried to save as much as he could. Even though there had been opportunities for his wife to do casual labour and earn a little money, he had never allowed her to do so, since he felt it was his obligation to provide for his family.

After two years, he had saved enough to start a new business, and he returned to the textile trade, mainly between Colombo and Vavuniya in the border region. But the business had become more difficult, and many other business people were taking advantage of displaced people like him. For example, he was rarely paid in cash. Instead, he would be given a cheque which, if it did not bounce, required a costly trip to Colombo to be cashed. Over a couple of years he lost large amounts of money and, in 1998, he finally decided to give up the textile trade and try something else. That was when he opened his small restaurant where he sells soft drinks, ice cream, bread, cigarettes, fruits and vegetables.

But even with modest ambitions, opening a small restaurant is expensive, as one must invest in a building and in stock. So, with his wife's agreement, he pawned her jewellery to raise money. Most of the time, his business does well, he says; but sometimes he finds it difficult to raise enough capital to buy the items he sells. If too many customers go away empty-handed too often, he knows that will further erode his income. He is now considering investing in poultry to earn more money for his business so it becomes a self-sustaining enterprise. Because of competition from the shops in town and the fact that his customers have little money to spend, he has to sell his goods for less than they are sold outside the camp, so he earns less profit. He accepts this as his personal problem, but to him it also reflects a serious structural problem: the outflow of capital from the camp to the town.

As a way of keeping money inside the camp, he thought of organising a weekly market, which would attract not only people in the camp, but also people from surrounding villages. He said he would like to be part of such an initiative, but his idea has gone nowhere, he says, since there is no appropriate forum in the camp in which such an idea can be discussed.

The fourth informant from this camp is a middle-aged man who lives with his wife and two teenage children in a small house and earns money through trade. He came from Mannar in 1990 during the general displacement.

After some time moving around, he settled in Vavuniya and established a small business. But after some time, he left for Puttalam, not because the military situation in Vavaniya was particularly unstable, but because the rent in Vavuniya was too high.[18] In Puttalam, he could settle in one of the camps and not have to pay rent. He could also maintain his business in Vavuniya while having some access to assistance. There was another reason for settling in Puttalam: education. Vavuniya offers a range of courses and higher education in Tamil, but there are also Muslim schools in Puttalam. Through the local school, one of his sons has obtained a scholarship to a Muslim college in the southern part of the country, where the Muslim community is strong. Both the boy and his parents are very happy about this opportunity and confident that he will be able to make use of his education to help his own people.

In a Resettled Community on Mannar Island

The village, home to some 300 families, is located close to Mannar town and not far from the main road connecting Mannar Town with Talaimannar, whence many people escaped to India in small boats, especially in the early years of the conflict. Since the distance between Talaimannar and India is so short, this area used to be an important link in the trade, both legal and illegal, between the two countries and to other parts of Sri Lanka. As it is also one of the few places with access to Jaffna by sea, the area continues to be heavily guarded by security forces. They try to prevent the smuggling of goods to the Tamil Tigers and to protect their own convoys of food and medicine against attack.

This is an old settlement, established by Arab traders more than 400 years ago. The layout of the oldest parts of the settlement is reminiscent of a small town, with houses and shops packed closely together along narrow streets. The newer parts of the settlement are dotted with small, temporary or semi-permanent dwellings hidden behind palmyra-leaf fences.

We met with the people of this community, who were farmers, fishermen and business people, on a number of occasions. But since the women often hesitated to take part in the men's discussion, we organised a separate meeting for the women in an adjacent room.

Some children and adolescents also participated in the women's discussion.

Like other Muslim communities in the north, in October 1990, the inhabitants of this village were instructed by the LTTE to evacuate their village and leave all valuables behind. They, too, were shocked by the order since they had always enjoyed good relations with the Tamils in the region, including the LTTE. But unlike most other Muslims we met, they did not leave immediately, but instead decided to see if they could negotiate the conditions of their departure with the LTTE. They did not approach the LTTE directly, but instead sent community representatives to the ICRC office to seek the agency's assistance in the negotiations. According to our informants, they succeeded in extending the deadline from 48 hours to 12 days, giving them time to plan and organise their move.

According to the villagers, the LTTE accepted their proposal because the area was an important transit site for the rebels' legal and illegal trade and so a degree of mutual dependency had developed. However, the villagers did not win the Tamil militants' approval to take more of their belongings with them. Like other displaced Muslims, they could only bring whatever few utensils, clothes and food they could carry in a shopping bag.

The representatives who went to meet the ICRC delegates were all members of the community MTB. The board also played a crucial role in planning and organising the departure, and three members of the board remained in the village until everyone else had left. This was important, they said, not only to ensure that everybody left safely but also to give some moral support during a dire situation.

The camps that were hurriedly being built in Puttalam to accommodate the many displaced Muslims were already overcrowded. Several villagers decided to move on to the Kurunegala region where there were a number of Muslim communities in which they hoped to, and did, find shelter.

Although most of the families eventually managed to find reasonable shelter either in camps or in other communities, they were keen to return to their home village. After seven months in 'exile', members of the displaced community were given a chance to go back to inspect their home village in anticipation of a possible return. Thirty-three males went back to the area and stayed for two months, living in a mosque. In mid-September 1991, all of their family members returned, among them, three members of the board, who wanted to play a leading role in the return.

According to the informants, more families had wanted to go back, but they were discouraged from doing so by certain political organisations. Many people have still not returned, either because the security situation is not optimal or because their land is occupied by the armed forces. Also, they lack the resources to repair or buy new tools, seeds, or equipment necessary for re-establishing their livelihoods. Some people, especially the younger displaced, have not returned simply because they have become accustomed to life in town. Others were severely traumatised by the expulsion from their home village and find it difficult to return to a place full of sad memories and still not free of the risk of new atrocities.

Indeed, the area is close to, and sometimes part of, the war zone, with the noticeable presence of the Sri Lankan Army, the LTTE and several other Tamil factions. In the early years after the return, there was a great deal of armed activity and pervasive suspicion. Although recent years have seen a reduction in the fighting, new forms of harassment have developed. For instance, several Tamil factions, some of whom have joined forces with the government against the LTTE, are extracting taxes from local communities to support their organisations. According to the villagers, all goods are now subject to tax; and each organisation has developed a monopoly on different items. This means that villagers are obliged to sell their products to the shop run by the organisation that controls the trade of that particular item. This arrangement mainly benefits the organisation, not the producers, who often have to sell at a low price, nor the consumers, who have to pay more.

Some of these organisations also decide which companies will get contracts to carry out work in the community, such as construction. Expenditures increase as external labour is brought into the village. This kind of intervention not only increases the cost of living, but also makes villagers acutely aware of the need to maintain good relations with everyone – a difficult task in such a highly politicised society. The strategy here is a delicate balance between avoidance, compliance and silence.

Villagers did not speak much about their relationship with the soldiers living among them, but since the area is known for its involvement in smuggling activities, and the villagers are probably suspected to have some contact with the LTTE, it is likely that the relationship is one of mutual wariness.[19] The villagers said that small platoons of soldiers march through the village almost daily. While we were having our meeting we watched one of these inspection squads pass quietly through the village.

The security situation has also directly affected the villagers' livelihoods since the government has imposed numerous restrictions on fishing. Sea fishing is only allowed during daytime, and only at a relatively short distance from the shore. These restrictions reduce the number and kind of fish that can be caught. To prevent smuggling and to make it easier to identify people at sea and avoid attacking civilians, soldiers collect the engines from the fishermen's boats every evening and keep them until early the next morning when the fishermen reclaim them.

Eventually, the villagers we spoke with brought up the subject of the pass system that was developed to monitor the movement of people, and thereby to detect the presence of LTTE cadres.[20] The villagers all have permanent passes, but when they leave the district, they must produce a letter stating the purpose of travel as well as the name and ID card number of each person travelling.[21] Depending on the region of origin stated in the identity papers, the villagers face greater or lesser difficulties on their journeys. A Jaffna origin, for example, immediately generates suspicion.

For the villagers, the pass system is not only time-consuming, involving long queues at checkpoints to have papers stamped and signed, it may also be costly, as the system has created a new source of income for corrupt officials. To get a pass, one has to pay.

When the families first returned to their village, there was no road to Mannar town, no public transportation and only a few shops. There was a boat connection to Kalpitiya, but the price was high: Rs250 per trip. In addition, the police had imposed restrictions on movement, both for security reasons and in an attempt to control the return. So even when there were opportunities to trade, it was not always easy to do so.

Few people could resume their pre-flight livelihoods, so most took advantage of whatever income-earning activities presented themselves. The returnees began cultivating the large areas of land that had been abandoned by those who had fled. They regarded this as a temporary situation, and intended to give the land back to the legitimate owners if and when they returned. Others gathered the cattle and goats that had also been abandoned by their owners and sold them to butchers or to the army. This was not only a profitable enterprise, but it also helped build good relations with the soldiers, which was essential for their survival. The informants told us that they spent a considerable amount of time negotiating with armed and civilian authorities to continue their economic activities. Aside from obtaining various permissions and passes, they also renegotiated the conditions of their work, including fishing times and the amount and type of imports and exports permitted, which also probably involved a certain amount of bribery.

Looking back, the villagers agreed that one of the difficulties in reviving the local community, at first, was that only a few families had returned. As soon as more people came back, they were able to build up a relatively good economy based on farming, fishing and a number of other activities. Some activities were new, such as onion production, which was an idea that the returnees had brought back with them from their stay in Puttalam. Others, such as the collection and sale of herbal plants used for medicinal purposes, were traditional, though long overlooked.

But the continued instability in the area led to a deterioration of social services, including education. The problem started when the villagers were first displaced and the children missed one year of school. When they returned, they resumed their education with the assistance of a volunteer teacher from the community. But as more and more families came back, the number of students increased and soon there were not enough qualified teachers. The community approached the local government for assistance, but because of the security situation, lack of resources and the perception that the area was 'remote', it was difficult to attract teachers. Finally, teachers were recruited from among the displaced Muslims living in Puttalam. The villagers assumed these teachers would stay since they were from the area, themselves; but in recent months, ten out of the 16 teachers left. The remaining six were responsible for more than 300 students.

The MTB convened a meeting to discuss possible solutions to the teacher shortage. Their first idea was to hire volunteers who would be paid a token Rs1,000 per month, just to make sure that the children could continue their schooling. The teachers' 'salary' was to be covered by the monthly fees paid to the MTB by members of the community; but, in the end, those funds couldn't cover the token salaries.

The MTB then devised a strategy that involved adding Rs1 to the price of a litre of kerosene. The local cooperative agreed and the plan looked promising – until the government increased the price of kerosene. Because the rise in kerosene prices coincided with a price rise for bread, vegetables and electricity, kerosene consumption plummeted. Once again, the community and the MTB had to come up with a new strategy.

Meanwhile, there was a dramatic increase in the school dropout rate. It was estimated that up to half of the children attended school irregularly. Given the difficulties in restoring their livelihoods, many families were becoming impoverished and were enlisting their children's aid in trying to earn an income. Some children began helping fishermen, working as casual labourers or selling firewood.

According to the informants, there is little interest in their plight among the Muslim elite in Mannar. Many Muslims left and are staying in other districts, so for a Muslim politician, or patron, there is less to gain, economically and politically, from investing in the Mannar area than investing in, say, Puttalam. In Puttalam, Muslims have acquired a political voice – they are even represented in parliament by a Muslim – partly because of their number and partly because there are more educated people there who have the skills to network effectively.

CONCLUSION

As explained in the section on methodology, the case studies were presented more or less as they were recounted to us in the field.

The activities undertaken by the displaced, regardless of whether they take place during or after displacement, occur in an unstable political, economic and social environment. This is important to bear in mind when trying to assess their effectiveness, because displaced persons may develop sound strategies in response to a particular problem and particular circumstances. But these circumstances, or external factors, often change rapidly and thus demand adjustments to the strategies even before the displaced person has managed to develop a sense of control over his or her situation. This means that the conventional image of the displacement, return and resettlement process as linear, proceeding from initial loss to recovery and development, is often both not linear and unpredictable, as the fourth case study illustrated. Even when the return and immediate reconstruction phase runs smoothly, the failure to end war and the resulting lack of security and dwindling resources may turn development into disintegration and dispossession.

A second aspect worth mentioning here is the social consequences of particular response strategies. As the cases demonstrated, people emphasised activities that aim to rebuild their livelihoods and achieve self-reliance. From a purely economic point of view, several of these efforts may lead to good results. But it is also important to look at how these changes in economic relations and practices influence and sometimes dramatically alter social relations, particularly at the domestic level. The case studies presented here showed changes in gender relations within the family, new marriage practices and new forms of community leadership. While these may sometimes contribute to the improvement of people's lives, they may also result in conflicts over authority and power, and the roles of particular social categories.

Another fact that emerged from our discussions with displaced communities was that the location of welfare centres and relocation villages near urban centres introduced entirely new consumption patterns within the community. These turned out to be not only a burden to the household economy, but sometimes also a factor in deciding whether or not to return. In that respect, a recurrent theme among the informants was the constant and systematic drain of capital from camp to town. Even when sound economic activities had been initiated, the net result was often negative, since consumption was concentrated in the urban centres. Several of the informants' stories suggested that their relative poverty was structural, in the sense that they were dependent on the kind of employment that local businessmen would offer them. In addition to struggling with the label of 'displaced' or 'refugee', they also became part of the local 'proletariat'.

Many strategies were developed to try to ensure that displaced children could continue their education. The Muslim community's emphasis on education serves both an economic end, in that education is a precondition for employment in Sri Lanka or abroad, and a cultural end, in that it helps the Muslim community to develop and nurture its sense of being a community with its own identity.

I have already pointed out that the experiences of the displaced Muslims can hardly be considered representative of internal displacement in Sri Lanka insofar as the circumstances under which they fled and were resettled were very different from those endured by the majority of displaced Tamils. But this does not mean that their case sheds no light on others. It is worth remembering when planning responses to displacement in other parts of the country that, more than ten years after their displacement, many displaced Muslims remain in temporary welfare centres or in other ways struggle to rid themselves of the 'displaced' label and to escape poverty. However, I also want to emphasise the presence of the 'cultural capital' that exists in any society. The cultural resources that the Muslim community possesses, such as the MTB and various practices that protect the most vulnerable members of the community, differ from those found in Tamil or Sinhalese communities. But they do exist in these other communities, and they should be identified and supported because they can give displaced communities a greater sense of ownership of and responsibility for the recovery process than most external, culture-blind approaches do. The challenge is how to combine effectively the displaced population's own response strategies with interventions planned by external actors.

ACKNOWLEDGEMENTS

I wish to thank Kathiravel Ranjan and Karthikeyini Sabaratnam, from the Danish Refugee Council, for assisting me in the field and for the stimulating discussions we had afterwards. I also thank the Rural Development Foundation, Puttalam, for sharing their information and views and for allowing their field officers to join us. Finally, I wish to thank all the informants who so willingly shared their experiences with us. While all these people have, in various and important ways, played a central role in the production of this chapter, the full responsibility for the interpretations presented above rests with me alone.

NOTES

1. There were an estimated 70,000–100,000 displaced Muslims in October 1990.
2. For a more detailed account of the changing identities and political strategies of the Muslim minority, see O'Sullivan (1999) and Ismail (1995).
3. The forced displacement of the Muslims was in many ways different from that of other groups in Sri Lanka. People had no choice about leaving or staying, the mass move occurred within a few days, and there was no immediate option for return. Unlike many other displaced Sri Lankans, the Muslims now live in a militarily secure area outside the war zone.
4. Statistics on the numbers of displaced in Puttalam vary, but several sources estimate about 12,500 families. However, data given in different surveys generally support the view that more than half the displaced population in Puttalam settled in the Kalpitiya area and immediately north and south of Puttalam town. They also suggest that about one-third of the displaced population remained in 94 welfare centres (as of 1999), nearly 55 per cent stayed in resettlement and relocation villages

scattered in 95 locations, and the remainder stayed with family and friends (Hasbullah et al. 1999).

5. In addition, I have conducted long-term field research among Sinhalese families who had been relocated in connection with the implementation of a development programme (Sorensen 1996).

6. The RDF was established in 1984 by a group of concerned Muslims in Mannar district who wished to help the poorer members of their own and neighbouring communities. In 1990, staff of the RDF had to leave Mannar together with all other Muslims. Many of them settled in Puttalam where they continue their work, focusing exclusively on the plight of other displaced persons.

7. To ensure that the interviews were not experienced as military-style interrogations, and because of time constraints, we did not tape the interviews. The accounts are thus not exact transcriptions, but rather summaries based on the material produced by the informants and on our own field notes.

8. My assistant was struck by the constant use of the word 'we' rather than 'I' by our informants, even in contexts in which 'I' would normally be used by Tamil speakers.

9. In most cases, the displaced who bought land on which to re-establish their communities gave their new village the name of the village they were forced to flee.

10. According to the Consortium of Humanitarian Agencies (CHA), the government offers displaced persons financial assistance of Rs7,000 for temporary housing, Rs1,000 for implements, Rs2,000 as a settling-in allowance, Rs4,000 as a productive enterprise grant and Rs25,000 for permanent housing (one US dollar equals Rs50–60).

11. The MTB usually consists of seven to eleven married males elected by the community, usually for a three-year term.

12. Brun notes how some Muslim families hesitate to accept the government's resettlement allowance because they fear that it might pose a hindrance if, at a later stage, they want to return, as they would be considered citizens of the new location (Brun 2000).

13. See Fuglerud (1999) for a discussion and comparison of the war and displacement-related changes in the dowry system among Muslims and Tamils in eastern Sri Lanka.

14. The countries of the Middle East have been major recipients of Sri Lankan migrant labourers. Because of their culture and religion, Muslim men and women from Sri Lanka comprise a large part of Sri Lanka's total labour migration to these countries.

15. The government runs most of the welfare centres, with some assistance from international and local organisations.

16. 'The majority of resettlement villages are located in the lands that are categorised as not suitable for cultivation or for settlements in the Puttalam District Land Use Map'. The problems mentioned include saline soil, flooding, pollution, sand dunes and marshland. According to the author, the displaced settled here because the land was inexpensive (Hasbullah 1999).

17. Many villages in his home area have long been involved in trade, and some in smuggling, between India and Sri Lanka. In fact, smuggling is considered by many to be the backbone of their economy. As the conflict intensified, smuggling was no longer simply an economic affair, but also a security issue, since trading also involves items going to and from the LTTE in the north.

18. The size of Vavuniya almost doubled during the 1990s (Balakrishnan 2000). Most of the new arrivals were displaced, though the military and police forces added significant numbers to the pre-war population.

19. On 30 January 2001, Tamilnet reported: 'Fishermen in Mannar complain that the Sri Lankan Navy arrests and beats them up regularly, accusing them of smuggling essential commodities banned under Colombo's decade-long embargo on the Vanni region' (www.tamilnet.com).

20. For a detailed account of the pass system in Vavuniya District at the time of writing, see CHA Newsletter, 2000. The regulations and practices undergo constant change, reflecting the existing security situation. However, the changes can also be interpreted as a way of making the presence of the state felt at all times and generating some uncertainty, which may, itself, reduce both mobility and the risk of unwanted LTTE personnel (Sorensen 2000).

21. Humanitarian agencies report that, in the north and east, many people do not have identification papers, including children who do not have birth certificates.

Latin America

8
Colombia: Creating Peace Amid the Violence. The Church, NGOs and the Displaced

Esperanza Hernandez Delgado and Turid Laegreid

The recent history of Colombia is a state of continuous violence punctuated by occasional short periods of peace. Struggles for political power, battles against social inequality and political marginalisation, land disputes, drug trafficking and intolerance for differing viewpoints have all, at one time or another, found expression in armed conflict. The fight for political power and full social and political participation within the country is also closely linked to forced displacement.

BACKGROUND

Some studies show that during the period of 'Classic Violence' (1948–53), over 2 million people were displaced by violent political confrontations between the country's two political parties and, to a lesser extent, by conflicts for the possession of land and for the control of local power (Oquist 1978).

The 50-year-old armed conflict that still rages in Colombia has its origin in the 1950s, when the government and insurgency groups battled for political power. Since the 1980s, paramilitary and self-defence groups have also taken up arms against the rebels. Caught in the middle is Colombia's civilian population, which has been used, mostly abused, by all combatants for their own ends. Through the decades, the original ideological rationale for the fighting has been lost amid unholy alliances with drug traffickers and peace negotiations played out while war efforts intensify.

The damage caused by the conflict is staggering. During 1999 alone, there were 430 massacres (Defensoria del Pueblo 2000), more than 220,000 crimes, of which more than 73,000 were offences against life and personal safety and nearly 100,000 of which were offences against private property, and 1,698 kidnappings (National Police 2000). Over 280,000 people were displaced that year because

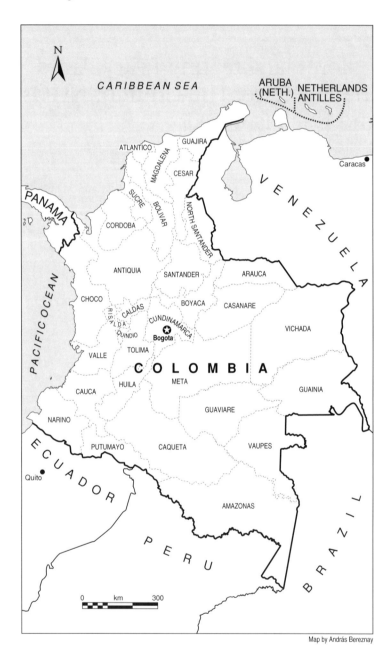

Map 8   Colombia

of the political violence (CODHES 2000). In the past 15 years, some 1.9 million people have been displaced because of the violence.

In 1995, under pressure from the church and national and international NGOs, the government acknowledged the magnitude of the displacement problem and elaborated a policy to prevent displacement and offer assistance to those already displaced. Law 387, adopted in 1997, recognised displaced persons' right to humanitarian aid in emergencies. It also provided for direct access to the state's social programmes with the aim of improving economic and social conditions to encourage return and resettlement. The law gives displaced persons access to government income-generation projects, the national agro-reform and rural development system, small business promotion, training and social organisation, programmes related to health and rural and urban housing, special programmes for children, women and the elderly, and urban and rural employment programmes organised by the Red de Solidaridad Social.

When announced, the offer generated enormous expectations among the displaced population. Those expectations, however, exceeded the state's capacity to meet them. Indeed, recent studies (Posada et al. 1998) suggest that the government's offer to assist the displaced is more theoretical than real, and still very much in the development stage. The policy does have potential, however, in that it envisions state resources being used to help the displaced rebuild their lives. But the policy emphasises that emergency humanitarian aid should be directed to the displaced to support them in their own individual and community responses to their displacement.

METHODOLOGY

The fieldwork for this study was conducted in the cities of Bucaramanga, Villavicencio and Barrancabermeja. Experiences from Bogotá, South Bolívar, Cúcuta and Catatumbo (North Santander) and Urabá have also been included. Urabá, Barrancabermeja, South Bolívar, Cúcuta and Catatumbo are all violent areas; the latter two have experienced a recent escalation of the armed conflict. Most of the displaced in these cities fled their homes because of the paramilitaries, although guerrilla groups also are responsible for a considerable amount of the displacement. Villavicencio is the exception: its proximity to the demilitarised area, where the government is holding peace talks with the Revolutionary Armed Forces of Colombia (FARC), makes Villavicencio a major reception area for the displaced who fled FARC abuses or threats.

Bucaramanga is a relatively calm city and a primary destination for the displaced coming from Magadalena Medio and Catatumbo. Montería is a stronghold of the paramilitary group 'Peasant Farmers Self-Defence Group of Córdoba and Urabá' (ACCU). The capital, Bogotá, hosts displaced persons from all over the country.

The study was conducted through in-depth interviews with displaced individuals, representatives of organisations formed by the displaced, representatives of accompanying organisations, Colombian NGOs and members of the Project Counselling Service (PCS) of Colombia. The findings are also based on direct observation and information gathered by the authors over several years.

SELF-PROTECTION STRATEGIES

Early Warning

In areas where there is still a high degree of organisation and intact social networks, there is a variety of ways, most of them informal, to warn communities about imminent danger. The armed actors, particularly the paramilitary forces, often start their incursions by going to villages with lists of people regarded as collaborators with the opposite group. When the armed actors start asking for particular persons, those asked will discreetly pass that information on to the individuals being sought. By watching and analysing the armed group's behaviour, those at risk can gauge if they have a chance to escape before the attacks begin.

We found highly developed early-warning systems in areas that were traditionally well organised. In Bucaramanga, for example, people used cattle horns to make far-reaching sounds that would warn others of the proximity of armed forces. Hidden messages in local radio broadcasts had also been used to warn people of danger.

Escape Routes

Flight amid the fighting is difficult and dangerous. Armed actors who have recently infiltrated an area will do everything they can to control transport and travel. Checkpoints and roadblocks are set up and all persons and goods travelling through them are carefully scrutinised. Community leaders from Catatumbo told us about one paramilitary group that checked personal identification against computerised lists at checkpoints in the region. The same group announced an explicit prohibition against leaving the area without permission. Anyone trying to leave would have to explain why and could not carry cash or goods exceeding a certain value. The paramilitary routinely executed persons who were believed to support the guerrillas or who had, in some other way, broken the paramilitary's newly imposed 'laws'. Checkpoints thus became an enormous obstacle for anyone who wanted to seek refuge in another part of the country.

The only way to avoid the checkpoints was by taking alternative routes, either by walking through woods, or travelling by boat on remote rivers. Peasant farmers often took advantage of their knowledge of the region by using well-hidden routes. Again, when a community had a tradition of being well organised, it also had the most systematic approach to finding and using safe escape routes.

Escaping to the Forest

Walking through rain forests for days on end is particularly hard for women, children and the elderly; and there is also some risk of being discovered. However, local NGOs report that there is still some 'colonisation' of forest areas, a response mechanism adopted by those who were displaced during the 1950s. Peasant farmers move their families into the jungle and begin farming on virgin land. While this strategy provides access to food and an easy return journey after the danger has passed, conditions in the jungle are harsh and there is no access to basic services. In addition, over the long term, farming in these areas can result in deforestation and the destruction of valuable natural resources.

Temporary Displacement Nearby

When communities perceive the risk of attack as short term, they will often seek protection in a neighbouring town and stay until the danger has passed and the armed groups have left their area. Individuals most likely to be personally targeted, such as community leaders and merchants, will perhaps remain displaced for a while longer until they feel it is safe for them to return.

For many communities, this strategy has ensured that individual and collective identities are maintained and that the loss of land and property associated with long-term displacement is minimised.

The 'return' will often be unaccompanied and spontaneous, with the attendant risk of being attacked. Indeed, new displacements are common. Some communities in volatile areas have become accustomed to almost cyclical displacements, leaving their homes once or twice a year. Others will simply give up and move to bigger cities.

Some families adopt a system of 'daytime displacement', in which they sleep in neighbouring villages, or set up temporary houses in the woods, and return to work their land during the day. Massacres and murders occur mostly by night; and it is easier to evade attacks during the day. Local NGOs report that this daytime displacement is less common now than it was a few years ago because of the severe escalation in the fighting and the higher incidence of attacks during daylight.

In Barrancabermeja, local social workers reported that in the aftermath of the 16 May 1998 massacres, the most affected neighbourhoods, which contained a high percentage of displaced persons, took collective actions to prevent new massacres. They set up a system whereby the most exposed persons would stay in different houses after 5 p.m. In an acute emergency, those people would run to one predetermined house to minimise their isolation and vulnerability.

Though the distance between home and refuge may be small, local displacement still disrupts a family's normal life and often forces changes in their subsistence strategies. The displaced must also endure shortages of food and perhaps shelter, as often the host communities are, themselves, struggling to survive.

Seeking Protection from the Combatants

The relationship between the (illegal) armed groups and the civilian population is quite complex. Immediate control of the population is generally based on fear and terror; but long-term political and social control will be dependent upon the armed group's ability to assume state-like responsibilities. The armed groups 'offer' improvements of infrastructure and 'law and order' mechanisms against petty crime and, of course, 'protection' against the enemy. In exchange, the civilian population is required to give tacit or explicit support to the ruling armed group, to accept its *de facto* political, social and military control and to obey the newly imposed rules of social conduct.

Some displaced youth are in danger of being recruited in the ranks of either paramilitary or guerrilla groups, either as informers or as combatants. Many young men and women see this as an opportunity to obtain protection, security and subsistence. Both the paramilitary and the guerrilla groups offer good salaries, clothing, food and lodging. However, by joining the armed group that is dominant in their area, these youth are also relinquishing their political independence.

In regions in which a particular armed group has held dominion for a long time, some communities have responded to attacks by opposition groups by fleeing to the mountains and declaring themselves resistors against the attackers. They are then guided and protected by the dominant armed group during their displacement. But this strategy is inherently dangerous, as the civilian population is thus linked with one group against another and is therefore stigmatised.

Avoiding Forced Recruitment of Children and Adolescents

Forced recruitment is a relatively new cause of displacement. In some areas, guerrilla groups or the paramilitary will forcibly recruit at least one son or daughter of each family in their area of control. Refusing to allow a child to 'join' the group will often result in punishment for the child or the family; killings are not uncommon. Sometimes the whole family decides to move to another town to avoid both recruitment and punishment. Other times, the family will send their children away to live with relatives in another town. Even though this inevitably leads to the disintegration of the family unit, this strategy may be the only way to preserve the life and freedom of the child. There are also considerable risks involved for the children, the family and the relatives who 'disobey' the armed factions and resort to this strategy.

Seeking Anonymity

In regions where fighting is intense, identifying oneself as a displaced person leaves one vulnerable to attack by one or several armed groups. Fear, then, drives the displaced to search for places in which they can hide their status as displaced persons, usually in medium to large towns and cities, even though this usually means they cannot benefit from state assistance provided to those individuals who have registered themselves as displaced. In Cúcuta, entire neighbourhoods have developed over the past few years, identified by local parishes and other local organisations as being populated entirely by internally displaced persons. But few of the inhabitants will admit that they are displaced; they would rather be labelled as migrants.

The state's registration system has been criticised by national and international NGOs because the information gathered during registration, including what group was responsible for provoking flight and why, can be used against the displaced. Local church representatives told us that some 400 people were assassinated in the city of Cúcuta during 2000. Most of the killings took place in displaced neighbourhoods, and most of the victims were displaced. Parishes in these neighbourhoods reported that individuals from specific towns and villages, presumed to be associated with one or another armed group, were targeted.

In such situations, *silence* becomes the most common, and most effective, protection strategy. Not to disclose, or to lie about, who you are and where you are from can increase the chances of survival, at least in the short run. But maintaining silence also prevents an individual from securing his/her basic human and civil rights, including access to public services and security. Public entities, like Red de Solidaridad Social, have traditionally only provided assistance or subsistence programmes to registered individuals or groups of individuals. External humanitarian actors, including international and national NGOs, have difficulty assisting a population that will not identify itself as displaced. By hiding their origin, and their needs, the displaced are copying the survival and subsistence mechanisms of 'ordinary' marginalised persons in Colombia.

Escaping to Neighbouring Countries

The borders between Colombia and Venezuela and between Colombia and Ecuador are quite porous, allowing for a constant flow of people and goods. Colombians will work and live on the Venezuelan or Ecuadorian side, and vice versa. Few of the people who do so have any legal status in their country of residence, but they are, to greater or lesser degrees, accepted in their adopted countries.

There have been several instances in which people have fled Colombia to seek temporary refuge in Venezuela or Ecuador, though they have not necessarily sought formal protection from the Venezuelan or Ecuadorian governments. In some cases, these individuals only wanted to use Venezuela for safe 'transit' to other places in Colombia. These movements have caused some consternation among human rights and refugee rights organisations because they blur the legal distinctions between refugees and displaced persons. The situation became even more complicated when Venezuelan authorities started to repatriate all Colombian *de facto* refugees and invented the term 'internally displaced in transit'.

Some groups established temporary 'secret' settlements on the Venezuelan side of the border, a short distance from their homes. The Colombian side of the border is the site of constant fighting, though no armed group has a permanent presence there. The displaced/refugees are well informed about the situation near their homes, so they cross the border and work their land whenever possible.

The Peace Communities in Urabá

The best-known organised self-protection movements in Colombia are the 'peace communities' (Comunidades de Paz) and Communities in Resistance (Comunidades en Resistencia) in Urabá.[1] These movements emerged after the first massive displacement occurred in 1997, following intense fighting between government forces and FARC that was accompanied by threats and massacres by paramilitary groups.

The initial objective of the movement was to keep the civilian population out of the armed conflict by declaring civilian autonomy *vis-à-vis* the armed groups. That autonomy involved organising the community democratically and formulating and adhering to self-imposed restrictions on carrying arms, passing information to armed factions, or in any other way supporting the armed groups. It was hoped that by doing so, those displaced living in camps in Pavarandó and Turbo would be able to return to their homes and future displacement would be prevented.

The peace communities negotiated with paramilitaries and guerrillas through third parties, mainly the church. The armed groups agreed not to attack the communities; similar agreements made with government troops were formalised. The community in Cacarica emphasised the government's responsibility for providing protection and security and negotiated an unarmed state presence (the so-called 'house of justice', which includes an ombudsman and an investigator from the Attorney-General's office).

Protection Tools

The peace communities designed symbols to designate the member villages and individuals. Signs were erected outside villages and 'camps', and members carry ID cards affirming that they belong to the community and that they do not carry arms and do not participate in the armed conflict. The ID cards have proven to be

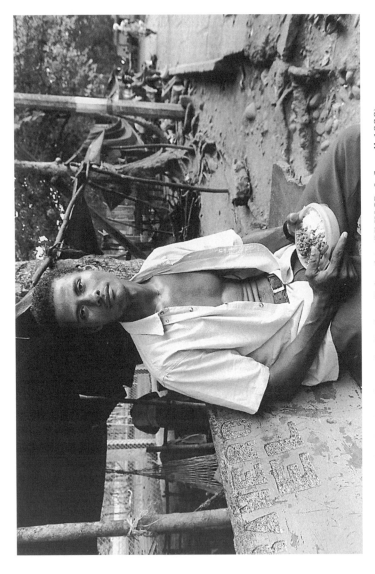

Photo 4   Camp for displaced people, Turbo, Colombia (UNHCR, J. Spaull 1998)

important assets for travel through the region as holders of those cards pass easily through the numerous checkpoints set up by each faction.

As another way of protecting themselves and their right to freedom of movement, members of the peace communities travel in groups and carry out work, such as planting, road repairs and fruit harvesting, collectively. Teams of missionaries and NGO staff also often accompany peace community members in their tasks, providing another level of protection.

Most of these communities are Afro-Colombian and enjoy particular rights as recognised minorities, the most important of which are collective land rights, including the right to use surrounding natural resources. *Titulación*, or the legal registration of collective property, is crucial for reclaiming their land once the displaced return. The communities were in the process of acquiring these rights at the time of their displacement. Negotiations with the Colombian Institute for Agrarian Reform (INCORA), the state entity that handles land reform, were conducted with the legal assistance of national NGOs.

Although many of the peace communities have suffered attacks by armed actors and continue to be threatened by the conflict raging around them, the initiative gave individuals the opportunity to be trained and allowed the displaced communities to return home in relative safety.

ORGANISED RESPONSES: ASSOCIATIONS OF DISPLACED PERSONS

Colombia has a rich tradition of popular movements, social organi-sations and NGOs. The first organisations of displaced persons emerged in the early 1980s. Initially, most were Bogotá-based; but in recent years a number of locally based displaced organisations have emerged, especially in medium and large towns and cities. One reason for this is that the Law on Displacement outlines the importance of local and regional mechanisms to handle the problems of displaced persons, the so-called Municipal and Regional Committees for Displaced People. Representatives of displaced communities or organisations have the right to participate in these committees, along with the municipality, local or regional ombudsman's office, police, military, NGOs, etc.[2]

Not surprisingly, the cities with the most severe security problems, such as Cúcuta and Barrancabermeja, host the fewest organisations for the displaced. In Bucaramanga and Villavicencio, where the security situation is less acute, the organised response is much more frequent and effective.

In Villavicencio, some organisations were composed of families who originated from the same area. In other organisations, it was need, usually for shelter, that had brought families from different areas and backgrounds together to seek assistance. In Bucaramanga, a group of displaced persons organised themselves into different committees to negotiate with the local authorities for access to land. When their appeals were rejected, they tried a different tack and simply settled themselves on an empty, but suitable, piece of land. The police were about to remove them from the site when the local ombudsman's office and a local NGO intervened on their behalf. They were allowed to stay.

Common to all these organisations is the presence of one strong, usually male, leader. In cases where the organisation was composed of families from the same area, the catalyst behind the formation of the association was usually the former community leader; in one case, the former mayor of the small town they had fled started the organisation.

Some of these organisations have succeeded in negotiating with local or central authorities for assistance. At times, however, assistance is provided only to cement a client–patron relationship. In at least two cases, the displaced organisations negotiated 'favours' in exchange for political support to specific candidates who were running for office in local elections. Interestingly, these organisations also later experienced severe internal divisions, resulting in two separate *juntas directivas* (leadership structures).

SELF-RELIANCE STRATEGIES

Shelter

Most displaced persons we spoke with had initially sought lodging with relatives or friends in their new location. But these host families were often also poor and marginalised. Many of them had been displaced long before by violence or had migrated to bigger towns and cities for economic reasons. In some cases, as many as six families shared a small house with only two rooms and two beds. Cramped and uncomfortable, parents would spend long hours out looking for work while children, lacking adult supervision, would begin to roam the streets. Many ended up in criminal gangs, especially in larger cities.

The women of the Popular Women's Organisation of Barran-cabermeja (OFP) who worked in the marginalised neighbourhoods of Barrancabermeja, observed that there were several phases of acquiring shelter. For the first three months after displacement, a family would stay with a host family. Then, the displaced family would look for other options. Some would rent a small place; but because most displaced have no steady income, they could not maintain this new arrangement in the long term. NGOs in Bogotá told us that a number of displaced people had become 'rental nomads': unable to pay rent, families figured they could remain in a dwelling for three months before being evicted for non-payment. They would then move on to another place, stay for a few months, be expelled, and so on.

A second option for this phase is claiming land and setting up huts and shacks. Sometimes, this is an organised event, with up to 30 families moving onto a large piece of empty land at night and settling in. More common is one family's spontaneous move onto the fringes of an already existing settlement. This phenomenon is so well known, some people now buy cheap land in order to rent it to displaced persons (*engorde de lotes*, or land speculation). Buyers anticipate that the value of the land will increase over time, since the displaced family will probably build a small house and cultivate the surrounding terrain. Sometimes, the family that rents the land and settles on it ultimately buys it.

A few families will have enough resources to buy wood to construct their shacks; most have to gather whatever material is available. In Cúcuta, we saw all kinds of materials used to build one shack we visited: paper, carton, clothing, plastic bags and some small pieces of wood. Since most of the areas on which the displaced settle are vulnerable to flooding and mud-slides, and even the most minimal infrastructure is lacking, the displaced and their dwellings are vulnerable to catastrophe.

The lack of basic infrastructure also means that sanitation is virtually non-existent. Each house will set up a provisional latrine, with the result that the settlement, as a whole, is exposed to disease and epidemics. In instances when the settlements had been collec-tively organised, we found that sanitation systems had been planned and were usually better, if not wholly satisfactory.

Still, there is some opportunity for upward mobility among the displaced over time. The little income that is gathered through occasional jobs may be used to upgrade a family's shack. After some years, a concrete floor may be poured. The luckiest among the displaced may end up with an entire house made of concrete.

A number of displaced persons may settle in public buildings, usually as second-phase accommodation. A small group will decide to move into a building, usually one that is government owned. In Bucaramanga, one displaced community settled in an abandoned railway station. Such communal responses to the need for shelter can, in turn, become the catalyst for greater organisation within the displaced community. However, overcrowding, a lack of essential services and a lack of adequate hygiene make living conditions within these buildings far less than adequate.

Begging for Food

In medium and large towns and cities, many displaced rely on begging to survive. In Bogotá, street beggars with signs saying, 'I'm a displaced person, please help' have become a common sight. This is one of the worst effects of displacement: it saps the self-esteem of displaced persons, many of whom were independent peasants before they were displaced.

Some displaced search for discarded food in markets and at butchers'. Often, it is the children's responsibility to loiter around markets to be first in line for leftovers, such as ears and intestines. Because they spend long days doing this to assist their families, children often do not attend school.

Ollas Comunitarias (Community Meals)

In many cities throughout the country, *ollas comunitarias*, or community meals, have become an important way for many displaced families to obtain daily meals. The most renowned is the OFP's *ollas* in Barrancabermeja, but meals are also served this way in Bucaramanga and Villavicencio. Although few *ollas* are totally self-sustaining (most receive some form of funding or subsidy from local or international NGOs), the first known *olla comunitaria* was initiated and run by displaced women with their own resources in Monteria.[3]

Seventeen peasant women in the Candelaria neighbourhood started the first *olla*, with the assistance of a woman from Lima, Peru, who knew of a similar system there. The women and their families, living in grinding poverty, decided to organise to help both themselves and the new displaced families that arrived each day. They formed a committee and started raising funds to support the *olla*. They ran neighbourhood parties and lotteries to raise money and obtained some free food in supermarkets and markets. When the first *olla* opened on 4 April 1994, 30 women and their families participated.

During the first four months, they organised a weekly *olla*, supported only by their local fund-raising activities and a 25-cent contribution from each family. Later, with support from several international NGOs (Oxfam, Swiss Aid and PCS), they expanded the *ollas* considerably. In 1999, about 1,000 persons received a daily meal via the *ollas*, and the women who started the service formed a women's association.

The concept has been copied with some success in Barrancabermeja and Villavicencio. Grassroots organisations are in charge of the formal administration of the *ollas*, but displaced families always do voluntary work. A coordinator will usually be paid a small fee; cooking and serving responsibilities are rotated among the displaced families.

Food can also be obtained at 'popular restaurants', a kind of soup kitchen. Meals there must be purchased, albeit for a very small sum.

Access to Health Services

Most displaced persons do not receive adequate health care, even if they are entitled to it under national law. The state does not have the capacity to provide adequate health care to the population, in general. But even where health services exist, bureaucratic red tape hinders most displaced persons from receiving the care they need. In addition, the displaced population is largely ignorant of what government services are available to them.

Some of the displaced have had access to pre-existing state services, like the SISBEN (a health system subsidised by the government). Others have received special attention at hospitals after being certified by the Red de Solidaridad Social.

Those who do not have access to public health care or NGO health programmes turn to local herbalists. This response is generally found in remote communities or in settlements where there is little or no government presence.

Access to Education

Theoretically, all children have the right to attend primary school in Colombia, but only a small percentage of displaced children receive a formal education. Many local schools deny access to displaced children because they do not 'belong', officially, to the municipality. Schools are often overcrowded or there is a lack of teachers, especially in rural areas, whence many teachers have fled because of the conflict. But there are practical and financial obstacles, too. Parents must provide transport, food, uniforms, pens, pencils, rulers, etc., and for most displaced, this is simply impossible.

One of the few education initiatives we heard about was located in Villavicencio. Rosendo, a displaced Afro-Colombian teacher from Chocó, started a school after his own children were refused enrolment by the local public school. He gave lectures himself and 'hired' other displaced teachers, all of whom worked the first year without a salary. Rosendo finally convinced the local municipality to pay the teachers, and the school is now accredited and providing primary education to some 250 displaced children.

Church and NGO programmes offer some training to displaced adolescents and adults with the aim of developing economic activities. Displaced persons have been trained in practical skills, such as baking, mattress making and the weaving of mosquito nets that have led to small-scale business opportunities.

SOURCES OF INCOME

According to the Consultancy on Human Rights and Displacement (CODHES), 42 per cent of displaced persons in Colombia were originally engaged in agricultural activities. Most wind up in medium to large towns and cities. Almost all the people we interviewed for this study reported they had great difficulty adjusting to urban life. Many complained that their lack of 'urban skills' made it almost impossible for them to find work.

El Rebusque

Almost none of the displaced persons we talked to had a regular income. Each family had to adhere to a variety of short-term strategies, or *rebusque*, a Colombian expression that means taking whatever opportunity comes along to earn a living. Casual paid labour, street vending and petty agriculture are among the most common strategies we found.

Paid Labour

Many displaced spend their days looking for daily or weekly work, which is almost always manual work at construction sites, market places, bus stations or at the ports.

Agricultural seasonal labour will, in many cases, offer the best pay for those who are able to obtain this kind of work. However, it usually means leaving the family alone for months at a time. In some cases, it also involves considerable risk, as this work is often situated close to the displaced person's original home where the armed elements responsible for the displacement may still be present.

Contrary to common belief, women have the greatest chance of earning an income, as the market for household-related work has not been affected by the conflict in the same way as work in the public arena has. Many displaced women and girls work as house servants or nannies. This work is not well paid, but will often lead to a steady, long-term income.

When a woman thus becomes the main breadwinner in the household, the man of the household will then have to assume traditional female responsibilities, such as raising the children, cooking and cleaning. Role reversals of this kind have had a profound impact on family relationships among the displaced.

Yet, for some women and girls, working outside the home has not led to increased independence. On the contrary, many have to stay at their employer's house for long periods at a time, often leaving their own children and family behind. Some of these women and girls also suffer abuse at the hands of their employers and are then stigmatised in their own community.

Informal Economy

Most of the people we interviewed had also earned money through petty trade. In the main streets, marketplaces or in neighbourhoods, displaced persons will offer *tinto* (tiny cups of black coffee), fruit, watches, home-made cookies, sweets or ice cream, cigarettes or toys on an informal basis.

In the poorest displaced neighbourhoods, where 'the poor are selling to the poor', as the local parish priest put it, we saw an informal trade creatively adapted to the local reality. With very little cash available among both customers and vendors, the goods were sold in tiny rations. Cooking oil, for example, was sold by the spoonful. The few families that had enough money to buy refrigerators sell ice blocks to their neighbours.

Petty Agriculture

Nearly all households with some income had invested in a few chickens or plants that would make a small contribution to the family diet. The occasional plantain, corn cob or a daily egg does not have a great impact on a family's nutrition, but it can provide an important psychological boost as a demonstration of some degree of self-reliance.

Prostitution

It is widely known that prostitution has become an important survival mechanism for many displaced women; however, it was difficult to discuss the issue with the displaced communities. Women's organisations working with displaced women confirm that prostitution is a serious and growing problem, especially in Bogotá, but also in other cities.

The women in Barrancabermeja wanted to draw attention to the grey zone between prostitution and having 'normal' boyfriends. Girls and women with no husbands to head their households look to boyfriends to provide for them. From the age of 12, girls may start looking for older men, and the sight of a 14-year-old girl with a 50-year-old man is not uncommon. The small gifts and occasional cash loans given by an older man can be the extra income a family needs. Sometimes parents push their daughters to find an older 'friend'. Not surprisingly, most of these couples are unstable. Many girls try to 'hook' a man by having his child. It is common for a displaced girl to have her first child when she, herself, is still a child, at age 14 or 15, and have another two by the time she is 18, often with different men.

CONCLUSION

Protection responses by the displaced are usually unplanned, given that it is generally an individual or a family that is reacting to an emergency. Self-protection responses are seen largely in violent areas where the armed conflict is escalating, rather than in cities. Organised responses prior to displacement take place only in regions where the armed conflict recently escalated and in which there had been some previous experience of social organisation. In areas controlled by an armed group, the community's predominant response is to submit to the group for protection.

Organised responses have, in many cases, been initiated by the church and by already existing community organisations. The lack of organised responses in some of the places studied could indicate that the community's social fabric had been rent by the conflict.

The types of responses are closely linked to the areas where the displaced originated. In rural areas and small villages, communication, information gathering and community organisation are easily accomplished. The social impact of organised responses is widely felt. Many basic needs are easily met by making use of the natural resources available. Traditional culture favours solidarity within the community.

In contrast, life in cities makes communication, the dissemination of information and organisation among the displaced more difficult. The culture of the individual is valued over that of the community, making it more difficult to get access to basic services.

That displaced populations look to the church or NGOs for assistance illustrates the inadequacy of responses offered by the government. It also indicates the confusion among peasant farmers when they find themselves in a strange, modern culture without the basic knowledge and skills required simply to access services that can help them meet their basic needs.

It would be valuable to conduct further regional studies of displaced populations to examine more closely their self-protection and self-reliance strategies and to identify the link between those responses and initiatives launched by the church and other organisations. The findings of these studies could then be the basis on which future interventions, both to prevent displacement and to assist those already displaced, are designed.

NOTES

1. There are several peace communities. The Cacarica Community 'Resistance Community' is composed of some 4,000 persons. The formation of these groups may not have been strictly self-help, since they were conceived, launched and are maintained as a joint effort of the communities, the church and national and international NGOs. The involvement of local church organisations (Diócesis de Apartadó and the Parish of Riosucio) and national organisations (Justicia y Paz and CINEP) has been particularly important. There is also little doubt that without the support of international organisations (humanitarian NGOs, Peace Brigades International, UN agencies, and diplomats) these initiatives may not have been able to survive.

2. In many municipalities, these committees have not been established, or they have had very little effect. In some places, the Committee for Displaced People is the same as the local security council, in which NGOs and displaced persons are not invited to participate.

3. Mireya Ramírez, of PCS, has worked closely both with the Montería and Barrancabermeja *ollas*. She contributed information on the history and functioning of the *ollas comunitarias*.

Europe

9
Georgia: Coping by Organising. Displaced Georgians from Abkhazia

Julia Kharashvili

Like many other countries that emerged after the break-up of the Soviet Union, Georgia experienced severe political and economic crises in the early 1990s that led to military conflicts. Fighting erupted in 1991–92 in South Ossetia (the Tskhinvali region) and in 1992–93 in Abkhazia. These conflicts have been exacerbated by the geopolitical interests of the Big Powers, the presence of oil in the region, and Georgia's location at the crossroads between East and West.

As a result of these conflicts, more than a quarter of a million people were forced to leave the territories of these regions; most of them were displaced from Abkhazia. Before the conflict, Abkhazia had a population of just over 525,000. Nearly 46 per cent of them were Georgians, 17.8 per cent Abkhazian, 14.6 per cent Armenian and 14.3 per cent Russian.

Despite intensive negotiations, no real political changes have been achieved in the region, although there is some hope for a resolution of the conflict in the Tskhinvali region (South Ossetia). Parties to the conflict and Russia have signed agreements on the return of displaced persons and refugees. The UNHCR is implementing a programme to support returnees there, and various international humanitarian organisations have launched development projects in the area. Armed forces from both sides of the conflict and representatives of the Organisation for Security and Cooperation in Europe (OSCE) are monitoring the cease-fire.

In Abkhazia, security in the Gali border district, which, prior to the war, was populated exclusively by Georgians, is intermittent, at best. The two warring sides, the Russian Federation and UNHCR agreed to a cease-fire, separation of forces and voluntary return of the displaced in 1994 and just over 300 people returned to their homes. But within a short time, all were forced to leave again, some were killed, and implementation of the accord was suspended. The

Map 9   Georgia

return of displaced persons to other districts in Abkhazia, such as Sukhumi, Gagra, Gudauta and Ochamchire, was not even discussed, as the returnees' security could not be guaranteed.

BACKGROUND

Georgia announced its independence in early 1990, before the collapse of the Soviet Union. Almost immediately after, tensions arose in areas populated by different ethnic groups. Nationalist ambitions, the fledgling government's lack of experience, economic and social uncertainties following the announcement of independence and separation from the Soviet Union, and the Kremlin's policy of 'punishing' the newly independent state all fuelled already existing enmities among different ethnic and political groups. Armed conflict escalated to full-scale war. Thousands were killed, hundreds of thousands were exiled and Abkhazia lost most of its population.

The Gali district is one of the richest agricultural regions in Georgia and was home to the largest number of ethnic Georgians in

Abkhazia. Since most of the population worked the land, the displaced from that area wanted to return under any circumstances, even despite numerous killings of civilians there. (Although the UN Observer Mission (UNOMIG) and peacekeeping forces from the Commonwealth of Independent States (CIS) monitor the security situation, they cannot guarantee total protection.) Since 1995, many displaced Georgians have returned to the Gali district spontaneously. Accordingly, the UNHCR office in Georgia has supported rehabilitation programmes in Gali through which schools and hospitals were rebuilt and returnees were given assistance to rebuild their houses. By April 1996, some 25,000–30,000 people were regularly crossing the Inguri river to work on their lands, trade and rebuild their homes in Gali (UN Report of the Secretary-General S/1996/284).

A process of normalisation, begun in 1997, was disrupted after fierce fighting broke out in Gali in May 1998. A second wave of displacement followed, in which some 40,000 people fled Gali, many of them for the second time, and headed for the Zugdidi region of Georgia. After they left Gali, their property, much of it rebuilt with assistance from UNHCR, was burned and their villages looted. In Zugdidi, the new influx of displaced persons led to a severe deterioration of the area's social and economic infrastructure, which was already strained to accommodate the displaced who had settled there earlier.

In 1999, Abkhazian authorities announced that they would accept the return of displaced persons who were residents of the Gali district. Some decided to return, at least temporarily, because of the poor conditions in the communal centres in Zugdidi. Many cross the 'border' along the Inguri river several times a month to tend their land in Gali, then return to Zugdidi. There are no economic investments in Gali, and international agencies and NGOs run no significant projects in the district because of the security threat.

The Georgian government kept intact the Georgian segment of the Abkhazian government that existed before the war and transplanted it to the territory of Georgia proper. Later, the Supreme Council of Abkhazia, composed of Georgian legislators elected before the war, was rebuilt in Georgia proper. As a result, three political powers are involved in resolving disputes between Abkhazians and Georgians: the central government of Georgia, the *de facto* Abkhazian authorities in Abkhazia and the exiled Georgian government from Abkhazia (the Autonomous Republic (AR) of Abkhazia Council of Ministers).

Despite the absence of more than half the population, elections were held in Abkhazia in 1996 and 1999 and a new parliament was elected. The Abkhazian parliament adopted a Constitution and declared Abkhazia an independent state, but the international community has not recognised its independence. To date, there have been no significant moves towards resolving the conflict and no improvement in conditions to encourage a mass return of the displaced.

METHODOLOGY

The data in this chapter were taken from published sources or collected by the author and her colleagues from interviews with displaced persons, humanitarian and government actors and colleagues.

Information was also culled from several past surveys. The 1994 study, 'IDPs in Georgia', was funded by the NRC and involved some 2,000 displaced persons living across Georgia. 'Psychosocial Examination of IDP Children and Women – Victims of Military Conflict on the Territory of the Republic of Georgia', a survey funded by OXFAM and conducted in 1995, involved some 650 displaced persons, mainly women, in four regions (Tbilisi, Gardabani, Borjomi, Mtskheta). The latest study, 'Current problems of IDP Women', was conducted in 2000 by the 'Sukhumi' foundation and the IDP Women's Association and was funded by the Dutch foundation, NOVIB, through the Interchurch Peace Council and the Institute of Democracy in Eastern Europe (IDEE) in Washington. One thousand women in Tbilisi, Zugdidi, Batumi, Kutaisi and Telavi were questioned for this survey. The respondents were selected through registration lists provided by the Ministry of Refugees and Accommodation of Georgia.

INITIAL DISPLACEMENT AND INITIAL RESPONSES

The first groups of displaced persons began arriving in Georgia proper in August/September 1992, mostly from the Gudauta region of Abkhazia and also from Sukhumi. They represented about 6.5 per cent of the total displaced population. Twice as many people fled Abkhazia during a second wave of displacement in October 1992, after the Abkhaz attack on Gagra, the second largest city in Abkhazia. More than 67 per cent of those who fled Abkhazia did so by crossing the Swaneti mountains on foot during September and October 1993. The remainder were forced to flee Abkhazia during late 1993–94.

The displaced urgently needed help with locating and reuniting family members, accommodation, basic food and medical care, medical assistance for those who were wounded during the fighting, and access to water and other facilities in communal centres. The Georgian government organised the first assistance programme for the displaced, providing financial allowances for displaced individuals (in 2000, this amounted to GEL12 for those displaced living on their own, GEL11 for displaced persons living in communal centres who did not receive bread, and GEL4.5 for displaced persons living in communal centres who received a daily bread ration (one US dollar equals approximately GEL2)). Those displaced persons who had no relatives living in Georgia were provided accommodation in public buildings.

The International Federation of the Red Cross and Red Crescent Societies (IFRC), UNHCR and several international NGOs quickly launched humanitarian assistance programmes for the displaced. Humanitarian assistance was distributed from special sites selected by the government. Assistance mostly consisted of food parcels, blankets, second-hand clothes and hygiene kits. Groups of volunteers among the local community collected used goods, such as clothes and medicines, food and milk for children, and donated them to people at the communal centres.

Footwear was especially in short supply: sometimes there were only one or two pairs of shoes per collective centre for distributing among all the residents. In a small village in the Racha-Lechkhumi region, a displaced woman who had been a handicrafts teacher in school before the war taught all the women in the communal centre to knit very thick socks that people could wear in dry weather as shoes. Because of her initiative, everyone living in the communal centre there could go outside in some degree of comfort.

Most displaced persons were first able to stay with relatives, generally in the western part of Georgia and in the capital or in communal centres. With the assistance of the Ministry of Refugees and Accommodation, some displaced persons found temporary refuge in hotels and hostels or in abandoned houses. People who were accommodated with relatives, friends and in other private living arrangements received humanitarian assistance if they registered with local authorities. The displaced living in communal centres also received humanitarian assistance and additional aid from other agencies.

Profile of the Displaced Population

Most of the displaced persons in internal Georgia are of Georgian background. People of other ethnic origins, especially Abkhaz, are usually of mixed ethnic backgrounds.

Almost all displaced persons in Georgia have Georgian citizenship. Some are also documented as Russian nationals, even though the Georgian government prohibits dual citizenship. Possession of a Russian passport allows many of the displaced to work in Russia and remit money back to their families in Georgia. In December 2000, the Russian government introduced a visa requirement for Georgian citizens, which means Georgians who want to travel to Russia must obtain permission from the Russian Embassy prior to travelling. This has made life much more difficult for those who were temporarily working in Russia.

Table 9.1   Ethnic composition of the displaced population in Georgia

Place of origin	Jewish	Ukrainian	Greek	Abkhaz	Armenian	Russian	Georgian
Tskhinvali region	52	7	1	0	67	28	9,072
Sukhumi	17	85	44	62	101	403	54,066
Sukhumi district	1	17	17	10	19	59	19,465
Gagra	3	17	5	8	38	146	25,409
Gudauta	1	4	2	3	9	18	6,747
Ochamchire	2	726	16	84	57	158	38,357
Tkvarcheli		6	2	17	8	31	3,464
Gali		26	18	21	31	147	82,845
Gullripshi	3	40	22	27	52	138	34,478

Source: UNDP (1998a).

There is a wide discrepancy, even within government surveys, of the number of displaced persons living in communal centres and those living in private accommodation during the mid-1990s. The differences in data can be partly attributed to the movement of displaced persons out of family accommodation and into the collective centres. Also, many displaced persons registered as both residents in private housing and in collective centres so they could receive more assistance.

MIGRATION AMONG THE DISPLACED

After displaced persons had settled in internal regions of Georgia, they tried to improve their circumstances by changing their living arrangements, usually moving from a communal centre to private accommodation or vice versa. People moved because of a lack of facilities, lack of space, problems with host families and/or the desire to move to another town or village. Some men who could not find jobs in Georgia migrated temporarily to Russia and other countries of the CIS. As a result, communal centres are mainly populated by women, children, the elderly and the disabled.

In the early years of the displacement, people generally moved from villages to towns, from western Georgia to Tbilisi and, within Tbilisi, from private accommodation into communal centres. Later, the reverse occurred: some residents of the Gali district who first settled in Tbilisi moved to western Georgia, particularly to Samegrelo, where they would be closer to their home villages. These moves often shadowed those of the international agencies and NGOs providing assistance to the displaced. From 1993 to 1997, most of these organisations worked from the capital; since 1998, most programmes have been implemented in the western region of Georgia.

Lack of facilities is one of the most common problems for displaced persons living in communal centres and in private accommodation. The displaced were settled in hotels, hostels, sanatoriums, schools, kindergartens, hospitals and shops. However, even those who were given comfortable accommodations in hotels had no kitchens and generally used electric or kerosene stoves. Dwindling supplies of electricity led to unregulated cutting of trees, and within a short time, some entire districts became deforested.

Shelters built for the displaced in 1998 did not meet minimum safety and hygienic standards and now require urgent repair. In some communal centres, inhabitants built cooking and sanitation facilities themselves, often violating fire and sanitary regulations in the process. Many villages have neither a sewerage system nor clean water. As a result, infectious illnesses spread quickly, as happened in Zugdidi in the spring of 1999 when a typhus epidemic broke out.

Until 1999, few displaced communities launched initiatives to improve the infrastructures in the areas in which they were living. Since then, several international NGOs, including IRC, OXFAM,

United Methodist Churches Relief Agency and Care and Counterpart International, have developed Community Participation Programmes through which the displaced and local communities together identify and then work to solve their most pressing problems. Projects are funded both from external and local sources, and most of the work is done by members of the displaced and the local communities. This process is generally more effective in rural communities, where displaced and local populations live together and where the displaced have access to land and community services.

PARALLEL STRUCTURES OF GOVERNANCE

After the Georgian population fled Abkhazia in the autumn of 1993, they restored the Georgian segment of executive power from Abkhazia to create a virtual government-in-exile with the intent of making it easier for people to trace relatives, find accommodations, benefit from humanitarian assistance and otherwise cope with their displacement. Each ministry or department of the central Georgian government allowed its counterpart from the AR of Abkhazia to use its facilities to register staff who had worked before the war for the same organisation in Abkhazia.

By retaining these structures of government, some of the displaced were able to continue to work, not just in the government bureaucracy, but also as teachers, doctors and other specialists. For example, the exiled Ministry of Public Health provided the displaced population with qualified medical assistance and distributed medicines among the most vulnerable persons. The creation of two polyclinics for the displaced in Tbilisi and several others in other areas, including Zugdidi and Kutaisi, allowed the disabled, newborn, pregnant women and elderly among the displaced population to be registered for special assistance. Although these polyclinics are not well equipped, they do have qualified professional personnel on staff.

Administrative structures from Abkhazia were also revived, so a displaced person who lost identity documents during flight could apply for new documents to the municipality of his/her city in exile. The displaced also have their own military commissariat, tax authority, police force and many other institutions and agencies.

The Supreme Council, which was the highest legislative body in the AR of Abkhazia before the war, was reconstructed in 1995 following a decision by the Georgian Parliament. According to an election law adopted shortly before the war, the Abkhazian minority in Abkhazia had a special quota for representation in the Supreme

Council. Representing 17.8 per cent of Abkhazia, they had 28 seats in the Supreme Council; Georgians, who represented 45.6 per cent of the population, held 26 seats. Eleven more deputies represented Abkhazia's other ethnic communities. The reconstructed Supreme Council consists of 24 deputies.

Both the Abkhazian Council of Ministers and the Supreme Council of the AR of Abkhazia in exile say they represent the displaced in Georgia, and the official Georgian government recognises them as representatives of the displaced community. Yet both bodies maintain a radical position regarding the conflict-resolution process, a position that is not shared by a large part of the displaced community. The government-in-exile's hard-line stance on Abkhazia has been an obstacle to many peace initiatives developed in Georgia proper and by the displaced population itself.

ACCESS TO INFORMATION

For populations psychologically shocked by the consequences of military conflict, access to information can be a route to recovery. Yet, from the earliest surveys, displaced persons complained of a lack of information and said they were often confused, and sometimes even further traumatised, by the deliberately false or misleading information they were given.

Since 1994, the exiled Abkhazian Radio and TV Company has been broadcasting to the displaced population several times a month in both Georgian and Russian languages. Since the company is controlled by the Supreme Council of the AR of Abkhazia, its coverage of both the displaced communities and events in the wider environment is highly politicised. However, the broadcasts, which include news, announcements of interest to displaced communities, and reminders of important dates and events connected with Abkhazia, help connect the displaced communities and maintain a sense of unity.

The newsletter *Apkhazetis Khma* (*Voice of Abkhazia*) is produced each week as an official newsletter of the government-in-exile and is distributed in Tbilisi and in regions of western Georgia. Each of the regions-in-exile – Sukhumi, Gagra, Ochamchire and Gali districts – tries to produce its own newsletter. Some eight newsletters and three magazines are published within the displaced communities; however, due to lack of funds, they do not appear regularly.

Several NGOs working with displaced persons and refugees also publish periodic newsletters and pamphlets. During the early years of displacement, the NGO Foundation of Development of Human Resources published a newsletter entitled *Psychological Consultation*, which was distributed free of charge in communal centres. The newsletter was intended to help the displaced overcome feelings of isolation in remote collective centres and help begin the process of rehabilitation.

A special magazine for war-affected children, *White Crane*, is published under the auspices of the United Nations Volunteers (UNV) and distributed free of charge in all displaced communities and in war-affected areas since 1995. The magazine aims to unite children from divided societies, promote mutual understanding and cooperation, give children the opportunity to express their feelings of loss and displacement, and provide informal education for children who cannot attend school or who did not receive appropriate formal education. The magazine reaches 11,000 children each month; and each month, thousands of young readers send letters, stories, poems and drawings to the magazine. Because the magazine's editor is, herself, displaced, the content genuinely reflects the problems, traumas and hopes of the children to whom the magazine is devoted.

During the last two years, several broadcasts targeting the displaced population were established. The Khroniconi radio station, for example, provides information to those displaced persons living in communal centres in the Zugdidi district.

INCOME-GENERATING ACTIVITIES

The unemployment rate in Georgia is 14.8 per cent; among the displaced population, the rate is much higher. Among those surveyed for this chapter, 31 per cent of family breadwinners are women and 19 per cent are men. Of the families interviewed 7 per cent receive income from other family members, most of them living outside the country, and 14 per cent of the families live on the government's allowance, only. (The government allowance is GEL12, or US$6, per month, which is rarely paid regularly.)

Wherever they are living, the displaced try to make use of any available land nearby. A teacher, his wife, who was a nurse, and their child had fled Sukhumi and were sheltered in Republic Children's hospital in a suburb of Tbilisi along with more than 50 other displaced families. The child had been seriously wounded during the war and was receiving treatment for his wounds at the hospital. After they heard Georgian President Eduard Shevardnadze declare that displaced persons were allowed to use free lands for family profit, the parents began to cultivate lands around the hospital. Within a few years, the parents had developed a small kitchen garden that provided the family with fresh fruits and vegetables. Such small plots are now at risk of disappearing as businessmen in Tbilisi try to privatise all lands.

Access to land is often dependent on the willingness of the local administration to help the displaced and lease them some land. Some of those without access to land have devised other ways to earn income through small-scale trade. In 1993–94, there was a bread shortage throughout Georgia. Consumers had to queue for bread for sometimes as long as eight to ten hours. Some displaced persons living in communal centres began selling part of their daily bread rations to local consumers. Although displaced women still engage in this trade, the practice is not as widespread, nor as lucrative, as it was during the height of the bread shortage. Now, displaced women sell cigarettes, nuts and other popular items.

Others in communal centres have benefited from income-generation projects run by organisations like OXFAM UK, International Rescue Committee (IRC), the NRC and other international NGOs. In several communal centres in Tbilisi, OXFAM UK developed an income-generation project through which women were given wool for knitting and were paid modest sums for the knitwear they produced. NRC developed a sewing project through which women received sewing machines and produced bedding. Later, the sewing machines were given to the displaced women. Women in the communal centres appreciated these types of programmes because they guaranteed a small, though constant, income and allowed women to earn money without leaving their families. But it was clear that these types of programmes were useful only as a short-term means of obtaining a minimal income.

Retraining for Greater Opportunities

By 1995, many displaced persons realised that they needed to improve their skills and their education so they would be able to compete for jobs. Data from surveys showed that although most women were highly educated (more than 45 per cent had university degrees; only 3 per cent had not completed secondary school), displaced women were not successful in competing for jobs in their professions. For many of them, their feelings of inferiority as displaced persons was an enormous psychological barrier against finding appropriate work or starting out in a new field. 'Adaptation schools', the brainchild of a group of displaced women, were set up to help displaced persons – mainly, but not exclusively, women – acquire the skills and knowledge needed to improve their lives. These schools were developed by the IDP Women's Association in Tbilisi in 1999 and, later, by the association Women and Business and the Women's Council from Abkhazia (in exile).

The curricula of these adaptation schools vary from school to school according to existing human resources and the needs of particular communities. But in addition to whatever educational programmes are offered, 'students' also have access to psycho-social counselling designed to help them overcome their lack of self-confidence and sense of hopelessness about the future.

The adaptation schools are based on the premise that displaced persons need more than short-term employment projects; they need to be able to plan for their futures, and that includes finding long-term employment. To that end, the displaced are taught how to research the needs of the job market, whether for goods or ideas, and learn new skills to enhance their own marketability. Courses offered in the schools include marketing, accounting, business management, law (related to small businesses and the rights of the displaced), tax legislation, computer skills and foreign languages.

Foreign language courses have been found to be particularly useful to professional urban women who have become displaced. In addition to promoting self-confidence and communication with others, foreign language lessons also represent an investment in the future.

Similarly, the IRC set up a system of 'business incubators' throughout western Georgia. Through these programmes, displaced and local community groups and individuals are given office space and supplies and free Internet access. In parallel, qualified programme staffs offer vocational training both for women and men from local and IDPs communities. The business incubators were set up in Zugdidi and Kutaisi, and in the central cities of Samegrelo and Imereti. Participants in the programme pay a modest sum for the services provided.

In addition, vocational training is provided for women who would like to learn handicrafts, cooking or modelling. Men can learn driving, electrical skills, car repair and other skilled and semi-skilled jobs.

The Importance of Micro-Credits

Of those women interviewed in various surveys, more than 86 per cent expressed a desire to start their own small businesses. An overwhelming majority of these women said they needed micro-credits and basic business training to do so.

Large-scale micro-credit programmes, targeted at both individuals and groups, were introduced in Georgia in 1998. While individual recipients of the loans clearly benefit, so far there is no indication that the community, as a whole, reaps any particular advantage from the small-scale businesses that are created out of the micro-credit scheme.

But in communities that are remote from centres for the displaced and that receive less attention and assistance from the government and NGOs, women have been organising communal agricultural businesses. Under this scheme, the group asks for credit that will be guaranteed by the community. Each member of the group has a stake in and a responsibility to the communal business. By pooling their resources, displaced individuals avoid the problem of not having any collateral against which a loan can be drawn.

Members of the displaced community in Khoni wanted to develop agricultural activities, but lacked the funds to do so. When the Danish Refugee Council (DRC) came to the centre offering small credits that required no collateral, many women decided to start small-scale farming ventures. From the credit they received, they bought cows and began producing *matsoni*, a type of yogurt that is very popular in Georgia. Within a short time, the women paid back the loan to the DRC and started making enough profits to be able to sustain themselves and their business.

With funding from the Haella Foundation of the Netherlands, the IDP Women's Association purchased pigs and gave them to a group of women living in the Rukhi Racetrack communal centre in the Zugdidi district. Profits earned from the sale of piglets were given to another group of women in the same community so they could start their own small-scale business. Other profits earned from the pigs were distributed among the members of the group.

Informal Trade

In the Zugdidi region of Georgia, most of the displaced are from the Gali and Ochamchire districts of Abkhazia. Some of the displaced managed to bring some livestock with them when they fled, but they were unable to move their farming activities to the Zugdidi region, since the soil there is not as fertile as it is in Gali. Indeed, some of the displaced prefer to go back to their villages in the Gali district to tend and harvest their crops there, in spite of the dangers involved in doing so.

Many families who lived in the Gali district owned their own nut plantations. During the annual nut harvesting period in September and October, thousands of displaced women cross the Inguri river to and from the Gali district to collect nuts from their plots in Gali and bring them to Zugdidi to sell. The women are willing to run the great risk of being robbed *en route* because the sale of nuts is their only guaranteed income for the winter. Indeed, it is one of the main sources of income for the displaced population in the area bordering Abkhazia.

Madonna S., from the Gali district, sells cheese in the Zugdidi market. She is the only breadwinner in her family. She received a small loan to broaden her business and invested in nuts. Then, she borrowed money from a sister living in Russia and bought citrus fruits in Abkhazia to sell on the Abkhaz-Russian border. For a small bribe, Russian peacekeepers and local soldiers at checkpoints allow women to cross the *de facto* border between Georgia proper and Abkhazia. Many former inhabitants of the Gali district are registered both in Gali, as local inhabitants, and in Zugdidi, as displaced persons, allowing them to travel through Abkhazia to pursue these kinds of small business ventures.

Beginning in November, groups of displaced women travel to and from Abkhazia to bring citrus fruits grown in Abkhazia out to interior areas of Georgia. The inhabitants of Abkhazia support this trade because most of them are not permitted to cross the border into Russia, and during the citrus harvest, Abkhazian women who want to sell their produce in Russia have to wait long hours at checkpoints manned by Russian peacekeepers. This small-scale, cross-border trade in nuts and citrus fruits has proven more beneficial to communities on both sides of the Abkhaz-Georgian 'border' than any attempt at diplomacy has been to date.

EDUCATION

More than 30 per cent of the total displaced population are children. A small number of children in communal centres do not attend school, largely because their parents cannot afford the cost of transportation, clothes and school materials, especially textbooks. Some parents said their children could not attend school because they were malnourished.

The number of children who do not attend schools varies from region to region. In Tbilisi, 2–3 per cent of displaced children cannot attend school, while in some villages of the Zugdidi district, 10–15 per cent of children do not attend classes during winter.

In Tbilisi, eastern Georgia and in the Imereti regions, most displaced children attend local schools, although some special schools and kindergartens have been established exclusively for displaced children. In the Zugdidi district, a large number of displaced children attend special classes that have been set up for them within local school buildings, held during different hours to the classes for local children. All the teachers in these schools for the displaced are themselves displaced.

The exiled Ministry of Education of the AR of Abkhazia supports the concept of a separate education system for the displaced. The schools set up for displaced children are less expensive than the local schools. Although primary education is free in Georgia, there are usually some incidental expenses involved, such as monthly donations to so-called 'class funds' and 'school funds'. In higher grades, parents have to pay for their children's education but displaced children can attend school for free. In the schools for displaced children, there are no extra expenses. The ministry also believes it is easier, psychologically, for displaced children to be among other displaced children than to be among local children. In some cases, the differences in income between displaced and local families can be a source of resentment and frustration for displaced parents and children alike. In addition, separate schools provide employment for about 1,500 displaced teachers.

Yet, while separate schools unify the displaced community and foster the desire to return to their homes, they also hinder adaptation to and integration into the local community. The quality of education in these special schools is often much lower than that in regular schools and the conditions worse.

University-age students have access to the Sukhumi branch of Tbilisi State University, the Sukhumi Institute of Subtropical Agriculture and the Sukhumi Institute, which were opened in exile. Some 11,000 displaced students can choose from a range of 22 courses; many of the lecturers are also displaced persons. More than 300 displaced lecturers and scientists work in the Sukhumi branch of

Tbilisi State University. The Student Union, created by displaced students, supports activities centred around peace-building, democratisation and reconciliation.

TREATING THE PSYCHOLOGICAL WOUNDS OF DISPLACEMENT

Children

Studies on how war affects children show that some 83 per cent of displaced children demonstrate signs of post-traumatic stress. Those severely traumatised during the military actions in 1992 and 1993 had no access to the kinds of psycho-social programmes that were launched just a few years later.

Immediately after the escalation of violence in Gali in 1998, the IDP Women's Association conducted an assessment of the psychological effects of war and displacement on displaced children. As a result of the assessment, the United Nations, including UN Volunteers and UNHCR, NRC and four other NGOs began a large-scale psycho-social assistance project for traumatised children in western Georgia. The programme included psychological games and art therapy for groups of children, individual consultations, and rehabilitation camps for displaced and local children. Project staff also focused on training local volunteers. Many of the children displaced from the Gali district of Abkhazia suffered displacement more than once in their young lives. For them, urgent assistance was needed to mitigate the trauma of war and displacement and to help them adapt to a new community. Most pre-school children from Gali spoke only Mingrelian, making it even more difficult for them to integrate into the local communities in Georgia.

At about the same time, UNICEF in Georgia set up the Helping Children in Distress programme, which included special training for teachers who work with traumatised children. Twenty psychologists and specialists were trained in psycho-rehabilitation; they, in turn, went on to train others in different regions throughout Georgia.

The Association Abkhazeti, which was founded by a group of young, highly educated displaced persons in Kutaisi, in the Imereti region, opened a rehabilitative Sunday school for children in 1996. The success of that programme encouraged the Association to become involved in other projects, including programmes that offered micro-credits to displaced persons who wanted to start their own businesses. The head of the organisation attended training courses abroad and became one of the nation's best trainers in micro-credit activities, fundraising and organisational development. Since it was founded, the Association Abkhazeti has become one of the most effective NGOs in the country.

Women

Despite the fact that many women now have the dual responsibility of raising a family and earning the family's income, women have adapted much better to their new situation than have displaced men. For most men, life in displacement means unemployment and a constant longing to return to their original homes in Abkhazia and Tskhinvali regions. The displaced community, in general, welcomes development programmes, but displaced women, in particular, seem most appreciative of these efforts.

Women living outside communal centres but in urban areas usually lack support for any entrepreneurial activities they may want to pursue and also lack the social network essential for adapting to their new surroundings. Women in their forties and fifties also suffer from low self-esteem. Before they were displaced, many of them had occupied fairly high positions in society. The change in their social status was a painful, humiliating blow.

In the absence of rehabilitation centres targeted to meet these women's needs, various NGOs and displaced women created mobile groups of social workers who travel through urban and rural areas to identify and assist these displaced women. Psychologists meet informally, often over coffee, with groups of displaced women to discuss their problems. Through role-playing, training and self-help activities, trust is established and the rehabilitation process begins.

Community Helpers

Members of the mobile counselling units also train helpers within the communities. When large-scale fighting erupted in 1998, NGOs well versed in treating trauma victims trained a large number of local volunteers from the Zugdidi region in psycho-social support activities. The volunteers all spoke Mingrelian, the local language that is also spoken in the Gali district, which was particularly useful when working with children who had just been displaced. Later, these volunteers created self-help groups within the displaced communities. In these groups, adolescents worked with groups of

Photo 5   An internally displaced person from Abkhazia selling medicines in a Tbilisi market, Georgia (UNHCR, A. Hollmann 1999)

children. The programme helped the younger children recover from trauma and gave a sense of value and confidence to the adolescents in the communities.

Medico C., who lives in Odishi village in the Zugdidi region, was trained as a community worker as part of OXFAM's community mobilisation programme. After some time, Medico, who studied at the university and has a small child, created a small kindergarten with a group of friends. The kindergarten became accredited by the state, which agreed to cover the cost of food for the children, but not teachers' salaries. Medico is now looking for support from private organisations so teachers can be paid and the kindergarten can remain open.

Community-based helpers also serve as liaisons between the displaced community and local authorities. This role is particularly important during the first stages of displacement, when the displaced do not understand either the local power structures or the local infrastructure. Helpers, social workers, or staffs of the mobile assistance units explain how to use local transportation and how to gain access to other services, such as health care and education.

When helpers start working in a new city or region, they visit the local administration and explain their work with the displaced population. By building good contacts with representatives of the local administration, the helpers make it easier for the informal leaders of the displaced communities to ask for assistance from the local authorities.

Displaced persons cannot participate in local elections and have no representation in municipal government. This has led to a situation in some places, including Tskhaltubo, Orsantia and Shamgona, where the majority population, which now happens to be composed of displaced persons, cannot participate in local decision-making processes. In Zugdidi town, which has the highest concentration of displaced persons in Georgia, a local NGO, Atinati, and the IDP Women's Association brought together representatives of the displaced community and the local administration. During several seminars, participants brainstormed about how best to involve the displaced community in decisions that may affect them. As a result of these sessions, a special commission was established, composed of members of both communities, to ensure that displaced persons have a voice in local affairs.

THE 'NEW APPROACH' INITIATIVE

The 'new approach' is a common initiative announced by the UNDP, UNOCHA, the UNHCR, the World Bank and the government of Georgia that aims to ensure equal rights and participation for displaced persons. One of the principal aims of the initiative is to identify successful strategies that can be easily replicated and can make a real difference in the quality of life among the displaced. The implementation of the initiative, which will include improved housing, broader income-generating activities and greater access to social services and education, began in 2001.

More than 260 organisations and individuals have already applied for grants ranging from US$25,000 to US$100,000 under the new initiative. Many new NGOs, associations and unions were formed by groups who decided to apply for grants together. Seventeen new NGOs, created by displaced persons, formed a common league to advocate for participation in the 'new approach'.

Pilot projects will be funded through the Georgian Self-Reliance Fund, which was established with support from key donors including the World Bank, the USAID, the UNHCR, the UNDP and the Swiss Agency for Development. The projects proposed include the development of farming and agricultural cooperatives, new housing for the displaced, credit unions and training in computers, business skills and handicrafts. Displaced persons proposed most of the programmes with the intent of developing new skills and new opportunities within the community. Indeed, the 'new approach' requires that NGOs participate not only as beneficiaries, but also as equal partners in choosing and monitoring the projects.

DISPLACED PERSONS IN THE BUSINESS AND CIVIL SECTORS

The 'new approach' initiative encouraged existing displaced business organisations and enterprises to apply for grants to develop and broaden their projects. In Kutaisi, the company Orgtechnique, one of the biggest enterprises created by displaced persons, employs up to a hundred displaced persons. The company mainly produces tea, cigarettes and stationery. It decided to widen its activities and to employ more people who will work on the re-cultivation of abandoned tea plantations in the Imereti region of western Georgia. It also plans to hire more displaced persons to produce prefabricated houses. Those houses will provide accommodation and land for the displaced now living in communal centres. Such initiatives, supported by the Self-Reliance Fund in Georgia, serve as models for replication in other districts of Georgia.

The process of self-organisation among displaced persons, both at the community level and in the form of NGOs, is another collective strategy for coping with displacement. Over the past decade, Georgia's civil sector has developed rapidly. This process began much later in the displaced community. The CIS Conference in Geneva has helped NGOs founded by displaced persons become constructive partners with the government of Georgia and effective advocates for IDP rights. More experienced NGOs helped fledgling organisations to develop. The Women and Business association, together with the exiled Women's Council from Abkhazia, designed a project that provides education and employment for displaced women living in communal centres. The Foundation of IDP Women 'Sukhumi', from Kutaisi, offers education to women's groups in the Imereti region. The Assist Yourself association published a booklet with useful information for displaced persons.

CONCLUSION

The displaced in Georgia demonstrate a wide range of response strategies on both the individual and community levels and to address short- and long-term problems. For instance, double registration and dual citizenship helped many people to survive during the emergency period. Learning to cooperate with local authorities has helped displaced NGOs and businessmen become more successful over the long term.

Some of the most vulnerable among the displaced, such as women, children, ex-combatants and disabled persons, developed their own strategies for adaptation and development. Women built small businesses and learned new skills with the aim of restoring normalcy to their families' lives.

Displaced children require the most and the most constant attention. Though there are rehabilitation programmes for children, including kindergartens, Sunday schools, rehabilitation and peace camps, clubs and even magazines created especially for them, children still suffer from the trauma of war and displacement and have difficulties integrating into their new surroundings.

During displacement, two motivations for activities predominated: keeping the community whole within Georgia in the hope of returning, as a community, to their homes; and allowing some opportunity for at least temporary integration into the local communities.

The displaced community has been able to protect its identity by:

- maintaining structures from Abkhazia, such as separate schools and other separate social services provided through the government-in-exile
- keeping communities together, especially in communal centres throughout Georgia
- maintaining a system of higher education.

During the initial phase of displacement, the government-in-exile and the Supreme Council of the AR of Abkhazia played a more positive role, giving the displaced community a voice in the central government. Over time, the displaced community became better organised and spoke for itself through civic activists, NGOs and community groups. Although displaced persons still do not have the right to participate in municipal and parliamentary elections, they can now more effectively advocate their rights and equal participation.

Initiatives like the 'new approach' are intended to help displaced persons survive both as members of a distinct community and as individuals among the local population.

Clearly the most effective response strategy for this displaced population is organising. Women organise groups and associations for mutual psycho-social support and to acquire micro-credits that can lead to the development of small businesses. NGOs are organising coalitions to participate successfully in different grants competitions. By creating their own associations for self-help and devising their own activities, the displaced have both empowered themselves and have demanded – and won – the attention of other NGOs, the international community and the Georgian government.

ACKNOWLEDGEMENTS

I would like to thank everyone who contributed to this survey: the IDP Women's Association (M. Pochkhua and L. Beria) and Foundation 'Sukhumi' (A. Gamakharia and M. Gelashvili), which shared material from recent surveys; Brian Keane (UNOCHA, Georgia) and Gigi Bregadze (UNHCR, Georgia) for constructive comments; representatives of the Ministry of Accommodation and Resettlement;

and representatives of NGOs and international agencies and organisations. My special thanks go to all the respondents who shared their stories and allowed me to publish them.

10
Yugoslavia: Displacement from Kosovo. From Patronage to Self-Help

Vladimir Ilic

Following NATO's military actions, displacement from Kosovo is generally associated with the forced migration of non-Albanian peoples that occurred in June 1999. But people have been migrating from Kosovo for decades; and that fact has had a profound influence on how and where the most recent displaced persons establish themselves after flight.

Although many of the ethnic Serbs who fled Kosovo for Serbia are willing to go back to Kosovo, and believe that will be possible in the future, most of them prepared for years, in some cases decades, to leave as part of a forced migration. They saved money, tried to create a network of connections among the local authorities, and bought houses, flats and/or land in central Serbia. As many as 4,073 persons from Kosovo moved to the town of Kragujevac in one five-year period (1976–81) (Helsinki Committee 2000:119). Inter-ethnic tension in Kosovo was the reason many Kosovo Serbs planned parallel strategies for surviving. In this way, they were unlike the refugees from Croatia and Bosnia, who were not prepared for migrating, but similar to the ethnic Albanians who lived in central Serbia and Vojvodina until the NATO bombing and who were also prepared for the possibility of forced migration.

Slavic Muslims and Roma also fled Kosovo. Most of the former migrated to parts of Serbia that were predominantly Muslim, namely, Montenegro and Sandzak. They are not part of this case study. The latter generally live in worse conditions than the displaced Serbs, but most of them do not want to return to Kosovo. In most cases, neither they nor their host families receive any financial support from outside sources.

BACKGROUND

For the past 125 years, the province of Kosovo has been the setting for serious inter-ethnic conflicts, caused mainly by a lack of

Map by András Bereznay

Map 10   Yugoslavia

economic development and overpopulation. Fighting flared dramatically during the periods when Kosovo was ruled by Turkey, the Kingdom of Serbia, and the Kingdom of Yugoslavia, and throughout the Italian occupation during the Second World War and the first years of communist rule in Yugoslavia. The conflict was exacerbated by the agrarian reforms of the 1920s, when privately owned land was mostly divided among settlers from Serbia only, and not among ethnic Albanians. A far higher birth rate among the Albanians than among the Serbs resulted in a greater demand for land and changed the ethnic profile of the province. In the latter half of the twentieth century, an increase in the number of desirable posts in the state administration and public services led to uncontrolled competition between the two ethnic groups. Forced migrations occurred periodically throughout the past century. Albanians were expelled to Turkey in the 1930s and Serbs were expelled to Serbia during the Italian occupation in 1941–42.

The communist government of Yugoslavia managed to control the conflict after the Albanians rebelled violently in 1944–45. The government tried to modernise the society by embracing a programme of agrarian reform, guaranteed ethnic equality, new employment in industry and public services, women's emancipation and greater social mobility. The Yugoslav federation invested in the economic and social modernisation of Kosovo by financing its economic development, education and health-care system. Apart from demonstrations by Albanian students in 1968, no obvious conflicts erupted until 1981.

But the modernisation drive created new structural grounds for ethnic conflict. Better health care meant fewer children died and a greater number were born. Serbs had represented one-third of Kosovo's population in 1931; by 1991, they represented only 11 per cent of the population. Broad autonomy for Kosovo produced many desirable new posts and sinecures in the provincial administration, which turned into a new source of competition between the two ethnic groups.

Some 80,000 ethnic Serbs left the economically underdeveloped province between 1961 and 1981. They settled in homogeneous enclaves in the suburbs of large towns in central Serbia, such as Kragujevac, Kraljevo, Nis and Smederevo. These sites became the destinations of large numbers of displaced persons during 1999.

In 1989, Belgrade set severe limits on Kosovo's autonomy. Troops were sent into the province to quell the ethnic Albanians' violent reaction to the measures. One year later, autonomy was suspended. Throughout the early 1990s, Kosovo was completely dominated by the regime in Belgrade. When Yugoslavia disintegrated, Kosovo Albanians asked for independence; the government replied by repressing them. While desirable posts in the provincial administration were given to Serbs, Albanians built parallel structures to meet their needs in governance, education and health security, and created a network of informal economic activities.

But this form of peaceful resistance ended by the close of the decade. In 1998, Kosovo was rent by brutal conflicts between the Serbian government and the ethnic Albanian Kosovo Liberation Army (KLA). The violence led to NATO's intervention and the bombing of Serbia and, simultaneously, to the forced migration of hundreds of thousands of Albanians, mostly to Macedonia and Albania, in the spring of 1999.

Since the Serbian capitulation in June 1999, Kosovo has been governed by the UN and occupied by forces led by NATO. The return of refugees brought new violence, this time targeted at non-Albanians, that is, Serbs, Roma and Slovenian Muslims. Provoked by fears of violence and destruction of property at the hands of the Albanians, some 210,000–220,000 persons left Kosovo and moved to other parts of Serbia and to Montenegro during this period. According to the UNHCR, some 190,000 settled in central Serbia and Vojvodina and over 30,000 settled in Montenegro (UNHCR 2000). About 19,000 refugees from Serbia and Bosnia can be added to this number of displaced. They had lived in Kosovo since the mid-1990s as part of the Belgrade regime's effort to alter the ethnic structure of the province. Many of these refugees left Kosovo in mid-1998 when armed conflict between government forces and the KLA broke out. Others waited to leave until the beginning of the NATO bombing on 24 March 1999. Most of the displaced population left Kosovo in June 1999.

Despite the threat of Albanian vengeance and the fear that the civil administration and the UN would not be able to guarantee their safety, some non-Albanians still live in enclaves in Kosovo. One, controlled by Serbs, is located in north-eastern Kosovo, around Kosovska Mitrovica, one is in the south-east of the province (Kosovsko Pomoravlje, around Gnjilane), and there are several isolated enclaves in central Kosovo, the largest of which contains, at most, 5,000 ethnic Serbs. In other parts of Kosovo, a few dozen or only a few elderly people remain. They are afraid to leave their houses for fear of being killed, and would die of starvation without assistance from humanitarian organisations.

Displaced Serbs

During the past decade, Kosovo was a paradise for the Serbs known as *kuferasi* who, because of their lack of skills, could not compete economically in Serbia but who were eager to earn money, property and political power. Many of these Serbs, and others who arrived in Kosovo after its autonomy was suspended, made a fortune in an environment marked by ethnic segregation, repression and corruption. Many administration and public services staff led a double life, staying in Kosovo during the workweek and spending weekends with their families in their homes in Serbia. These people regarded Kosovo only as a place to get rich, and they were ready to leave long before the Yugoslav army withdrew from the province.

Other non-Albanians had also known for years that change in Kosovo was inevitable. They prepared to leave well before the armed conflicts began by building houses and buying land in Serbia, sending their children to schools outside Kosovo, and building a network of connections in Serbian towns.

Displaced Roma

Although not the focus of this chapter some comments are required on the Roma. According to the UNHCR, the ethnic profile of the displaced population is approximately 76 per cent Serbs. The 19,500 Roma make up approxiamtely 11 per cent (UNHCR/Commissioner for Refugees of the Republic of Serbia 2001). The latter figure is undoubtedly an underestimate, since there is a strong tendency among Roma in all the Balkan countries to declare themselves as members of other ethnic groups, given the widespread prejudice against Roma throughout the region. Since they believe they will not be welcome in Serbia, Roma often try to immigrate illegally to the countries of the European Union.

Roma were poor and ready to do the 'dirty' jobs when the government in Belgrade controlled Kosovo. Even before the NATO bombardment, Kosovo Albanians considered Roma to be collaborators and traitors because they worked for Serbia's public services. When the UN peacekeepers (KFOR) entered Kosovo, the Albanians said that Roma had the job of removing any traces of mass killings claimed to have been perpetrated by the Serbian forces in Kosovo.

The status of Roma is far lower than that of any other ethnic minority in Kosovo, and among the displaced population, as well.

Most of the Roma living among the displaced population are sheltered in their own enclaves in illegally built settlements in central Serbia, particularly in Vojvodina. Since the Roma families who offered them lodging are often not registered as residents themselves the displaced Roma from Kosovo cannot demand the documentation from the authorities that could ensure at least minimal assistance from the state. The Roma's irregular status means they can only receive assistance from some foreign humanitarian agencies; otherwise, they are on their own. Their survival strategies are limited by the poverty of the Roma who accepted them and by the tensions and conflict within the Roma communities.

According to the Committee for the Protection of Roma's Human Rights, Roma living in camps in Kragujevac often have to squeeze as many as 20 people into a four-square-metre room and sleep on concrete floors (*Return* 1999). During winter 1999–2000, Roma babies died of cold and hunger (Domonji 2000). Those Roma living in the suburbs of Veliki, Mali Bedem, Dudara and Deponija rely on each other and on the assistance provided by humanitarian organisations.

The largest number of displaced Roma ended up in Vojvodina, in the northernmost section of the country. Central Serbia was not a real option for the Roma since local populations there were hostile towards displaced persons from Kosovo, in general, and towards displaced Roma, in particular. Vojvodina was attractive because it is relatively wealthier than the rest of the country, and because there were numerous Roma communities, composed of previous settlers from Kosovo, already entrenched there.

The Roma's language and religious heterogeneity makes it difficult for them to adjust to their new surroundings. In the slums in Zrenjanin and Kikinda, the newly displaced Roma are supported by Roma who had fled from Kosovo earlier. Members of the latter group are Muslim and speak Albanian. For years, these Roma have competed with native Roma, who speak Serbian and are Orthodox, for jobs in the city sanitation department or as gravediggers at the cemetery. This conflict among Roma intensified as the newcomers arrived from Kosovo. With more job-seekers around, wages fell.

In the northern city of Subotica, the situation is even more complicated. There had already been some tension between the Catholic Roma, who speak Hungarian, and the Orthodox Roma, who speak Serbian. A large group of Muslim Roma, who speak

Albanian, exacerbated the friction by trying to engage in illegal trade near the Hungarian border. Before long, the previously antagonistic native Roma groups discovered they had a common enemy: the newly arrived Albanian-speaking Roma.

AN ECONOMY IN COLLAPSE

Serbia is in a state of total economic collapse, with average monthly salaries at US$40 and with an unemployment rate of 30 per cent. A week's worth of food for a family can cost four to five times the average monthly salary. The health-care system, stretched to breaking point, suffered another blow in the summer of 2000, when the Serbian Ministry of Health adopted measured that forbade patients from buying medicines in private drugstores. Hospitals carry out only urgent surgery. There is a constant shortage of gasoline; and public transport is unreliable, at best. Electricity is in short supply, since the electric power system was partially destroyed during the NATO bombing; and the government has no money with which to buy gas from Russia, which a large part of the population uses for heating. The government's policy of supporting low prices on basic foodstuffs, such as bread, milk, meat, flour and cooking oil, has led to permanent shortages of these items. Independent researchers in Belgrade say that almost half the population is involved in some kind of illegal economic activity (Centre for the Study of Alternatives 2000).

RESEARCH METHODOLOGY

The main intent of the research was to reveal the real heterogeneity of this population under its apparent homogeneity. Observations were conducted not only in the parts of central Serbia where the majority of displaced persons is concentrated, such as Krusevac and Smederevo, but also in Vojvodina (in the areas around Novi Sad, Subotica, Zrenjanin and Kikinda) and in the suburbs of Belgrade (Borca, Kaludjerica, Veliki i Mali Zbeg, Deponija).

In addition to collecting first-hand material, I used data from different humanitarian organisations, Serbian organisations for human rights and for refugees and displaced persons, such as the Helsinki Committee of Serbia and the Humanitarian Centre for Integration and Tolerance, specialised newspapers for refugees and displaced persons, and earlier research data about migrations from Kosovo. The use of these resources served not only to bolster my own findings, but to verify the authenticity of the oral statements given by the displaced with whom I spoke. This was necessary because displaced individuals are not only afraid and embittered, they are also insecure and often do not make any distinction between research done for NGOs, such as the NRC, and surveys conducted by the state. In many cases, I could not reassure potential respondents that they would suffer no ill consequences by participating in this study.

Since the vast majority of displaced persons had anticipated migrating from Kosovo and had prepared for that eventuality by setting up private accommodations in Serbia, the study focuses on the displaced persons who found refuge in private houses rather than in collective centres. Most of these people headed for central Serbia because the whole of south Serbia was perceived to be threatened by the growth and spread of the Albanian population.

Research Problems

A person who lives in a refugee hut in Mirijevo or in a homogeneous settlement of displaced persons in the suburbs of Kraljevo or Kragujevac sees a researcher as someone who will not be of any practical use. Rather, as a compatriot and an associate of NGOs, the researcher is regarded as responsible for the displaced person's departure from Kosovo. At the same time, those who made a fortune during, or otherwise participated in, the ethnic discrimination of Albanians in Kosovo do not want to give any information for obvious reasons.

Thus, the primary research problem was not in interpreting the data, but in eliciting information from people who were suspicious of the researcher. Tension between the Serbs from central Serbia and the displaced Serbs from Kosovo made the task that much more difficult. The latter were convinced that they were betrayed by the former simply because the 'native' Serbs wanted to save themselves from more NATO bombing.

EARLY MONTHS OF DISPLACEMENT

Migration from Kosovo following the NATO action was spontaneous and chaotic: a convoy of private cars and tractors, military and official state vehicles that quit the province at the same time. Serbian authorities tried to keep some people in Kosovo by not permitting their vehicles to enter Belgrade and northern Serbia and by insisting on issuing documents to those who wanted to register in other towns. To local Serbs, the Kosovo Serbs were privileged, perhaps guilty of causing the bombing because they were staunch supporters of Slobodan Milosevic, and fundamentally different. The population of central Serbia saw in the displaced population a great opportunity to make money: the displaced were charged 50 per cent more for gasoline for their convoys than the local population were charged.

Less than 20 per cent of the displaced population from Kosovo found shelter in collective centres in Serbia; the vast majority stayed in private dwellings with relatives or friends. Anticipating the imminent crisis, some Serb families in Kosovo tried to move their children and elderly to central Serbia in 1998. The state resisted by refusing to allow Kosovo-based children to attend schools in Serbia. But by spring 1999, schools in Kosovo had closed because of the NATO bombing and most of the non-working, non-Albanian population moved in with previously displaced Serbs in central Serbia. When the mass migrations began in the second part of June 1999, those who had to stay behind for military duty or work already had a support system in place in Serbia.

Some displaced persons returned to Kosovo during July and August 1999 to try to fetch any property they could bring with them to Serbia. Others tried to make arrangements with their Albanian neighbours to protect and/or sell their property. These visits were limited to the eastern half of Kosovo, as western Kosovo, known as Metohija, was considered too dangerous for non-Albanians.

A MODIFIED CULTURE IN A NEW ENVIRONMENT

The Serbs who had arrived in Kosovo after autonomy was suspended benefited from a system of patronage through which they obtained choice jobs and lodgings. Their patrons were the eminent members of the Socialist Party of Serbia, members of the provincial committee and municipal committees, who also worked for periods as high-level officials in private companies. Thus, their influence spanned many spheres of life.

After migration, the networks of patronage that had been developed over the previous ten years began to unravel, since the heads of rival Serb factions in Kosovo also left the province. Although abandoned by their patrons, the displaced Kosovo Serbs tried to maintain a sense of homeland and neighbourhood while settled in camps and private lodgings during their first months in Serbia. In 2000, this sense of community gradually began to fade, too, as families started moving in search of work or places in which to build homes. People who participated in this study said that those who moved lost their connections with their former neighbours. Solidarity among the displaced from Kosovo, they said, would not last.

Changes have occurred within the displaced family unit, as well. Kosovo Serbs were far more patriarchal than those Serbs living in Serbia. Adult males dominated women and children, and families led an insular life, partially because of the risk of physical assault by Albanians. Although the local populations in Serbia have not been particularly welcoming to the displaced Serbs now living among them, the displaced from Kosovo no longer fear for their lives. Female and younger members of families move around more freely, though they still seem to adhere to the strict morality with which they were raised.

Among those who have settled in collective lodgings, most of the young males left after only a few weeks or months to look for jobs in other cities and towns, often in the suburbs of Belgrade. Their departure was regarded as temporary by the rest of their families and, in most cases regular contact was maintained between those who left and those who stayed behind in the collective shelters. However, wives and elderly family members are suspicious about how much money those who left for the cities are earning and how they spend the money. Wives left behind in central Serbia while their husbands stay in Belgrade to work do not fear that their husbands will leave them and their families; family connections are strong. But there is some fear that the husbands will neglect their families and spend money and time with other women in some kind of parallel life.

Temporarily displaced persons living in the Belgrade suburbs usually remain unregistered, since the authorities had not wanted them to settle in Belgrade, and earn their living almost exclusively through illegal activities (trading in gasoline, foodstuffs and foreign currency) or by manual labour as unregistered workers. This temporary arrangement means that elder family members, both in collective centres and in private lodgings, are now being supported by the young: a complete reversal of the patriarchal system in which they grew up.

PROBLEMS AND RESPONSE STRATEGIES

Unlike earlier refugees who arrived in Serbia from Croatia and Bosnia, the displaced from Kosovo have fewer problems in obtaining identity documents, since they are citizens of Yugoslavia, and can therefore exercise their rights to education and health care. Yet since they had to flee quickly, many have no papers; and there has been no official contact with Kosovo. The Serbian National Council of Kosovo tries to organise temporary returns of displaced persons so they can reclaim their documents, but travelling in Kosovo is not safe. In addition, authorities have determined that persons who left Kosovo after 1 April 2000 cannot obtain identity documents, refugee IDs or any humanitarian assistance (the Red Cross will not give them monthly food rations or hygienic packages, nor can they have free medical check-ups).

Those without valid documents must go to Belgrade to resolve their problem with the Committee for Refugees (Komarevic 2000). But the displaced in need of documentation do not go to Belgrade before consulting with people in their families and their home communities. These people then contact someone influential among the displaced population in Serbia to try and get assistance in solving their problem. These 'connections' are members of the former sub-elite and elite in Kosovo, including ex-ministers. The highest echelons of Kosovo Serbs (leading officials of the Socialist Party of Serbia in Kosovo) mostly live in Belgrade and do not normally communicate with their displaced compatriots. Others of lesser rank can inform them of the circumstances of the displaced population, but they do not assist ordinary displaced persons in any way.

Constraints on Self-Help

Given the state of Serbia's economy, displaced persons find it difficult to support themselves through the legal market. Though many have tried, nearly all have failed.

Some displaced persons in Kragujevac and Kraljevo tried to earn money by distilling brandy. Since the price of fruit was high, the producers used sugar to stretch the fruit during production. The result tasted bad, but everyone – both the displaced population and the local population – could afford it. When more people started producing the brandy, a shortage of sugar developed on the legal market. The price of sugar on the black market became so high, it became unprofitable to distil the brandy. The distillers did not blame the government for the sugar shortage; rather, they blamed the local black-marketeers who, they felt, were taking advantage of the situation to make a profit.

January 2000 was a cold month and there were periodic restrictions on the use of electricity throughout the country. One family of Kosovo Serbs in Kraljevo decided to invest money in candle moulds, wicks and paraffin to make candles. They calculated that the candles could be sold for a competitive price with a considerable profit. The main advantage of this business was that it could be done at home and all four adult members of the family could work. A large amount of the family savings was used to buy the paraffin on the black market in one of the suburbs of Belgrade. At some expense, the head of the family travelled to Belgrade to buy the materials. When he arrived, the seller, a black-marketeer from Belgrade, raised the price they had previously agreed to in a telephone conversation. The seller reckoned that the buyer would not go back to Kraljevo empty-handed. But the buyer refused to buy at the higher price. Three times the buyer travelled to Belgrade and three times he returned home empty-handed, refusing to pay the higher price. The fourth time, the buyer relented and paid the higher price, unhappily, and brought the material back to Kraljevo. He and his family started making candles the next day.

Two days later, before he sold his first batch of candles, the temperature rose, the restrictions on electricity use were lifted and the demand for candles plummeted. The family was eventually forced to sell its stock of paraffin to a local buyer at great financial loss.

The Illegal Economy

Some of the wealthier displaced persons retained business connections in illegal trade with northern Kosovo, then controlled by the people close to the Milosevic government in Belgrade. In that part of Kosovo, there is freedom of movement, an established link with the central Serbia, connections with Albanian traders from central Kosovo, and no taxes. Merchandise from Serbia moves freely to Kosovo. Although most of the profit from this trading went to representatives of the Milosevic regime (Nojkic 2000), some displaced persons were still able to make a living this way.

Poorer displaced persons who lodged with relatives and friends first made their living by selling black market cigarettes. Often, local black-marketeers hired the displaced to work as their 'retail dealers'. But within months, the displaced abandoned the trade as tensions developed between the displaced traders and the local black-marketeers. The displaced now mainly work in the illegal food trade with Montenegro. But the lack of capital and unreliable railways make transport of perishable items, like citrus fruits and meats, difficult, if not impossible.

The Legal Economy

The poorest group of displaced persons cannot earn an independent income because there is little demand for their labour and because they are not involved in the patronage network of homeland clans.

A large number of displaced persons are peasants who now have no land to tend. Although those displaced persons from Kosovo who arrived earlier complain that there are not enough agricultural labourers around, the newly arrived are not hired to work the fields. The elderly among them are not regarded as productive labourers; many of them suffer depression and are not inclined to search for work. The younger family members prefer illegal trading or physical work in the cities, rather than working on the land, primarily because of opportunities to find additional work in the cities. The displaced who arrived from Kosovo earlier also generally grow cereals and crops such as corn, sunflowers and sugar beets, which require fewer labourers than other crops.

The local population and the displaced population also have different work ethics. Fewer displaced persons are prepared to do extremely low-paid, menial work than are the poorest among the local population. But it is also clear that displaced persons are brutally exploited in both the legal and illegal sectors of the Serbian economy. A displaced person, hired as a waiter in a privately owned restaurant, will often be paid only half of what a local resident would be paid.

Well-educated displaced persons often cannot compete for good jobs in Serbia. The University of Pristina has always had a reputation for lower standards of teaching and examining than the other universities in Serbia. Because of this, the professionals among the displaced population are unlikely to get work in the private sector and are probably not prepared to look for it. In addition, there are many women with university degrees who have had no work experience. Female participants in the study explained that they were housewives because there had been no need for them to work in Kosovo.

TENSION BETWEEN THE DISPLACED AND LOCAL COMMUNITIES

In values and culture, the Kosovo Serbs have more in common with Kosovo Albanians than with Serbs from central Serbia and Vojvodina. This fact has made displacement in Serbia a bleak experience for Kosovo Serbs. After fleeing the threat of physical violence in Kosovo, the displaced were greeted with coldness by the local Serb communities and were exploited by private employers and landlords. To the local population, the Kosovo Serbs enjoyed a privileged life during the past decade, since some of them became wealthy on a system of ethnic segregation and abuse. This attitude, betraying more than a little jealousy, is no doubt fuelled by the new competition for jobs and resources (Helsinki Committee 2000:166). In Kraljevo, for example, some 20,000 displaced persons settled in a town with a population of less than 100,000.

Local Serbs have complained that a great number of displaced individuals living in private accommodations who are capable of working, do not look for jobs. They also claim that housewives of displaced Serbs rarely cook, but serve re-heated food or that adult males sleep all day. There was no way to confirm from the study whether these behaviours were true and the consequences of the trauma of forced displacement or simply a continuation of the way the newly displaced lived before migrating.

The animosity between the two communities, and even between different strata of the displaced, is mutual. A migrant from Pristina said: 'I can hardly wait to go back home. The authorities in Serbia have had benefits, there was everything, and our people who come from down there with a lot of money, they aren't clean. Many of them have made a fortune in a dishonest way' (Helsinki Committee 2000:155). Researchers found that an overwhelming 72 per cent of respondents in Kragujevac are not satisfied with the treatment they receive in Serbia. Those with a positive attitude towards their treatment in Serbia are generally those who own property outside of Kosovo (Helsinki Committee 2000:160).

PROPERTY ISSUES

In 1989, the government issued a law declaring that any real estate transactions had to be approved by the state. Many displaced persons now living in Serbia want to sell their houses and possessions in Kosovo to Albanians there, but this is considered a national betrayal by the population of Serbia and many of the Serbs from Kosovo, as well. In August 2000, the Serbian Ministry of Finance issued a decree annulling all real estate deals made since KFOR arrived. To comply with the decree, displaced persons would have to return the money they received from Albanian buyers. But for the vast majority of the displaced population, returning to or selling their property is not an option: Albanians have either already taken possession of or destroyed their holdings.

THE POSSIBILITY OF RETURNING

There is practically no chance that displaced persons will return to Kosovo in the near future. According to the International Helsinki Federation, when Serbian forces withdrew, about 250,000 persons fled, leaving behind more than 1,000 others who were murdered and more than 100 destroyed Orthodox churches and monasteries. Life in the Serbian enclaves that remain is extremely insecure. People seek constant protection from the UN Mission in Kosovo (UNMIK), as all basic human rights, including the fundamental right to live, are violated. Serbs must endure insults, physical violence, stoning and attempted murder when they try to leave their homes. Basic medical care is provided for Serbian inhabitants in the enclaves; but if someone is seriously ill, he/she must risk a dangerous journey to a large medical centre. The unemployment rate in Kosovo is almost 100 per cent; only those employed in education and medical services work. The legal system does not function: crimes against members of ethnic minorities are not prosecuted (International Helsinki Federation 2000; UNHCR 2000).

According to a poll conducted by the Helsinki Committee of Serbia in two settlements of displaced Roma (one near Novi Sad and the other near Belgrade), out of the 164 persons questioned, only 1 per cent said they would go back to Kosovo unconditionally; half would not return under any circumstances. Displaced Roma are apparently less tolerant than displaced Serbs: when asked about their attitude towards a multi-ethnic Kosovo, 87 per cent of them said they would agree to live only among Serbs (Helsinki Committee 2000:164).

Regardless of the fact that many displaced persons had prepared to leave Kosovo, most would gladly return home, but only under certain conditions. According to a poll conducted by the Helsinki Committee in Kragujevac among 205 displaced Serbs, 89 per cent would like to return to Kosovo, but 62 per cent of them emphasised they would only return if the Serbian army and police returned, too. Of the respondents 75 per cent expressed their distrust of KFOR; while 62 per cent said that peace would only be achieved in Kosovo if the Serbian army and police return. Forty-nine per cent of the respondents said flatly that a multi-ethnic Kosovo is an impossibility.

CONCLUSION

The primary problems of the displaced persons living in Serbia are shelter, poverty and unemployment. Displaced persons want to live in homogeneous settlements and, as a result, prices of real estate in central Serbia are higher than in other parts of the country. Difficulties in obtaining permission to build are sometimes eased with the help of relatives or influential individuals. But as time goes by, the strength of the connections between the displaced in Serbia and any remaining contacts in Kosovo diminishes. Those displaced will have to find other ways to cope in their new surroundings than through the system of patronage to which they had grown accustomed in Kosovo.

The problem of unemployment is less about the work ethics of the Kosovo Serbs than it is about the collapse of the Serbian economy. Competition with the local population in the labour market is a source of animosity between the local and the displaced communities. To a greater or lesser extent, too, the Kosovo Serbs, who had depended on the patronage system both when they lived in Kosovo and in the early months after their migration, retain the attitude that they will receive assistance from others. They are, as a result, less inclined to develop self-help strategies.

Although confronted with an uncertain and insecure future, many of the displaced from Kosovo believe they will one day return to Kosovo under the protection of the Yugoslav army and police. This belief provides a great deal of psychological comfort. But it is a hope not shared by Roma, who do not want to go back to Kosovo, even though they live in far worse conditions in Serbia than most of the rest of the displaced population there.

11
Conclusion
Birgitte Refslund Sorensen and Marc Vincent

Researching and understanding the role of response strategies adopted by victims of forced displacement is an emerging priority for the humanitarian community. Although social anthropologists have been studying the effects of conflict on individuals and communities for years, it has only been recently that the humanitarian community has devoted serious attention to the issue of how internally displaced persons cope with their changed circumstances. Humanitarians are developing an appreciation that, beyond the imperative to help, there is a need to find the most appropriate way to help in a rapidly changing and complex environment.

While research into the responses of local communities is gaining momentum, understanding the responses of people forcibly displaced requires more than additional resources and research: it also requires *a change of attitude*. It would be easy, for example, to look at the results of this study and fall into a humanitarian logic that emphasises the logistics of delivering aid over understanding the more complicated issues of short- and long-term social impact. Continuing along this path, it may be argued that there were no real surprises from what many humanitarian field workers would intuitively guess to be the responses of individuals, families and communities to forced displacement. First, one seeks safety; then, one finds food and shelter; then, if not displaced again, one starts trying to rebuild one's social life. Eventually, one may even adapt to the new reality. That intuition, though, is only a fraction of the story.

In recent international discussions on internal displacement held in New York and Geneva, there has been a tendency to perceive the internally displaced only as victims of displacement and targets of humanitarian assistance. In other words, we look through a one-dimensional lens and see the displaced at one point in time, in only one context, rather than as rounded human beings with various histories, ambitions and resources. And as the Angola and Sri Lanka chapters remind us, there are several axes of identity aside from being displaced, and these all influence the impact of displacement as well as the response strategies devised by individuals. We must see and understand the response to displacement because, without putting an overly positive spin on what is still a traumatic upheaval, the variety, ingenuity, and persistence that is portrayed in these case studies must be recognised and appreciated. Once we have agreed to change our lens, then the next priority is to see how the humanitarian community can contribute to existing mechanisms without upsetting the delicate balance and making things worse.

This research has identified the gaps in our understanding rather than providing answers to all our questions. The subject matter is so vast, with so many different variables, that conclusions are all but premature. Instead, we would like to begin to identify what may more accurately be called 'interesting revelations'.

PREPARATION FOR DISPLACEMENT

Focusing on security and protection strategies has allowed us to observe something, which turns the humanitarian perception of internally displaced persons as helpless victims on its head. The degree of preparation among some of the internally displaced prior to displacement came as something of a surprise.

In many cases, awareness of the probability of displacement and the degree of preparation appeared to be dependent on prior experience. In some cases, such as in Kosovo, Serbs prepared for flight as long as a decade before they left their homes by purchasing property and sending their children to school in Serbia, an indication of an early and perceptive risk assessment. In most other cases, the awareness that displacement will take place and the necessity of preparing for it indicated the steep learning curve among the internally displaced. Comments from Burundi illustrate that those who survived the first instance of flight had better chances of surviving subsequent displacements because they were better able to identify the risks and develop contingency plans.

An important aspect of preparing for displacement was the identification of essential supplies to take along. In Burma, potential victims prepared for departure by packing important possessions each night and pre-positioning food supplies along escape routes. In the Sudan, preparation for the next stage of displacement was so routine that the displaced regularly dismantled parts of their own homes, before the bulldozers completed the job, so they could re-use the valuable building materials at their next settlement. Preparedness and risk assessment was also reflected in changing attitudes towards goods and belongings, where mobile assets and personal skills became increasingly appreciated after the first experience of losing everything.

Another area of preparation revealed in the studies is the importance of knowing which route to take to avoid hostilities and to obtain protection and support. As the studies of Angola, Sri Lanka and Colombia demonstrate, information regarding safe routes and havens are obtained from a variety of sources, including self-organised civic groups, informal networks based on kinship, community or ethnic identity and the authorities. Decisions regarding the timing of flight were equally important, as these would partly determine access to relief, labour and other resources at the destination.

The chapters on the Sudan and Burundi also emphasise the importance of information networks among the displaced and potentially displaced. In the Sudan, information was clearly a strategic tool important enough, according to the authors, for families to gain access to the police and security forces so they could increase the warning period. In Burundi, the internally displaced recognised that their survivability increased after multiple displacements because their information networks improved.

When displacement occurred regularly or was of a cyclical nature, information networks and early action were extremely well developed. This was the case in Colombia, where the potentially displaced relied on both traditional warning systems, such as cattle horns, or on more sophisticated hidden messages in radio programmes to warn others of the presence of armed actors. Those at risk of displacement also had predetermined safe havens.

What does the early preparation tell us? First, it shows that situation analyses and risk assessments are ongoing activities among most populations living in a conflict environment and that such analyses are used to prepare the best possible response to whatever may arise. Second, it demonstrates that the level of analysis and preparation can influence the effects of displacement and the degree of dependency that a displaced person or group may experience or, to put it positively, the level of self-reliance and control they may exert over their own lives.

Although these strategies often mitigated the impact of displacement and increased the survivability of the displaced, they were not always successful. As the authors of the Colombia chapter point out, despite well-organised preparation and planning, many individuals abandon the attempt to avoid or localise displacement and choose greater security and anonymity in urban centres, instead.

THE CENTRAL ROLE OF FAMILY, COMMUNITY AND OTHER NETWORKS

The ability to rely on existing social structures, such as the family, the village, the community or other extended social networks, was of paramount importance to the displaced.

While it is intuitive that the *family* and the immediate social network would be the main pillar of response, evidence shows that the nature of the support was as varied as its success was mixed. Among its positive functions, the family often provided an intimate structure that supported individuals in situations where prevalent cultural and social norms had to be transgressed to make ends meet. In many cases, the family appeared to be the only sphere in which displaced individuals could find trust, safety and support. In addition, the family often served as an economic unit, though not the only one, in which different family members exploited their individual skills and particular opportunities to improve the family's overall circumstances.

But the family is not unaffected by conflict. In some cases, displaced families suffered severe strains, either as a result of the changing roles of some of its members or due to restricted access to resources, which, in turn, limited their ability to assist displaced members of the family or to continue functioning as a social unit.

Sometimes, the wider community was able to act together to support its members. The support varied from providing moral support, as in Sri Lanka where great importance was placed on having all previous members of a village live together again, to economic support, where previous self-help mechanisms were revived to support the most marginalised and vulnerable. In the Sudan, the group provided defence against 'outside threats' and developed more organised assistance, such as communal funds, to the benefit of all its members.

The cases examined in Uganda, Sri Lanka and Burundi all point to a remarkable cultural and social resilience and continuity despite years of upheaval. However, subtle changes to social structures and cultural practices also seemed more pronounced. In some cases, these changes were the result of mixing with other communities. For example, in Angola, the authority of the *soba* remained unchallenged if the village stuck together after escape and during their

Photo 6   Large numbers of Sri Lankan civilians have been repeatedly displaced by the ongoing conflict (UNHCR, M. Kobayashi 1999)

temporary settlement. But if the displaced found shelter in a host community the traditional authority of the *soba* was diminished as the host community's own *soba* assumed responsibility. The subtle changes that resulted from contact with other value systems also, however, had positive effects, as in Sri Lanka, where intermingling with the Sinhalese host community led to a realisation among the displaced of the value of education.

Changes to social institutions and practices were not only a consequence of encounters with different groups; they also resulted from the necessary adjustments to new socio-economic conditions. The most severe strains on social structures seemed to be within the context of the family. Displacement involved substantial changes in gender roles and responsibilities. Several authors noted that men seemed to suffer more from losing their homes and employment because that loss had direct consequences on their sense of identity and dignity. The strains were reflected in men's destructive behaviour, ranging from growing alcohol abuse to direct challenges to women's increased role as breadwinners. For women, displacement prompted a range of emotions, from despair as to how they would be able to provide for their family, to enthusiasm about their newly won freedom and new opportunities, to frustration about the new burdens they must shoulder and the continuing obstacles erected by the surrounding society.

Changes in marriage structures and dowry systems, which partly reflected the wider changes in economic structures and access to capital, also affected families. The changes in marriage patterns not only corresponded to transformations in gender relations, but also, and perhaps more important, they were indicative of a shift in the roles, responsibilities and relationships between generations. The studies in Sri Lanka, Uganda and Burundi reported an increase in the number of child marriages. When parents could no longer afford to make a financial contribution to their children's marriage, their influence in decisions regarding partners was sometimes reduced and, likewise, the young couple tended to concentrate more on their own household than on the extended family. Yet other parents took a keen interest in their children's marriages, as it could provide their way out of poverty and a life as 'displaced', assuming they could find a suitable partner for their child.

The changing and sometimes precarious role of the youngest members of society was also illustrated in the many reports on children and youths involved in prostitution, crime or who provided cheap labour.

The revision of intergenerational relations was also clear in the context of local authority structures, where the young generation, and women, assumed growing responsibilities and influence. As the material from Sri Lanka shows, the presence of humanitarian organisations, with their emphasis on capacity-building projects, sometimes directly influenced this process, as those youths with better communication skills were more suitable mediators between the community and external agencies. In a few cases, the youths' new role was appreciated as it promised greater support for the community. But in many others, their new role was perceived as undermining traditional social structures and caused anxiety and tensions.

There was also evidence of new alliances that were outside traditional structures and that, in some cases, actually crossed existing conflict lines. In Georgia, for example, the non-displaced Abkhaz depended to a certain extent on displaced Georgians to provide access to a market for the nut and citrus trade. Illegal trading or sanctions-busting by the Serbs also proved that commercial networks sometimes have stronger resilience than political allegiance.

Several of the cases pointed to the importance of other networks, such as those for business or trade. These networks were used to protect the assets of people while displaced, but made their most significant contribution during the early re-establishment phase, when they enabled displaced persons to resume their economic activities by giving access to economic markets and credits, and provided them with an alternative to relief assistance. On the negative side, such networks also sometimes excluded certain groups of displaced people from getting access to markets and employment, and maintained other forms of exploitation, such as low pay and over-pricing goods, which was evident in Uganda and Kosovo.

In some cases, governance structures were kept almost intact, but not without some adaptation. In Georgia, the complete transfer of national infrastructure from Abkhazia is quite astounding, even when tempered with the understanding that the Georgian government has a clear political motivation for maintaining 'a government in exile'. Nevertheless, the government, health and education infrastructure proved durable and important as the skeleton upon which response mechanisms were built. A similar pattern can be discerned in Sri Lanka, where, in most instances, the religious Mosque institution continued to play a central leadership role during the different phases of flight, 'exile' and return. In fact, the successes of a displaced community appear to be closely linked to the availability of effective and accountable community organisations and leadership.

Another interesting lesson learned from the examination of community initiatives and networks was that while it is common to see internally displaced populations as highly localised groups, their response strategies revealed that they think and act locally, regionally, nationally and sometimes even internationally.

THE IMPORTANCE OF EDUCATION

Because it is often viewed as a step towards an improved future, most displaced populations considered education important. Access to education for many of the displaced who came from rural areas was already limited prior to displacement. In some cases, the displaced based their decision on where to seek safety according to the availability of education for their young. Most displaced were also willing to accept adverse conditions or family separation to provide their children access to education. When education was not available, displaced groups often organised classes themselves, keenly aware that each month that went by without schooling would adversely affect their children's future.

The importance of education reinforces one of the main themes of the study: that the internally displaced are not limited in ambition. They struggle, as everyone else, to take advantage of new opportunities. The value placed on education also illustrates the willingness of the displaced to learn new skills. It is important to recognise, however, that the general interest expressed in education is fuelled by several factors. In many cases, it appeared that women were most prepared to take advantage of the chance to learn new skills. This may reflect their past marginalisation regarding access to education, a general awareness of the need for better education to meet their new responsibilities, or a more determined wish to change their social role and position. In Georgia's 'adaptive schools', the opportunity to develop new skills to improve income was almost formalised.

On the other hand, the value placed on education demonstrated a shift in the priorities of the youth and the corresponding concern among adults about the loss of other skills, such as farming skills, which would have been valuable for return. The apparent choice of

Sudanese youth to stay in urban settings rather than return to their previous roles shows how traditional social structures are threatened by displacement.

CULTURE AS AN INFLUENTIAL FACTOR

We were also interested in learning whether the displaced had similar reactions to their situation, regardless of their cultural backgrounds, or whether their responses were designed according to pre-existing cultural norms and practices. Not surprisingly, there were no decisive answers; reactions showed a combination of the two. Most case studies suggested there was little choice: people did what they had to do based on what was available. Admittedly, the focus of the study was on 'what' the displaced were doing rather than 'why' they were doing it. Nevertheless, the prominence of social networks as the only alternative, non-institutional support structure meant that culture did, indeed, figure prominently in responses to displacement.

Moreover, it was evident that while the activities showed a remarkable consistency from case to case, their particular meaning and wider social consequences differed. It was also clear that no matter where they were, the displaced try to make sense of their experiences. In Burma, for example, the author describes the Karen as being almost resigned to displacement, regarding it as part of their social history. In Sri Lanka, many of the displaced Muslims suffered because they could not understand why they were forced to leave their homes. The studies in Burundi and Uganda, on the other hand, demonstrated how religion provided a useful interpretive framework and set of practices that helped people to come to terms with their experiences and to reintroduce a certain level of normalcy in their lives.

The author of the chapter on Afghanistan begins with the assertion that ethnic bonds, traditional ties and social networks defined responses. Groups organised into kin-based structures responded differently to groups that live in semi-feudal, land-based networks, partly because of real differences in their attachment to land and the nature of social networks, and partly because of the different meanings attached to sedentary life and mobility. Several of the studies examined how economic activities were judged both from an economic and a moral perspective, where issues of appropriateness were high on the agenda. While all displaced groups prioritised economic security, such security could not be isolated from wider concerns about dignity and redeveloping a social identity, as these were often threatened by displacement. In the end, it became clear that responses to displacement are culturally influenced.

By looking at who makes the decisions concerning response strategies, we approach the same question from a slightly different perspective. In most cases, traditional leaders, who are often the guardians and interpreters of culture, decided when to leave and where to go. This was certainly true of Burma, Afghanistan, Angola and Uganda. Even in economically more developed societies, such as Georgia and Serbia, decisions seemed to be more of a group process than individual choices. This would appear to support the assertion that responses to displacement are more determined or framed by culture and social structure than they are by an individual experience of displacement.

Finally, some of the cases revealed that perceptions of the local political culture also influenced responses. When the displaced believed that the government or the surrounding society should offer assistance to them, they hesitated to take the initiative in meeting their own needs. To assume such responsibilities was understood to be unjust and, in a sense, to undermine the political and social structures of society.

ALARMING PATTERNS

The aim of this publication was to document the many and creative ways in which displaced people try to make the best of their situation and, by doing so, to assert themselves. This conclusion has tried to summarise these activities and efforts and so, we hope, contribute new and positive insights. However, as has already been pointed out, most response strategies entail many trade-offs and their impact is not always positive. One of the circumstances likely to affect internally displaced populations and the development of post-conflict communities is the drastic restructuring and reconfiguration of society.

Another is the rural-to-urban movement of many internally displaced people. While almost all the case studies presented here stressed that people who had been displaced from a rural area tried to maintain a link to their lands, many eventually ended up in urban or semi-urban areas because of the promise of greater safety and economic opportunities. But as the studies showed, the reality in these urban areas was best characterised as life on the margins or at the bottom. Displaced people often ended up in temporary squatter settlements, with only insecure incomes from the informal economic sector or from criminal activities, and with few, if any, rights. From the point of view of the nation state and the international community, this suggests growing problems of urbanisation. From the point of view of an internally displaced person, it suggests that displacement may not be simply a temporary decline in living standards, but a more permanent, structurally enforced plummet to the bottom of society. These conclusions remind us that we must continuously commit ourselves to finding durable solutions.

IMPLICATIONS FOR FUTURE HUMANITARIAN RESPONSE

International law treats internally displaced persons as citizens of a country; therefore, they are protected by existing human rights and humanitarian law. The legal perspective puts ultimate responsibility for caring for the internally displaced squarely into the hands of states. But states are often at least partly to blame for the displacement, either by playing a direct role in displacement or by refusing assistance to the displaced. Some states have been willing to provide assistance and protection but have been unable to do so because of a lack of resources or lack of access.

At the moment, many UN agencies, intergovernmental organisations, and NGOs work with the internally displaced.[1] Each approaches the issue according to its mandate. While all are contributing to the response, none are meeting 100 per cent of the needs of the internally displaced. Some organisations are involved in assistance, some in protection, some in a combination of activities. Their capacities vary widely. As a result, gaps have opened within the institutional framework.

The results of this research are far too preliminary to provide information and analysis that will change humanitarian field practice, but, without question, they support the current trend. Frameworks such as humanitarian principles, People-Orientated Planning or the Sphere Project, used by intergovernmental organisations such as the UN and NGOs, prioritise understanding of local response mechanisms before acting. They also demand that the internally displaced be involved in making decisions and that the division of labour among agencies allows for greater flexibility.

The findings of these studies indicate ways in which this process can be supported. It has been demonstrated that the displaced are often much better prepared than the humanitarian community gives them credit for. Without overstating or oversimplifying the case, humanitarian organisations prefer to rely on their own analysis of a situation rather than give credence to local analyses – often with disastrous consequences. Instead, humanitarian organisations should make an effort to listen and learn from local analysts. They should support local actors in developing feasible contingency plans. The UNHCR and a district-level NGO consortium in Sri Lanka, for example, worked together to improve people's preparedness should they be forcibly displaced again.

To learn from and support local analyses requires the ability to listen, which is something the humanitarian community should do more of. OXFAM's programme, again in Sri Lanka, provides a good model. Using a variety of participatory methodologies, OXFAM conducted listening surveys among the displaced communities in northern Sri Lanka. While the 'listening exercises' resulted in a greater understanding of the problems, needs, aspirations and capacities of people in conflict, they also resulted in tangible changes to policy. These changes included revising the non-food assistance package to be more gender sensitive, and shifting from short-term humanitarian relief towards longer-term investment in community development, sustainable livelihoods and conflict resolution (Harris 2000).

The studies, especially those in Georgia and Angola, illustrate an extremely varied set of economic activities in which the displaced are engaged. Assessing how the displaced respond will help develop a rich array of possible income-generation projects and identify the negative responses that can damage the social network or the environment. The research also illustrates a wide range of good practices that may be adaptable to other situations. The communal kitchens in Colombia or the adaptive schools in Georgia spring to mind here. Activities should, of course, be appropriate and sustainable, especially given what we now know about displaced persons' concern with issues of identity and dignity.

The area of domestic relations and shifting gender and generational roles requires further analysis and assessment. The observation that women are more readily employed in Colombia and in Sri Lanka and that they are assuming the role of village heads in Burma because of their ability to negotiate with the military are interesting developments. But there is a down side: role reversals are shown to result in domestic violence, as reported in Uganda, or in increased incidences of child labour and exploitation. What these cases underscore is the importance of addressing changes and tensions in the life of the family and extended family, especially since they play a central role in sustaining the displaced.

The humanitarian community can also play a greater role in facilitating access to documentation. The value of documentation is often underestimated, yet without proper documentation, the enjoyment of most civil rights is impossible. Documentation is essential for freedom of movement, especially when movement involves crossing checkpoints. The absence of documentation forces the displaced to take more circuitous routes to safety or limits the distance of flight. Documentation is also crucial in facilitating access to social services, obtaining compensation or tracing family members. The dangers associated with having the 'wrong' documentation were also well documented in Sri Lanka, Colombia and Angola, where armed actors used documentation as a control mechanism. In extreme cases, the displaced became targets of attack, since possession of certain identification papers was perceived as proof of political allegiance.

Access to documentation is almost entirely dependent on national officials, a dependency that can, in itself, be another source of insecurity if the displaced are in the territory of an authority other than the one that issued the documentation. It would be worthwhile to investigate whether the humanitarian community could more regularly facilitate access to, or even provide, some form of documentation for the internally displaced. Clearly, it is a highly sensitive issue; but seeking ways to use documentation as an affirmation of the neutrality of civilians may yield positive results. Again, the well-organised and developed responses in Colombia, such as the issuance of ID cards by the peace communities in Uraba, may be replicable or modified for use elsewhere.

Closely related to the subject of documentation is the issue of registration. The humanitarian community has, in recent years, been paying greater attention, and dedicating more resources, to registration. As a protection tool, it can counteract the anonymity of the displaced, which, under certain circumstances, can make it more difficult for authorities to abuse the rights of the displaced. There are occasions when anonymity is itself a protection tool; in those instances, the desire to remain 'hidden' must not be compromised. Nevertheless, improved methods of registration would be advantageous for several reasons. Effective registration can help ensure an accurate assessment of the scale of a displacement crisis, can help in information-gathering exercises and may even allow for preliminary interviews to gain a better understanding of the conditions facing the displaced. Most important, registration must be done with sensitivity, avoiding any risks to the displaced.

Another mechanism that deserves more support from the humanitarian community is negotiating in an attempt to prevent displacement. Case studies in Burma and Colombia illustrated the variety of delicate techniques, including negotiation with armed elements, acceptance, or silence that the displaced employed to gain some control over their fate. The same patterns emerged in return settings, such as in Sri Lanka, highlighting the importance of the complex and long-term social negotiation processes that must take place so the return or resettlement will be durable.

NEED FOR MORE RESEARCH

The original premise of this research was that, despite a significant increase in awareness, there was still relatively little understanding of how internally displaced persons coped with displacement. Following the research, it is easier to be more precise. Like many other aspects of the international response to internal displacement, there are significant gaps in research.

There is a growing body of literature on the worldwide crisis of internal displacement and greater awareness of the conditions that confront internally displaced persons. But there is still a significant lack of knowledge about the response mechanisms of the internally displaced, especially during those periods when they are beyond the reach of humanitarian organisations – the period between actual displacement and the time when victims reach safety and security. In other words, we know very little about the pre-flight and flight stages of displacement.

This gap in our understanding can be attributed to several factors. It is not easy to study internally displaced persons. To understand response mechanisms during conflict one must conduct research in the midst of a conflict. In other situations researchers face hostile governments and national authorities. These facts alone probably discourage most researchers from focusing on the early phases of displacement. Furthermore, as demonstrated in several cases in this study, the internally displaced often fear that providing information for studies can compromise their security, so they are not particularly welcoming to researchers, especially those from outside their own communities.

Another factor to explain the lack of emphasis on the pre-flight and flight stages is that until now, research on the internally displaced has concentrated on the periods during which the humanitarian community is most involved, that is, the assistance and return phases. This is evident in the amount of research on refugees that focuses on how victims of displacement respond to exile and camp life, or the appropriateness and impact of humanitarian assistance.[2] It is also evident in the amount of research that can be found on return and resettlement such as the research conducted by the World Bank and the UNDP, and in the action-orientated research of the War -Torn Societies Project.[3]

There is no doubt that these are all positive contributions that widen our understanding of communal processes and response mechanisms. But it is essential to focus on the pre-flight and flight stages of displacement to learn more about how internally displaced persons live in this most vulnerable of phases.

Focusing on pre-displacement and the period immediately after also broadens our understanding of possible preventive actions. Since displaced communities appear to go through a process of choosing possible actions and reactions, understanding their choices may help identify areas of positive intervention to prevent displacement. This is the case in Afghanistan where the emphasis now is on 'stabilising' populations to avoid displacement.

At the other end of the spectrum, despite the focus on the return and resettlement stages, little is known about the long-term social consequences of displacement and resettlement. This is partly because large-scale internal displacement is a fairly new phenomenon, and partly because of the tendency to concentrate on a time-span that corresponds with that of most humanitarian projects, namely up to five years. Little research has been conducted into how displacement affects people's livelihoods over a longer period or how new social structures are formed. We do know that displacement often affects an individual's status in the surrounding society, and the social consequences of displacement can last for a generation or longer. We also know that being accepted into a new community or rebuilding a community that has suffered, both physically and psychologically, the atrocities of war, takes much longer than the time it takes for the humanitarian actors to declare that the situation is 'back to normal'.

Indeed, this book suggests that, contrary to common belief, people may not necessarily return home once the main causes for displacement have been removed. Many have constructed new houses and built new livelihoods in their place of 'exile' and find it impossible or unattractive to give up what has become their home. Others who do return find that 'home' has become unfamiliar. Studying displaced people's longer-term strategies of mobility and locality will help humanitarian organisations to avoid basing their assistance on false assumptions about 'home' and 'belonging'.

On the scholarly and political level, it would be worthwhile to study the link between displacement/resettlement and the wider processes of state/nation building. As the cases in Burma, Sri Lanka, Kosovo, the Sudan and others showed, displacement and resettlement are inextricably linked with competition for scarce resources, power and representation within nation states.

Also, while women, youth and children often appear in the literature on humanitarian emergencies as 'vulnerable groups', they played a prominent role in all the case studies presented here. The future social position of these groups and their relationship to other members of society also deserve more and continuous scholarly attention.

Observing and acknowledging the ingenuity and resourcefulness of the internally displaced, as demonstrated in their response mechanisms, is the first step towards abandoning the humanitarians' self-image as benefactors. It should also underscore the importance of designing actions not according to preconceived notions, but according to the way internally displaced persons live their lives, in all their complexity.

NOTES

1. For a summary of the institutional involvement of various organisations, please refer to the annex in the IASC Protection Paper (available on the ICVA web site and at www.idpproject.org).
2. On the impact of humanitarian assistance, see, for example, the writings related to the Sphere Project and minimum standards.
3. See, for example, the work of Michael Cernea and his risk and reconstruction model, or the Post-Conflict Unit at the World Bank. The UNDP, along with the Brookings Institution, has also devoted significant resources to the issue of resettlement.

Contributors

Nina M. Birkeland is a research fellow at NTNU (Norwegian University of Technology and Science), Trondheim, Norway.

Geneviève Boutin, currently a consultant with the UNDP in Congo Brazzaville, is pursuing her doctoral research on IDP and refugee resettlement in the Great Lakes region at the Graduate Institute of International Studies in Geneva, Switzerland.

Chris Cusano started working with Burma's displaced people in 1993. Today he serves as Profile Editor at Ashoka: Innovators for the Public, in Washington, DC.

Esperanza Hernandez Delgado is a teacher, researcher and consultant. She has a law degree from the Universidad Autónoma de Bucaramanga, Bucaramanga, Colombia, and degrees in public law and political studies from the Universidad Externado de Colombia, Santafe de Bogotà, Colombia, and the Pontificia Universidad Javeriana, Bogotà, Colombia.

Grant Farr is a professor and the chair of the Department of Sociology at Portland State University, Portland, Oregon.

Alberta Uimbo Gomes is the director of ADRA in Huambo, Angola.

Vladimir Ilic is currently a professor in the Sociology Department at Belgrade University.

Karen Jacobsen is a Visiting Assistant Professor and the Director of the Refugees and Forced Migration Program, which is jointly administered by the Fletcher School of Law and Diplomacy and the Feinstein International Famine Center, at Tufts University in Boston, Massachusetts.

Julia Kharashvili is currently working in the United Nations Volunteers office in Tblisi as national community facilitator working with IDP communities. She is also elected chairperson of the IDP Women's Association in Georgia.

Sue Lautze is Director of the Livelihoods Initiative Program at the Feinstein International Famine Center, at Tufts University in Boston, Massachusetts.

Turid Laegreid is currently working at the NRC Headquarters in Oslo. From 1998 to 2000 she was the NRC Resident Representative in Colombia. She is a political scientist, with a former research background with the Norwegian Institute of International Affairs (NUPI), Oslo, Norway, on conflict resolution and UN peacekeeping operations.

Salvatore Nkurunziza is the Coordinator of Action Aid, Ruyigi in Burundi.

Ambrose Olaa studied history and sociology at Makaere University in Kampala and is currently a Community Development Officer in Kitgum district.

Abdal Monim Kheider Osman is a PhD student at the Tufts University School of Nutrition, Boston, Massachusetts.

Birgitte Refslund Sorensen is Associate Professor at the Institute of Anthropology in Copenhagen, Denmark. In 1999–2000 she worked as a Training and Programme Advisor for the Danish Refugee Council, Sri Lanka.

Marc Vincent is currently the Coordinator of the Global IDP Project, an undertaking of the NRC. Based in Geneva, the Project works towards improving the international response to the protection and assistance needs of internally displaced persons through information analysis, publications and training.

Bibliography

INTRODUCTION AND BACKGROUND

Andrade, Filomena (forthcoming) 'A Life of Improvisation! – Displaced People in Malanje and Benguela' in Robson, P. (ed.) *Communities and Reconstruction in Angola*, Development Workshop Occasional Paper No. 1.

Brookings Project on Internal Displacement (2000) *Report of the International Colloquy on the Guiding Principles on Internal Displacement.* Washington, DC: Brookings Institution. 21–23 September.

Cernea, Michael (1997) 'The Risks and Reconstruction Model for Resettling Displaced Populations', *World Development*, Vol. 25, No. 10.

Cernea, Michael and Christopher McDowell (2000) *Risks and Reconstruction: Experiences of Resettlers and Refugees.* Washington, DC: The World Bank.

Davies, Wendy (ed.) (1998) *Rights Have No Borders: Internal Displacement Worldwide.* Oslo: Norwegian Refugee Council.

Hampton, Janie (1998) *Internally Displaced People: A Global Survey.* London: Earthscan Publications.

International Committee of the Red Cross (October 1999) 'The People on War Report', *ICRC Worldwide Consultation on the Rules of War.* Geneva: ICRC.

Jesuit Refugee Service (2001) *War Has Not Changed Our Spirit: Experiences of Forcibly Displaced Women.* Rome: JRS. February.

Lautze, Sue and John Hammock, MD (1996) 'Coping with Crisis: Coping with Aid, Capacity Building, Coping Mechanisms and Dependency, Linking Relief and Development', *Report to the UN Inter-Agency Standing Committee.* December.

Muggah, H. C. R. (2000) 'Conflict-induced Displacement and Involuntary Resettlement in Colombia: Putting Cernea's IRLR Model to the Test', *Disasters*, Vol. 24, No. 3.

Robson, Paul (forthcoming) *Communities and Reconstruction in Angola*, Development Workshop Occasional Paper No. 1.

Schmeidl, Susanne (1998) 'Comparative Trends in Forced Displacement, 1964–96', in Hampton, J. (ed.) *Internally Displaced People: A Global Survey.* London: Earthscan Publications.

Sorensen, Birgitte Refslund (1998) 'Self-help Activities Among Internally Displaced People', in Davies, W. (ed.) *Rights Have No Borders: Internal Displacement Worldwide*. Oslo: Norwegian Refugee Council.

Stremlau, John (1998) 'People in Peril: Human Rights, Humanitarian Action, and Preventing Deadly Conflict', *Report to the Commission*. Washington, DC: Carnegie Commission on Preventing Deadly Conflict. May. (http://www.ccpdc.org/pubs/peril/peril.html)

United Nations Commission on Human Rights (1993) Comprehensive study prepared by Dr Francis M. Deng, Representative of the Secretary-General on the human rights issues related to internally displaced persons, pursuant to Commission on Human Rights resolution 1992/73. UN document E/CN.4/1993/35. Geneva: UNHCR.

—— (1996) 'Report of the Representative of the Secretary-General, Francis M. Deng, submitted pursuant to Commission on Human Rights, Resolution 1995/57, UN document E/CN.4/1996/52'. New York: United Nations. 22 February.

United Nations High Commissioner for Refugees (UNHCR) (1997) *The State of the World's Refugees 1997–98: A Humanitarian Agenda*. Oxford: Oxford University Press.

—— (2000) *Refugees and Others of Concern, 1999 Statistical Review*. Geneva: UNHCR Registration and Statistical Unit, Programme Coordination Section. July.

United Nations Office for the Coordination of Humanitarian Affairs (UNOCHA) (1999) *Guiding Principles on Internal Displacement*. New York: UNOCHA.

CHAPTER 1 – ANGOLA

Bender, G. J. (1978) *Angola under the Portuguese: The Myth and the Reality*. Nairobi/Ibadan/Lusaka: Heinemann.

Birkeland, N. M. (2000) 'Forced migration and *deslocados* in the Huambo Province, Angola', *Norwegian Journal of Geography*, Vol. 54, No. 3.

Bordo, S. (1990) 'Feminism, post-modernism and gender scepticism', in Nicholson, Linda (ed.) *Feminism/Postmodernism*. New York and London: Routledge.

Central Intelligence Agency (CIA) (2001) 'Angola', *The World Factbook 2000* (www.cia.gov/cia/publications/factbook/geos/ao.html).

Cohen, R. and F. Deng (1998) *Masses in Flight: The Global Crisis of Internal Displacement*. Washington, DC: Brookings Institution.

Helle, D. (1998) 'Enhancing the Protection of Internally Displaced People', in Davies, W. (ed.) *Rights Have No Borders: Internal Displacement Worldwide*. Oslo: Norwegian Refugee Council.

Hodges, T. (2001) *Angola from Afro-stalinism to Petro-diamond Capitalism*. Oxford/Bloomington/Oslo: Indiana University Press/Fridtjof Nansens Institute.

IRIN (United Nations Integrated Regional Information Networks) (2000a) 'Angola: IDP transit centres in Central Highlands closed' (www.reliefweb.int/irin).

—— (2000b) IRIN news on 22 September 2000 (www.reliefweb.int/irin).

—— (2000c) 'Angola: WFP warns of imminent break in food pipeline', 15 December 2000 (www.reliefweb.int/irin).

—— (2001) 'Angola: Humanitarian update', 21 February (www.reliefweb.int/irin).

Medécins sans Frontières (MSF) (2000) 'Angola rapport, MSF/Leger Uten Grenser' (www.leger-uten-grenser.no/artikler/artikkeltekster/angola-rapport).

Munslow, B. (1999) 'Angola: the politics of unsustainable development', *Third World Quarterly*, Vol. 20, No. 3.

Norwegian People's Aid (2000) 'The political/military situation in Angola' (www.angola.npaid.org/political-situation.htm).

Norwegian Refugee Council (NRC) (2000a) 'Internal Displacement in Angola', *The Global IDP Database*, 6 July 2000 (www.idpproject.org).

—— (NRC) (2000b) *Workshop on the Guiding Principles on Internal Displacement*. Luanda/Geneva: Norwegian Refugee Council.

Russo, J. (1993) 'Economia–dos caminhos trilhados aos desafios do futuro', transcription of session given at the conference *Conheça Angola – sessão no 4 – Huambo*, Luanda 21–25 Septembro de 1993 no Cinema ALFA 2. Presentation given by Dr Joaquin Russo, moderator: Eng. Fernando Pacheco (Unpublished).

Sorensen, Birgitte Refslund (1998) 'Self-help Activities among Internally Displaced People', in Davies, W. (ed.) *Rights Have No Borders: Internal Displacement Worldwide*. Oslo: Norwegian Refugee Council.

United Nations Development Programme (UNDP) (1999) 'Angola', *Human Development Report 1999*. Luanda: United Nations Development Programme.

United Nations Office for the Coordination of Humanitarian Affairs (UNOCHA) (1999) *Handbook for Applying the Guiding Principles on Internal Displacement*. Geneva/Washington, DC: UNOCHA/ Brookings Institution.

—— (2000a) *Angola: Relatório sobre a Avaliação Rapida das Necessidades Críticas*, versão final. Luanda: UNOCHA.

—— (2000b) *UN Consolidated Inter-Agency Appeal for Angola*. Luanda/Geneva: UNOCHA.

Vines, A. (1998) 'Angola', in Hampton, J. (ed.) *Internally Displaced People – A Global Survey*. London: Earthscan.

—— (1999) *Angola Unravels: The Rise and Fall of the Lusaka Peace Process*. New York/Washington, DC/London/Brussels: Human Rights Watch.

Wille, J. (2000) *Social Capital and Humanitarian Mine Action*. Oslo: University of Oslo.

CHAPTER 2 – BURUNDI

Bennett, Jon (2000) 'Forced relocation in Uganda, Rwanda and Burundi: Emerging policy', *Forced Migration Review*, Vol. 7.

Buyoya, Pierre (1998) *Mission Possible: Construire une paix durable au Burundi* (Témoignage recueilli par David Gakunzi). Paris: L'Harmattan.

Chambers, Robert (1997) *Whose Reality Counts? Putting the First Last*. London: Intermediate Technology Development Group Publishing.

Deng, Francis M. (1994) *Profiles in Displacement: Burundi*. UN document E/CN.4/1995/Add.2. New York: United Nations.

L'État du Monde 1995, F. Maspero, Paris.

L'Etat du Monde 1999, F. Maspero, Paris.

Government of Burundi (1989) *Rapport de la Commission Nationale chargée d'étudier la question de l'Unité Nationale*. Bujumbura: Government of Burundi.

Humanitarian Law Consultancy (1997) *Burundi's Regroupment Policy: A Pilot-study on its Legality*. The Hague: Humanitarian Law Consultancy.

Kay, Reginald (1987) *Burundi since the Genocide*. Washington, DC: Minority Rights Group.

Kriner, Stephanie (2000) 'Famine Threatens Controversial Burundi "Regroupment" Camp', *Staff Write for DisasterRelief.org*. Internet: DisasterRelief.org.

Lemarchand, René (April 1998) 'Genocide in the Great Lakes: Which Genocide? Whose Genocide?', *African Studies Review*, Vol. 4, No.1.

Lemarchand, René and David Martin (1974) *Selective Genocide in Burundi*. Washington, DC: Minority Rights Group.

Ministère en Charge de la Réinsertion et de la Réintégration des Déplacés et des Réfugiés (MRRDR) (2000) *Données Nationales des Personnes Déplacées Intérieures*. Bujumbura: Government of Burundi.

Malkki, Liisa H. (1995) *Purity and Exile: Violence, Memory, and National Cosmology among Hutu Refugees in Tanzania*. Chicago and London: University of Chicago Press.

Norwegian Refugee Council (NRC) (2000) *Internal Displacement in Burundi: Updated Profile*. Geneva: Norwegian Refugee Council. June.

Proceedings of the 1985 International Conference on Rapid Rural Appraisal (1987), Khon Kaen University, Thailand.

United Nations Development Programme (UNDP) (2000) *Human Development Report 2000*. New York: UNDP.

United Nations Office for the Coordination of Humanitarian Affairs (UNOCHA)/Burundi (1999) *Choosing Hope: The Case for Constructive Engagement in Burundi*. Bujumbura: OCHA.

—— (2000) *Affected populations in the Great Lakes region*. Nairobi: OCHA. May.

United States Committee for Refugees (USCR) (1998) 'Burundi: A Patchwork of Displacement', in Cohen, R. and F. Deng (eds) *The Forsaken People: Case Studies of the Internally Displaced*. Washington, DC: Brookings Institution.

CHAPTER 3 – SUDAN

Anderson, G. Norman (1999) *Sudan in Crisis: The Failure of Democracy*. Gainesville: University Press of Florida.

Corbett, J. (1988) 'Famine and Household Coping Strategies', *World Development*, Vol. 16, No. 9.

Deng, L. B. (1999) 'Famine in the Sudan: Causes, Preparedness and Response: A Political, Social and Economic Analysis of the 1998 Bahr el Gazal Famine', Discussion Paper 369, Institute of Development Studies. Brighton: University of Sussex.

Deng, Francis (1995) *War of Visions: Conflict of Identities in the Sudan*. Washington, DC: Brookings Institution.

de Waal, A. (1988) *Famine that Kills: Darfur 1984–1985*. London: Save the Children Fund UK.

Duffield, M. (1993) 'NGOs, Disaster Relief and Asset Transfer in the Horn: Political Survival in a Permanent Emergency', *Development and Change*, Vol. 24.

Grawert, Elke (1998) *Making a Living in Rural Sudan: Production of Women, Labour Migration of Men and Policies for Peasants' Needs.* New York: St. Martin's Press.

Hamid, Gamal Mahmoud (1996) *Population Displacement in the Sudan: Patterns, Responses, Coping Strategies.* Staten Island: Center for Migration Studies.

Human Rights Watch (1996) *Behind the Red Line: Political Repression in Sudan.* New York: Human Rights Watch.

Keen, David. (1991) 'A Disaster for Whom? Local Interests and International Donors during Famine Among the Dinka of Sudan', *Disasters*, Vol. 15, No. 2.

—— (1993) 'Famine, Need Assessment and Survival Strategies in Africa', Oxfam UK Working Paper. London: Oxfam.

—— (1994) *The Benefits of Famine: A Political Economy of Famine and Relief in Southwestern Sudan, 1983–1989.* Princeton: Princeton University Press.

Kibreab, Gaim (1996) *People on the Edge in the Horn.* Lawrenceville: Red Sea Press.

Loveless, Jeremy (1999) 'Displaced Populations in Khartoum: A Study of Social and Economic Conditions' for Save the Children Denmark. September 1998–April 1999. Unpublished Report for Channel Research Ltd.

O'Ballance, Edgar (2000) *Sudan, Civil War and Terrorism 1956–99.* New York: St. Martin's Press.

Post, Johan (1996) *Space for Small Enterprise: Reflections on Urban Livelihood and Urban Planning in the Sudan.* Amsterdam: Thesis Publishers.

CHAPTER 4 – UGANDA

Atkinson, Ronald R. (1999) *The Roots of Ethnicity: The Origins of the Acholi of Uganda.* Kampala: Fountain Publishers.

Gersony, Robert (1997) 'The Anguish of Northern Uganda: The Results of a Field-based Assessment of the Civil Conflicts in Northern Uganda', Report. Kampala: USAID.

Joint Forum for Peace (2000) 'Support for Reconciliation and Long-term Peace Efforts in the Acholi Community, Northern Uganda', Report. Kitgum district.

Kitgum District Psychosocial Support Programme Quarterly Report (July–December 1999, December 1999–March 2000, April–June 2000)

Museveni, Yoweri Kaguta (1997) *Sowing the Mustard Seed: The Struggle for Freedom and Democracy in Uganda.* London: Macmillan Publishers Ltd.

Obonyo, Caroline (1999) 'Field Practice Report: June–September 1999'. Kampala: Makerere University.

CHAPTER 5 – AFGHANISTAN

Agence France-Presse (AFP) (1999) 'Taliban welcome gradual UN return to Kabul'. Internet 13 March.

Bashir, Mohammad (2000) 'Civilians Flee as Taliban Close in on Northeastern Afghan Town'. *Agence France-Presse* Internet August.

Doctors Without Borders (1999) 'Cholera Hits Afghanistan'. Internet 26 August.

Human Rights Watch (HRW) (1998) 'The Massacre in Mazar-i-Sharif'. Internet November.

Lazaroff, Cat (2000) 'Drought in Afghanistan Threatens Millions', *The Lycos Network.* Internet 6 June.

Rubin, Barnett (1999) 'Afghanistan Under the Taliban', *Current History*, January, Vol. 98, No. 625.

Shorish-Shamley, Zieba (2001) 'The Plight of Women and Health Care in Afghanistan', *Women's Alliance for Peace and Human Rights in Afghanistan.* Internet.

United Nations Children's Fund (UNICEF) (2001) Afghanistan Proposal for Emergency Assistance to Drought and Conflict IDPs, March–August 2001.

United Nations Commission on Human Rights (UNCHR) (1999) 'Report of the Secretary-General on the Situation of Women and Girls in Afghanistan'. Internet 14 July.

United Nations Department of Public Information (UNDPI) (1999) 'Mission in Panjshir Valley Confirms 100,000 Displaced'. Internet 3 September.

United Nations General Assembly (1999) 'Interim Report on the Situation of Human Rights in Afghanistan, prepared by the Special Rapporteur of the Commission on Human Rights'. UN Document A/54/422. New York: United Nations. 30 September.

United Nations Office for the Coordination of Humanitarian Affairs (UNOCHA) (1999) *Afghanistan Weekly Update*, No. 337. Internet 2 November.

—— (2000) 'Crisis of Internal Displacement: Status of the International Responses through IASC Members and their Partners'. Internet 6 July.

United Nations Resident Coordinator Office (UNRCO) for Afghanistan (2000) 'Hazarajat Baseline Study (Part 1) Interim Report'. Internet March.

United States Agency for International Development (USAID) (2000) 'Afghanistan Complex Emergency Information Bulletin No. 1', *ReliefWeb* (Internet).

United States Committee for Refugees (USCR) (1995) *World Refugee Survey 1995*. Washington, DC: USCR.

—— (1996) *World Refugee Survey 1996*. Washington, DC: USCR.

—— (1997) *World Refugee Survey 1997*. Washington, DC: USCR.

—— (1998) *World Refugee Survey 1998*. Washington, DC: USCR.

—— (1999) *World Refugee Survey 1999*. Washington, DC: USCR.

—— (2000) *World Refugee Survey 2000*. Washington, DC: USCR.

United States Department of State (1999) 'Afghanistan Country Report on Human Rights Practices for 1998'. Internet 26 February.

World Food Programme (WFP) (1999) 'WFP Assistance to Internally Displaced Persons, Country Case Study of Internal Displacement, Patterns of Displacement in Afghanistan'. Internet October.

CHAPTER 6 – BURMA

Amnesty International, Myanmar (1999) *The Kayin State: Militarisation and Human Rights*. London: Amnesty International. June.

Asia Watch (1993) *A Modern Form of Slavery: Trafficking of Burmese Women and Girls into Brothels in Thailand*. New York: Human Rights Watch.

Asian Human Rights Commission (AHRC) (1999) *Voice of the Hungry Nation: People's Tribunal on Food Scarcity and Militarisation in Burma*. Hong Kong: AHRC.

Beyrer, Chris (1999) 'The Health and Humanitarian Situation of Burmese Populations along the Thai–Burma Border', *Burma Debate*, Fall, Vol. 6, No. 3. New York: Open Society Institute.

Burma Ethnic Research Group (BERG) (1998) *Forgotten Victims of a Hidden War: Internally Displaced Karen in Burma*. Chiang Mai: BERG.

—— (2000) *Conflict and Displacement in Karenni: The Need for Considered Responses*. Chiang Mai: BERG.

Deng, Francis (1998) *Guiding Principles on Internal Displacement*. UN document E/CN.4/1998/53/Add.2. New York: United Nations.

Eh Na, Saw (November 1998) 'Effects of the Relocation Programme on Villagers in Palaw Township, Tenasserim Division, Burma'. Unpublished.

Hinton, Peter (1979) 'The Karen, Millenialism and Accommodation', in Keyes, C. (ed.) *Ethnic Adaptation and Identity: The Karen on the Frontier with Burma*. Philadelphia: Institute for the Study of Human Issues.

Htoh Lwi War (1999) 'Htoh Lwi War Reports: September 1998–March 1999. T'nay Char Township, Pa'an District'. Unpublished.

Images Asia (1997) *Migrating with Hope: Burmese Women Working in the Sex Industry in Thailand*. Chiang Mai: Images Asia.

International Labour Organisation (ILO) (1998) 'Forced Labour in Myanmar (Burma). Report of the Commission of Inquiry appointed under Article 26'. Geneva: ILO.

Karen Human Rights Group (KHRG) (1999) 'Caught in the Middle: The Suffering of Karen Villagers in Thaton District', KHRG No. 99–07 (www.khrg.org). September.

—— (March 2000) 'Starving Them Out: Forced Relocations, Killings and the Systematic Starvation of Villagers in Dooplaya District', KHRG No. 2000–02 (www.khrg.org).

Karen Information Centre (KIC) (1998) *Newsletter*. August.

Karen National Union (undated) 'Karen History in the Karen National Union (KNU) Narrative' (www.karen.org/history/knunarr.htm).

Keyes, Charles (ed.) (1979) *Ethnic Adaptation and Identity: The Karen on the Frontier with Burma*. Philadelphia: Institute for the Study of Human Issues.

Kweh Klo, Saw (1999) 'Mone Township-Khlerlwihtooh District, Report on Village Conditions'. Unpublished.

Kweh Say, Saw (1996) 'Report on Conditions in the Free-fire Zones of Mudraw District and Mone Township'. Unpublished.

Nyapaythwet (1999) 'Propaganda: Another Side of the Coin', *Burma Issues Newsletter*. Bangkok: Burma Issues. March.

Renard, Ronald (1980) *History of Karen–T'ai Relations from the Beginning to 1923*. Doctoral dissertation. Hawaii: University of Hawaii.

SKS (1999) 'Economics and Development in Mone Township', *Burma Issues Newsletter*, May, Vol. 9, No. 5. Bangkok: Burma Issues.

Spiro, Melford E. (1967) *Burmese Supernaturalism: A Study in the Explanation and Resolution of Suffering*. Englewood Cliffs: Prentice Hall.

—— (1982) *Buddhism and Society: A Great Tradition and its Burmese Vicissitudes*. Berkeley: University of California.

Stern, Theodore (1968) 'Ariya and the Golden Book: A Millenarian Buddhist Sect Among the Karens', *Journal of Asian Studies*, Vol. 27, No. 2.

Tun, Saw Moe K. (1998) *Education for the Development of the Marginalised Karen in Burma*. Bangkok: Burma Issues.

Walker, Anthony (ed.) (1981) *Farmers in the Hills: Upland Peoples of North Thailand*. Singapore: Chinese Association for Folklore.

CHAPTER 7 – SRI LANKA

Balakrishnan, N. (2000) 'Resettlement, Rehabilitation and Reconstruction – The Vavuniya District', in de Silva, K.M. and G.H. Pieries (eds) *Pursuit of Peace in Sri Lanka: Past Failures and Future Prospects*. Kandy: International Centre for Ethnic Studies; Washington, DC: The United States Institute of Peace.

Brun, Cathrine (2000) 'Spatial Practices of Integration and Segregation among Internally Displaced Persons and their Hosts in Sri Lanka', *Norsk Geografisk Tidsskrift*, 54.

Fuglerud, Øivind (1999) 'Space and Movement in the Sri Lankan Conflict', *Working Paper 1999*, Vol. 2. Oslo: Centre for Development and the Environment.

Hasbullah, S. H. (1996) 'Refugees are People'. Proceedings of a workshop. Colombo: Northern Muslims' Rights Organisation.

Hasbullah, S. H. with S. H. M. Rizni and A. G. Anees (1999) 'Preliminary Findings on the Living Conditions of the IDPs in Puttalam District'. Unpublished.

Ismail, Qadri (1995) 'Unmooring Identity: The Antinomies of Elite Muslim Self-representation in Modern Sri Lanka', in Jeganathan, P. and Q. Ismail (eds) *Unmaking the Nation: The Politics of Identity and History in Modern Sri Lanka*. Colombo: Social Scientists Association.

McGilvray, Dennis (1999) 'Tamils and Muslims in the Shadow of War: Schism or Continuity?' in Gamage, S. and I. B. Watson (eds) *Conflict and Community in Contemporary Sri Lanka: 'Pearl of the East' or 'Island of Tears'?* New Delhi: Sage Publications.

Mauroof, Mohamed (1972) 'Aspects of Religion, Economy and Society among the Muslims of Ceylon', *Contributions to Indian Sociology*, Vol. 6.

O'Sullivan, Meghan (1999) 'Conflict as a Catalyst: The Changing Politics of the Sri Lankan Muslims', in Gamage, S. and I. B. Watson (eds) *Conflict and Community in Contemporary Sri Lanka: 'Pearl of the East' or 'Island of Tears'?* New Delhi: Sage Publications.

Schrijvers, Joke (1998) 'Internal Refugees in Sri Lanka: The Interplay of Ethnicity and Gender', *The European Journal of Development Research*, Vol. 9, No. 2.

—— (1998) '"We were like coconut and flour in the pittu": Tamil-Muslim Violence, Gender and Ethnic Relations in Eastern Sri Lanka', *Nethra*, Vol. 2, No. 3.

Seneviratne, H. L. and Maria Stavropoulou (1998) 'Sri Lanka's Vicious Circle of Displacement', in Cohen, R. and Francis M. Deng (eds) *The Forsaken People: Case Studies of the Internally Displaced*. Washington, DC: Brookings Institution.

Sorensen, Birgitte Refslund (1996) 'Relocated Lives: Displacement and Resettlement within the Mahaweli Project, Sri Lanka', *Sri Lanka Studies*, No. 3. Amsterdam: VU University Press with UNRISD, Geneva.

—— (1998) 'Women and Post-Conflict Reconstruction: Issues and Sources', *War-Torn Societies Project,* Occasional Paper No. 3. Geneva: United Nations Research Institute for Social Development.

—— (1999) 'State Autonomy and Political Rebuilding After Conflict: Positioning Gender', in Degnbol-Martinussen, J. (ed.) *External and Internal Constraints on Policy Making: How Autonomous are the States?* Occasional Paper No. 20. Roskilde: International Development Studies, Roskilde University.

—— (2000) 'Territorialisation of the Nation, and Internationalisation of Territory in Sri Lanka'. Unpublished.

United Nations High Commissioner for Refugees (UNHCR) (2000) *Remembering the Displaced: Celebrating their Courage, Resilience and Determination.* Colombo: UNHCR.

United States Committee for Refugees (USCR) (1994) *People Want Peace: Repatriation and Reintegration in War-Torn Sri Lanka.* Washington, DC: USCR.

—— (1996) *The People in Between: Sri Lankans Face Long-Term Displacement as Conflict Escalates.* Washington, DC: USCR.

—— (1997) *Conflict and Displacement in Sri Lanka*. Washington, DC: USCR.

Van der Wijk, Dieneke (1997) *The Human Side of Conflict: Coping Strategies of Women Heads-of-Households in Four Villages in Sri Lanka and Cambodia*. London: Oxfam UK.

World Food Programme (WFP) (1999) *WFP Assistance to Internally Displaced Persons. Country Case Study on Internal Displacement: Sri Lanka, Displacement in the North and East*. Rome: WFP.

CHAPTER 8 – COLOMBIA

Consultoría para los Derechos Humanos y el Desplazamiento (CODHES) [Consultancy on Human Rights and Displacement] (2000), *Human Rights and Displacement Consultancy Bulletin*, 28. 22 February.

Defensoria del Pueblo (2000) *Massacres occurred in Colombia 1998–1999*. Bogotá: Defensoria del Pueblo.

National Police (2000) *Revista Criminalidad 1999*. Bogotá: Police Rotary Fund.

Oquist, Paul (1978) *Violence, Conflict and Politics in Colombia*. Instituto de Estudios Colombianos, Bogotá.

Posada, Marcela Salazr, Esperanza Hernandez Delgado and Ana María Durana (1998) *Identification of the State Attention Programmes for the Population Displaced by Political Violence in Colombia*. Bogotá: International Committee of the Red Cross. July.

CHAPTER 9 – GEORGIA

Assist Yourself (1999) Information-Education Bulletin Tbilisi: Assist Yourself.

Hansen, Greg (1998) *Humanitarian Actions in the Caucasus: A Handbook for Practitioners*. Providence: Thomas J. Watson Jr, Institute for International Studies, Brown University.

International Centre of Education and Information (1996) 'The Women's Movement and Social Problems in Georgia', conference materials. Tbilisi: International Centre of Education and Information.

International Federation of Red Cross and Red Crescent Societies (2000) *Vulnerability and Capacity Assessment*. Tbilisi: IFRC.

Kharashvili, Julia (1999) 'IDPs in Georgia', *Media Caucasica*.

—— (1999) 'Women Work for Peace in Georgia', *International Women's Day for Peace and Disarmament*.

—— (1999) 'Georgia: Helping Children in Distress', *Out Loud*.

—— (2000) 'Women and Reconciliation', *Newsletter of the Centres of Pluralism*, No. 13.

Kohen, J. (ed.) (1999) 'Problem of Sovereignty: The Georgian-Abkhaz Peace Process', *Accord: an International Review of Peace Initiatives*, 7.

MacFarlane, Neil, Larry Minear and Stephen Shenfield (1996) *Armed Conflict in Georgia: A Case Study in Humanitarian Action and Peace-keeping*. Providence: Brown University.

Ministry of Labour of AR Abkhazia (1998) Various statistical data.

Norwegian Refugee Council (NRC) (1994) 'IDPs in Georgia', a survey. Tbilisi: NRC.

OXFAM (1995) 'Psychosocial Examination of Children and IDP Women – Victims of Military Conflict on the Territory of the Republic of Georgia', a survey. Tbilisi: OXFAM.

Union of Wives of Invalids and Lost Warriors (1999) 'War and Women's Social problems in Georgia'. Conference materials. Tbilisi: Union of Wives of Invalids and Lost Warriors.

United Nations (1996) Report of the Secretary-General concerning the Situation in Abkhazia, Georgia S/1996/284. 15 April.

United Nations Development Programme (UNDP) (1998a) *Handbook for IDPs*. New York: UNDP.

—— (1998b) *Human Development Report – Georgia*. Tbilisi: UNDP.

—— (1998c) *Looking Ahead*. Tbilisi: UNDP.

—— (1999) *Human Development Report – Georgia*. Tbilisi: UNDP.

United Nations High Commissioner for Refugees (1999) *Global Appeal*. Geneva: UNHCR.

Ves Mir (1998) 'Georgians and Abkhaz: The Way to Reconciliation'. *Ves Mir*.

CHAPTER 10 – YUGOSLAVIA

Balla, B. (1972) *Kaderverwaltung*. Stuttgart: F. Enke.

Centre for the Study of Alternatives (2000) *Report*. Belgrade: Centre for the Study of Alternatives. September.

Cvejic, S. and V. Ilic (1994) 'Nacionalizam na Kosovu – sekundarna analiza', *Socioloski pregled*, Vol. 28, No. 4 ['Nationalism in Kosovo – a secondary analysis', *Sociological Review*].

Domonji, Pavel (2000) *Response*, No. 263. Belgrade: The Humanitarian and Information Centre for Refugees and Promotion of Civil Society. 2 March.

ECRE/ICVA Reference Group on former Yugoslavia (2000) *The Protection of Refugees and IDPs in Serbia: An Advocacy Information Report*. Internet May.

Helsinki Committee (2000) *Helsinki Committee Report.* Belgrade: Helsinki Committee for Human Rights in Serbia. February.

International Committee of the Red Cross (ICRC) /International Federation of the Red Cross (IFRC)/Yugoslavia Red Cross (YRC) (2000) *Report.* Internet May.

—— (2000) *IDP's and Refugees' Living Conditions.* Internet 31 May.

Ilic, V. (2000) 'The Serbian opposition during and after the NATO bombing', *Potential for Changes, Helsinki files*, No. 2. Belgrade: Helsinki Committee for Human Rights in Serbia.

International Helsinki Federation (2000) *Report.* Vienna: International Helsinki Federation. 26 July.

Komarevic, M. (2000) 'Prijava da, a li ne i pomoc', *Response.* Special issue. Belgrade: The Humanitarian and Information Centre for Refugees and Promotion of Civil Society. 31 August.

Lazic, M. (October 1999) 'On potential for changes among social groups', *Danas.* Belgrade: Danas. 30–31 October.

Nojkic, Randjel (2000) Interview, *Response.* No. 288. Belgrade: The Humanitarian and Information Centre for Refugees and Promotion of Civil Society. 30 August.

Petrovic, R. and M. Blagojevic (1989) *Seobe Srba i Crnogoraca sa Kosova i Metohije (Migrations of Serbs and Montenegrins out of Kosovo and Metohija).* Belgrade: SANU.

Politika (Politics) (1999) 'Osnovano drustvo "Stara Srbija"'. Belgrade. 6 November.

Return (1999) Belgrade: The Humanitarian and Information Centre for Refugees and Promotion of Civil Society. June–July.

Tomic, O. (1999) 'Kragujevac pred humanitarnom katastrofom', *Republika (Republic).* No. 220.

United Nations High Commissioner for Refugees (UNHCR) (2000) *South-Eastern Europe Information Notes.* Internet 15 June.

United Nations High Commissioner for Refugees (UNHCR/Organisation for Security and Cooperation in Europe (OSCE) (2000) *Report.* Internet June.

United Nations High Commissioner for Refugees (UNHCR)/Commissioner for Refugees of the Republic of Serbia (2001) Registration of Internally Displaced Persons from Kosovo and Metohija, 31 December.

United Nations Office for the Coordination of Humanitarian Affairs (UNOCHA) (2000) Internet 27 April.

Vlajkovic, J., Jelena Vlajkovic, Jelena Srna, Ksenija Kondic and Milan Popovic (1999) *Psychology of Refugees*. Belgrade: Institute for Psychology.

CONCLUSION

Anderson, M. B. (1996) *Do No Harm: Supporting Local Capacities for Peace through Aid*. Boston: Collaborative for Development Action, Local Capacities for Peace Project.

Cernea, Michael and Christopher McDowell (2000) *Risks and Reconstruction: Experiences of Resettlers and Refugees*. Washington, DC: World Bank.

Cernea, Michael (1997) 'The Risks and Reconstruction Model for Resettling Displaced Populations', *World Development*, Vol. 25, No. 10.

Cohen, Roberta and Francis Deng (1998) *Masses in Flight: The Global Crisis of Internal Displacement*. Washington, DC: Brookings Institution.

Cohen, Roberta and Francis Deng (eds) (1998) *The Forsaken People: Case Studies of the Internally Displaced*. Washington, DC: Brookings Institution.

Davies, Wendy (ed.) (1998) *Rights Have No Borders: Internal Displacement Worldwide*. Oslo: Norwegian Refugee Council.

Hampton, Janie (ed.) (1998) *Internally Displaced People: A Global Survey*. London: Earthscan Publications.

Harris, Simon (2000) 'Listening to the Displaced: Analysis, Accountability and Advocacy in Action', *Forced Migration Review*, Vol. 8, August.

Kane, June (1999) *War-Torn Societies Project: The First Four Years*. Geneva: War-Torn Societies Project.

Knudsen, John (1991) 'Therapeutic Strategies and Strategies for Refugee Coping', *Journal of Refugee Studies*, Vol. 4. No. 1.

Lautze, Sue and John Hammock, MD (1996) 'Coping with Crisis; Coping with Aid, Capacity Building, Coping Mechanisms and Dependency, Linking Relief and Development'. *Report to the UN Inter-Agency Standing Committee*. December.

Lumsden, David (1999) 'Broken Lives? Reflections on the Anthropology of Exile and Repair', *Refuge*, Vol. 18, No. 4.

Ogden, Kate (2000) 'Coping Strategies Developed as a Result of Social Structure and Conflict: Kosovo in the 1990s', *Disasters*, Vol. 24, No. 2.

Sorensen, Birgitte Refslund (1998) 'Self-Help Activities Among Internally Displaced People', in Davies, W. (ed.) *Rights Have No Borders: Internal Displacement Worldwide*. Oslo: Norwegian Refugee Council.

United Nations Office for the Coordination of Humanitarian Affairs (UNOCHA) (1999) *Guiding Principles on Internal Displacement*. New York: OCHA.

Waldron, Sidney (1998) 'Working in the Dark: Why Social Anthropological Research is Essential in Refugee Administration', *Journal of Refugee Studies*, Vol. 1. No. 2.

Annex 1: Burundi – Matrix of Coping Strategies (Ruyigi)

	Infants (0–3 yrs)	Children (4–14 yrs)	Young women	Young men	Orphans	Adult women	Adult men	Widows	Elderly/ Handicapped	Total
Protection strategies	0	10	30	70	10	20	50	10	0	22
Subsistence strategies	20	30	80	60	10	30	40	10	0	31
Self-reliance	0	10	80	70	0	30	50	10	0	28
Access to education	0	40	20	50	10	60	60	20	0	19
Public participation	0	20	20	30	10	70	90	50	20	34
Documentation needs and citizenship	0	0	10	20	0	10	20	10	0	8
Family unity, identity, culture, dignity and pride	80	60	20	70	60	80	50	40	60	58
Property issues	0	0	20	50	10	60	60	20	0	24
Health conditions and access to health services	20	40	50	70	20	30	50	40	20	38
Total	13	23	37	54	14	37	46	21	11	

See Chapter 2, p. 77, note 5.

Annex 2: Burundi – Conflict and Population Displacements Timeline of Political Developments/Population Displacements/International Response

1972 … /… 1993	1994 1995	1996 1997 1998	1999	2000
• Alleged coup attempt by Hutu dissidents. • Massive army repression, in particular, at eliminating Hutu intellectual class. • An estimated 150,000 killed (mostly Hutus). • June: First free election; President Ndadaye (FRODEBU) elected with a large majority; he is the first Hutu President of Burundi. • October: Ndadaye assassinated by extremist army elements	• Large-scale massacres of Tutsis in retribution for the president's assassination; estimated number of dead over 50,000. • In response, army represses Hutu communities. • Coup is incomplete; FRODEBU remains in power. • Burundi ruled by a succession of weak and divided administrations. • Unrest continues. • Hutu rebels launch attacks from the Kibira forest, Kivu (Zaire) and Tanzania.	• July: former dictator Pierre Buyoya returns to power with the support of the army. • As a military strategy to regain control of rebel-held territory, authorities forcibly regroup 250,000 civilians in provinces of Karuzi, Kayanza, Muramvya. • By end of 1997, most regroupment camps dismantled. • Following loss of bases in Kivu, rebels regroup in Tanzania and focus operations on SW, in particular the provinces of Makamba and Bururi. • Small-scale regroupment continues in response to localised destabilisation. • June: Parties, but not armed opposition, meet in Arusha to discuss peace plan. • Agreed cease-fire is not respected.	• Negotiations continue in Arusha but progress is very slow. • Instability increases around Bujumbura. • Repeated rebel attacks inside the city and in suburbs. • Forced regroupment of over 400,000 in Bujumbura Rurale.	• Peace talks resume under leadership of Nelson Mandela. Armed opposition join talks in July. • Negotiator's team hopeful that peace plan may be signed by late August. • Regroupment camps in Bujumbura Rurale dismantled by early August.

1972 .../... 1993	1994	1995	1996	1997	1998	1999	2000
• An estimated 200,000 flee their homes (majority of them Hutus, flee to Tanzania). Most of them still remain in camps or towns along the border.	• About 200,000 (mostly Tutsis) flee their homes and seek army protection in camps around towns. • Large numbers of Hutus seek refuge in neighboring countries (Zaire: 150,000; Tanzania: 250,000). • Up to 400,000 additional people congregate in spontaneous IDP sites inside the country. • Undetermined numbers of Hutus seek refuge in rebel-held Kibira forest.		• About 250,000 civilians forced into regroupment camps. By the end of 1997, they either return home or join existing IDP camps. • Following conquest of Zaire by Kabila-led alliance, most refugees in Kivu return to Burundi and swell IDP camps in NW, particularly in Cibitoke province.		• Over 100,000 people move to newly formed camps in Makamba and Bururi provinces.	• New crisis in DRC provokes a wave of returns. • Northern provinces stabilise and people return to their hills in Cibitoke and Bubanza provinces.	• People leaving regroupment camps either return home or move to IDP camps (not visited yet). • New camps in Ruyigi following unrest.

UNHCR provides assistance to Burundian refugees in Tanzania and Kivu.
Assistance also provided to Rwandan refugees in Burundi between 1994 and 1996, and refugees from DRC as of 1996 and until today.

1972 .../.../...	1993	1994	1995	1996	1997	1998	1999	2000
	• Activities of UN agencies limited to providing relief to IDPs living in camps. Operations constrained by unrest and insecurity. • Special Representative of SG initiates mediation attempts between parties.			• UNDP/UNOPS launch project to assist local Ministry in charge of Resettlement and Reintegration. • Resettlement projects funded by UN and implemented by NGOs in relatively stable provinces.	• Adoption of Griffith Memorandum and common position on regroupment: only short-term assistance to regroupment camps; policy is condemned. • Other resettlement assistance continues.	• CAP and 'Choosing Hope' argue for 'constructive engagement' in Burundi. Argument is that long-term 'development' assistance should be provided to those in living in relatively stable provinces.	• UN agencies condemn forced regroupment in Bujumbura Rurale. • Short-term assistance provided to accessible camps. • Most operations halted after murder of 2 UN officials in Ruyigi.	• Programmes for assistance to resettlement and reintegration resume as of May. • Short-term assistance provided to regroupment camps in Bujumbura Rurale. • Most camps closed by autumn 2000.

Index

Compiled by Sue Carlton